LIVING AGAINST AUSTERITY

A Feminist Investigation of Doing Activism and Being Activist

Emma Craddock

BRISTOL
UNIVERSITY
PRESS

First published in Great Britain in 2021 by

Bristol University Press
University of Bristol
1-9 Old Park Hill
Bristol
BS2 8BB
UK
t: +44 (0)117 954 5940
e: bup-info@bristol.ac.uk

Details of international sales and distribution partners are available at bristoluniversitypress.co.uk

British Library Cataloguing in Publication Data
A catalogue record for this book is available from the British Library

ISBN 978-1-5292-0575-6 paperback
ISBN 978-1-5292-0570-1 hardcover
ISBN 978-1-5292-0572-5 ePub
ISBN 978-1-5292-0571-8 ePdf

Cover design: blu inc, Bristol
Front cover image: flowerphotos / Alamy Stock Photo

This book is dedicated to my granny, who sadly cannot be here to witness the publication of my first book but who always believed this would happen and encouraged me throughout my studies to keep working. I promised you that I would do it, and I have.

Contents

CONTENTS

List of Abbreviations

BME	black and minority ethnic
NSM	new social movements
NSMT	new social movement theory
PCSO	Police Community Support Officer
RMT	resource mobilisation theory
SMT	social movement theory

Acknowledgements

The research this book is based on would not have been possible without the input of my amazing participants who generously gave me their time to speak about their experiences and warmly welcomed me into their groups. You are inspiring people who all do more than 'enough' and change the world for the better by your presence and actions. I have no doubt that you will continue to do so and am very blessed to consider many of you my friends. I hope that this book does justice to the complexities of the research context and that my story of our stories is of some use to you all. Thank you especially to Pete Wakeling for continually showing maturity, generosity and care in your friendship and activism. Thank you also to others whom I will not name in order to maintain anonymity; I hope you know who you are.

Thank you to all my friends and family who have supported and encouraged me during my research and the (long) process of writing this book. I thank especially my parents, friends both offline and online, who have provided guidance, laughter, empathy and encouragement throughout, and colleagues past and present who have supported me through the process of discussing ideas and reading article drafts (thank you Simon Cook for being my 'critical friend'!). Thank you to my oldest friend, Naomi de la Tour, for always believing in me.

Thank you to my PhD supervisors, Nick Stevenson and Anne-Marie Kramer, who provided the best team I could have wished for and who continue to be a great support. Thank you also to Steve Fuller who initially sparked my academic curiosity and has continued to be an academic sparring partner over the years. Your pragmatic encouragement at various points of this long journey is appreciated.

I am extremely grateful for the funding I received from the ESRC (grant number ES/J500100/1) for the original research project.

Thanks to God for the opportunities and blessings You have provided me, for the support and wisdom of my close friends and church family, and for Mog, the best feline company during writing (although I had to delete his additions!).

Finally, a heartfelt thank you to the incredible women in my life who show me the beauty of female friendship and whom I am proud to stand alongside as a feminist.

An Introduction to Local Anti-Austerity Activist Culture

Emma (researcher)	That's the Notts Uncut banner
Morris (participant)	Yeah, I made that banner.
Emma	Oh did you, is it a big bed sheet?
Morris	(laughs) It is a big bed sheet. I remember I needed something to do. It was just after my dog had died and I was really heartbroken so I said 'oh I need a banner to make'.
Emma	To keep you busy?
Morris	To keep me busy. And I remember sitting in my, and having this and I was making it, I was looking after my brother's cat at the time and if you look at it close there's all paw, bloody cat walked across the paint, there's all paw prints down here on it. (laughs)

> My mother's mother she told me there's a rug that she made for me being born and you can tell halfway round it my grandfather got made airman in the mine which is a much more responsible job with much more money, because she actually bought wool to use. So it's all fabric in the inside and then the outer is yarn. And it's, I had it for years and it's just like this significant moment shown up in the detail of something, but it's the difference between you can afford to buy materials and you can't. (Mel, participant)

The above quotations are excerpts from two separate interviews with two research participants – Morris, a white middle-aged working-class man, and Mel, a white woman in her 50s, with disabilities. Both refer to the act of making something, drawing our attention to the process as well as the product. Looking closely reveals a deeper meaning. The first excerpt details several facets of the process of doing activism and being an activist; how activism is a meaningful activity for Morris into which he can channel his emotions and that he can draw on at times of emotional distress, as well as being a source of humour and fun. His story about the banner-making reveals the shared meanings, experiences and insider knowledge that exist surrounding its creation. Mel's comment similarly reveals insider knowledge about the shared meaning of the rug that has been passed down in her family history, as well as the interaction between the symbolic and the material – with the rug representing the 'difference between you can afford to buy materials and you can't'.

At first glance, it is easy to miss such nuanced and rich meaning, but to do so misses a vital part of the fabric that makes up our experiences, identities and the patterns of meaning that we create in our life histories and everyday lives. There is something distinctly human about these moments that stands in stark contrast to the dehumanising discourse and impact of neoliberal capitalism, which is a strand threaded through the narratives about anti-austerity activism in this book. As Jasper (1997: 9–10) asserts, 'who are we humans, who protest so much? Most prominently, perhaps, we are symbol-making creatures, who spin webs of meaning around ourselves'. It is these webs that constitute 'culture' and the task of the researcher is to analyse them not as 'an experimental science in search of law but an interpretive one in search of meaning' (Geertz, 1973: 5). Such an approach invokes a broader notion of culture as 'not a thing but a dimension, not an object to be studied as a dependent variable but a thread that runs through, one that can be teased out of, every conceivable form' (Alexander, 2003: 7).

This book aims to unravel the rich tapestry of anti-austerity activist culture, developing a cultural and feminist analysis of the messy and complex processes of making and practising this culture, with a focus on the experiences of 'doing activism' and 'being activist', a distinction first identified by Bobel (2007). The phrase 'being activist' reflects how the activist identity and its meanings are embodied. In this respect, 'activist' is not merely a descriptive label. 'Being activist' both evokes traditional philosophical notions of 'being'; the nature and essence of a person, and encapsulates the active and evolving process involved that the term 'being *an* activist' cannot adequately capture. Drawing on Calhoun and Sennett (2007) and Thompson (1963), I deliberately use the words 'making' and 'practising' to emphasise the active processes and effort involved; as Calhoun and Sennett (2007: 5) assert, 'culture is practice: embodied, engaged, interactive, creative and contested'. Thompson's conceptualisation of the *making* of the English working class emphasises the importance of agency and relationships in making cultures, as well as the need to pay attention to particular contexts. Paying close attention to the everyday experiences of anti-austerity activism, and listening to the voices of those involved, makes visible the previously invisible, developing new insight into the motivating and sustaining factors of activism, as well as the constraining elements of this culture and the barriers that exist to becoming politically active outside mainstream political channels. Significantly, it reveals how such barriers are gendered, uncovering power relations between activists, these often being neglected by studies that focus on movements that seek to resist elite power.

While arguments against austerity have become more mainstream with the rise of Jeremy Corbyn as Labour leader, it is important to remember that this resistance began outside party politics and, in some respects, involved resistance *to* party politics, as Chapter 3 demonstrates. Drawing on ethnographic research conducted between 2011 and 2013, this book tells the story of this grassroots resistance, focusing on a specific local context in order to provide an in-depth description and understanding of anti-austerity activism during this period. It therefore tells the story of a distinct moment in British history when a strong resistance to austerity was nowhere to be found within party politics and the multiple crises of the economic and political realms opened up space for political participation outside mainstream channels of engagement. This moment has been recognised as epoch-making; Castells et al (2012) note that we have entered a world with very different social and economic conditions than before the financial crisis of 2008. By focusing in detail on individuals' everyday lived experiences and meanings of political engagement, exploring the affective and cultural dimensions of activism, this book tells the stories of those on the sidelines, of individuals and local communities who are so often written out of history and forgotten. As Solnit (2005: 35) asserts, we need to pay attention to actions that occur away from the main political stage, 'from the places that you have been instructed to ignore or rendered unable to see, come the stories that change the world, and it is here that culture has the power to shape politics and ordinary people have the power to change the world'.

Having outlined the value of an in-depth, cultural approach to studying activism, this chapter will outline the key themes of the book including the central role of emotion in political engagement and the relationship between gender and social movement activism. It will then provide a brief overview of the research project this book draws on, focusing on a feminist approach to doing research, and an outline of the book's content and structure. However, before that, we return to the beginning – the moment when the 'age of austerity' began.

Where it all began: the financial crisis and austerity

Crisis: To separate or cut, to make fixed, settled or stated […]
refers to a sharply defined, climactic event, possibly dangerous,
but in any case decisive (Rosalind Williams, 2012: 25)

The financial crisis of 2008 marked the beginning of a seismic shift in economic, political and social history. The first quake, starting with the collapse of Lehman Brothers in the US, sent shockwaves throughout the financial sector, and the Western world as a whole. It was followed closely by repeated aftershocks. Appearing to begin underground with cracks and shifts in the financial sector, unseen to the public eye, the culmination of high-risk decisions and lending within the context of unregulated global capitalism was the biggest economic disaster to occur since the American Great Depression of the 1930s. Unlike an earthquake, however, this disaster was human-made.

The UK government's immediate response was to contradict the neoliberal ideology of minimal state intervention in markets by bailing out the failing banks, using state funds to stabilise the financial sector. The resulting public deficit took centre stage, while the banks and millionaire bankers sidled off into the wings. Rather than making any serious attempt to tackle the problems of unregulated global capital, which, combined with increasing individualisation, had resulted in a culture of selfish, high-risk decision-making by those in charge of financial markets, the focus was on reducing the deficit by cutting public expenditure. Austerity was now the main agenda. The UK was reimagined as a household that had spent more on its outgoings than its income allowed. To rebalance the books, cutbacks had to be made.

In the autumn of 2010, the UK's chancellor, George Osborne, announced a programme of austerity to be imposed across the country, involving widespread and deep cuts to public spending. Between 2010 and 2015, £35 billion of cuts were made, with a further £55 billion to be cut by 2019 (Gentleman, 2015). The Institute for Fiscal Studies (2014) stated that 'colossal cuts' to public spending would take government spending to its lowest point since before the Second World War, and that by the end of this process 'the role and shape of the state will have changed beyond recognition'. Austerity enables a drastic shrinking of the welfare state and an increase in privatisation and financialisation, turning citizens into consumers of previously public services. Thus, austerity is more than a solution for managing government debt, it is an ideological extension of neoliberalism – as will be demonstrated throughout this book.

In response, there was an international surge in collective action that sought to challenge not only austerity but also the wider neoliberal capitalist system that underpinned it, including movements such as the Spanish Indignados, the American Occupy, and UK Uncut. These movements reframed austerity as an ideological attack on the poorest in society, highlighting the growing inequalities between the richest 1 per cent and the other 99 per cent, and addressed issues of political representation by drawing attention to the democratic deficit. Thus, anti-austerity politics is as much about reconfiguring democracy as it is about defending social protections of the past, such as state welfare (Della Porta, 2015). Shannon (2014: 13) remarks that 'living in an age of multiple crises creates multiple possibilities for the widening of antagonisms between privilege and power, on the one hand, and the dispossessed, on the other'. This notion is no better summed up than by Occupy's pitting of the 99 per cent − 'ordinary' citizens − against the 1 per cent − 'fat cats' who were deemed responsible for the financial crash but faced none of the consequences.

A central feature of political reactions to austerity is the widespread sentiment that austerity is an infringement of human dignity, demonstrated by the slogan of the 15M movement (a Spanish precursor to Occupy): 'We are not products in the hands of politicians and bankers'. This emphasis on the lived and felt experiences of human beings, as opposed to products and objects of a capitalist system, is reflected by movements' emotional framing of austerity as an affective, lived condition. Brown et al (2013) suggest that such movements should be understood as a response to a 'crisis of care'. They contend that movements approach this crisis by criticising the government's lack of care for its citizens and by seeking to demonstrate how alternative social relations based on care are possible. In this respect, moments of crisis can open up spaces for reimagining possible, better, futures. Shannon (2014: 2) asserts:

> When historical moments of crisis hit − when people's expectations are undercut by austere social realities − they shake the faith in capitalism that allows it to be continually reproduced in our daily lives. People begin to see that the way that we've organised our lives is one option, but that other possibilities may also be on the table. While global movements have also arisen in times when capitalism has not been in crisis, in the current, historical moment, crisis was a primary spark.

In other words, people (and especially the dispossessed) start to see that, actually, there *is* an alternative. As Holloway (2010) explains, cracks in capitalism begin to show, revealing the possibility for agitation to widen these cracks. Brah et al (2015: 5) demonstrate the 'double-sided effects of dispossession, including the opportunity to create new social bonds and forms of collective struggle against the suffering, immiseration and violence of austerity politics'. By focusing on the cultural and affective dimensions of movements, the processes taking place in these alternative spaces are revealed.

Although large-scale studies of European anti-austerity movements exist (Della Porta, 2015), there is a need for in-depth 'thick description' (Geertz, 1973) of anti-austerity activist cultures to explore the lived and felt experiences and meanings of political engagement. Such in-depth exploration has previously been carried out in the context of lifestyle activist cultures, such as Portwood-Stacer's (2013) study on anarchist culture, revealing the practices that maintain group boundaries and the role played by the activist identity. However, the context of anti-austerity activism problematises the role or even existence of an activist identity, given the populist framing of the movements' participants as 'ordinary' people, or the '99 per cent'. Questions about the role of the activist identity are confounded by the tendency for anti-austerity movements, such as UK Uncut, to be made up of loose horizontal networks that have no official membership.

Further questions are raised about the role of affective aspects of political engagement, such as solidarity, as well as how such activism is sustained over a period of time within such horizontal networks; a strong collective identity has traditionally been seen as a key way of sustaining political participation, particularly during difficult times. A question arises, then, about what motivates and sustains individuals who are participating in anti-austerity activism, especially when we consider that at the time of the research that this book draws upon (2011–13), four years had passed without any success in combating public spending cuts, and at the time of writing, nearly a decade has passed – yet anti-austerity activism continues. In order to answer these, and other, questions, I contend that it is vital to develop an in-depth, focused exploration of the ways in which individuals become and remain active during such times of crisis, and in particular, the affective and cultural dimensions of everyday political engagement.

The affective dimension of political engagement

There has been a recent emphasis placed on the role of affect within social movements, which involves a distinction being made between emotion, feeling and affect. Here, it is argued that:

> Feelings are *personal* and *biographical,* emotions are *social* [...] and affects are *pre-personal* [...] An affect is a non-conscious experience of intensity; it is a moment of unformed and unstructured potential [...] Affect cannot be fully realised in language [...] because affect is always prior to and/or outside consciousness. (Shouse, 2005: 1, 5)

Such definitions and understandings of affect build upon Spinozist–Deleuzian ideas and clearly demarcate emotion from affect. However, an obvious criticism of this approach is that the fluid nature of 'affect' results in the concept being too abstract and vague. More problematically, this distinction between affect and emotion serves to narrow our definition and understanding of emotion, privileging affect. Here, a contrast is drawn between 'a mobile impersonal affect and a contained personal emotion', which 'can operate as a gendered distinction' (Ahmed, 2014: 207), echoing the gendered dichotomy of reason and emotion. Further, the focus placed by this recent affective turn on exploring 'how mind is implicated in body; reason in passion', ignores many years of feminist work that has challenged the mind/body and passion/reason dualisms (Ahmed, 2014: 206). Because of this, I will not be distinguishing between emotion and affect but instead referring to both under the term 'affective', which I will use to refer to a more general cultural approach that explores the construction of meanings and the role of emotions and their effects within political engagement.

Social movements and emotions

Since the late 1990s, there has been a growing emphasis placed on the central role played by emotions in protest (Jasper, 1997; Jasper, 2011; Goodwin et al, 2000, 2001; Flam and King, 2005). Despite this expanding body of literature, cultural studies of social movements have tended to focus on the cognitive, reflecting the persistence of the traditional emotion versus reason dichotomy where emotions are presupposed to be irrational. Challenging the assumption that emotion and thinking are two separate and even opposed functions, Jasper (2014: 23) argues that 'rather than the opposite of thought, emotions are forms of thinking, and as such are a part of culture mixed together with cognitive propositions and moral principles and intuitions'. Jasper highlights the need to consider the moral dimension of protest and how this interconnects with the emotional, a relationship that has not been sufficiently recognised. Yet, as Calhoun (2001: 50) asserts, 'one of the advantages to taking emotions seriously is to see better how moral norms and injunctions come to have force'. In this respect, emotion is understood not solely as subjective but also social and active – 'doing' things, as Ahmed (2014) suggests.

A key area in which emotion 'does things' is that of sustaining social movements during latent periods. While social movement research tends to explore emotions in relation to how individuals are recruited to social movements, it is argued that we need to pay attention to the role of emotion during movements' latent as well as active periods. Linking lived experiences to the emotional dimension of activism, Brown and Pickerill (2009: 27) state that 'there is a need to understand how participants emotionally experience their actions, how action is embodied, and how meaning is constructed out of those experiences and feelings'. This focus on the affective dimension of political participation widens the focus of research from rationalistic approaches that focus on strategy and the effectiveness of movements to looking at questions of why and how individuals become and remain politically engaged, where emotion plays a central role.

Emotions are therefore central to understanding the meanings shaped and shared by activists, raising questions about their absence from cultural approaches to social movement studies. I agree with Jasper's (2014: 26) contention that this gap reflects lingering 'fears of the passions'. Further, as I alluded to earlier, the move to affect instead of emotion perhaps also reflects this remaining connotation of emotion as irrational and an illegitimate area of study. It is notable that this emotion/reason dichotomy is linked to the dichotomies of female/male and private/public, where the former is denigrated and the latter is deemed superior. Because of how such binary categories have historically been naturalised, their influence tends to be unrecognised in the everyday. This is reflected by how mainstream social movement theory (SMT) has traditionally neglected gender, which is another key theoretical strand of this book.

Gender and social movement activism

The neglect of gender in SMT has been identified by feminist theorists (Charles, 1993; Roseneil, 1995; Einwohner et al, 2000). It is argued that the gender-neutral discourse traditionally employed in this literature obscures the role of gender in social movements. Instead of creating common ground, conceptualisations of universal, abstract individuals 'mask domination' by ignoring differences (Fraser, 1992: 113). Phillips (1991: 57) contends that 'impartiality is not just a matter of abstracting from difference in order to identify a lowest common denominator. The very idea that there *is* a lowest common denominator […] turns out to be weighted in favour of certain groups.' Crucially, she argues that the 'abstract individual' is a patriarchal category, and that to accept this abstract, disembodied, individual is 'silently accepting his masculine shape' (1991: 36). Bourdieu (2001) explains that social life is implicitly gendered and that the effects of this are masked by society's 'doxa' (what is taken for granted), which conceives masculine domination as neutral.

Taylor (1999: 9) highlights that gender hierarchy is created through organisational practices and that we should therefore expect gender and its intersections 'to be as much an organizing principle of protest groups as it is of institutionalized ones'. Likewise, Einwohner et al (2000: 683) contend that 'social movements are gendered on all of these levels: individual, interactional, and structural'. Therefore, Kuumba (2001) proposes using a 'gender lens' to incorporate the structure of gender into all elements of analysis of social movements in order to make gendered differences and their implications visible. The area of gender and social movements has therefore developed over the past 20 years, most recently culminating in an *Oxford Handbook of U.S. Women's Social Movement Activism* (McCammon et al, 2017).

However, this literature has tended to focus on the US context and/or explicitly feminist social movements. As the problem of the implicitly gendered abstract individual highlights, we need to look closely at perceived gender-neutral contexts in order to reveal the hidden gendered power relations that exist. It is important, then, to pay attention to gendered differences in movements that are not explicitly feminist or overtly concerned with gender. Anti-austerity activism in the UK presents a unique opportunity to explore the cultural and emotional dimensions of political engagement, their interaction with the material dimension and the role of gender in movements that are not explicitly feminist but where gendered concerns are still relevant, given austerity's disproportionate impact on women. Such a study is vital given that, at the time of writing, only 32 per cent of MPs are women and the UK government neglected the statutory requirement to consider the equalities impact of its policies when austerity measures were drafted in 2010, resulting in women and ethnic minorities being disproportionately affected (Pearson and Elson, 2015).

Nottingham represents an intriguing research context for exploring the gendered dimension of anti-austerity activism. While the gendered nature of the cuts is reflected by feminist activism in some localities such as Bristol, where, in May 2015, a group of young women organised a march of thousands against austerity (ITV News, 2015), within Nottingham at the height of anti-austerity activism (2011–13), there was a distinct feeling that groups such as the People's Assembly (a movement that, along with the local branch of UK Uncut, is one of the biggest anti-austerity groups in Nottingham, and the research site this book draws on) did not adequately address women's concerns, resulting in women not relating to such activism.

Similarly, Maiguashca et al's (2016) analysis of feminism within the People's Assembly demonstrates that where gender is paid attention to (and, notably, it does not feature prominently in the People's Assembly's documented ideological vision), women's experiences of gendered oppression are conceived in economic terms only. This book explores the local People's Assembly's neglect of the gendered dimension of austerity and barriers to political participation, arguing that the movement prioritises class politics over gender, partly owing to the dominance of white working-class men. It also outlines the ways in which local women responded – by forming their own community groups to combat the gendered impacts of austerity through provision of practical support to women affected by the cuts. This response provokes debate about the potential and problems of such approaches, with the risk that social actors who provide such support become 'complicit with the imposition of austerity' (Bramall, 2013: 136). Thus, reflecting the wider tension that exists between resisting and reinforcing neoliberal capitalist values is a thread that runs throughout this book, which seeks to represent the complexity and ambivalence of anti-austerity activism.

The research project: a feminist approach

Feminists have sought to move women's voices and experiences from the margins to the centre of research, ascribing them the status of legitimate knowledge and challenging the androcentric foundations of the social sciences. Although there is no single feminist methodology, it is argued that the combination of certain features demarcates 'feminist research practice' (Hesse-Biber, 2007). These include an understanding that gender inequality exists, a commitment to political change through research, a concern with the subjective, lived experiences of participants, an emphasis on knowledge building as a relational process, which requires researcher reflexivity, and an acknowledgement of the positionality of the researcher and the power dynamics between researcher and the researched, all of which influence the knowledge produced. In order to move away from connotations of passive research 'subjects', I use the term 'participants' to refer to those who took part in the research, emphasising their subjectivity and active participation in constructing knowledge. While this may place too much emphasis on the researched and thus seemingly mask the power imbalance that will inevitably exist between researcher/researched, given that I acknowledge and will explore this imbalance, combined with the positive connotations of participant, I believe that this is the most appropriate term to use.

Research aims

The overall aim of the research was to produce an in-depth understanding, or 'thick description' (Geertz, 1973), of local anti-austerity activist culture and individuals' experiences and meanings of anti-austerity activism. This involved exploring the 'making' and 'practising' of activist culture within a specific context, paying close attention to the affective dimension of political engagement. The research started with a general interest in the cultural and affective dimensions of political engagement at the local level. As Maddison (2007: 392) asserts:

> The cultural lens brings into focus a far wider range of social movement activity, including those activities that take place quietly, 'behind the scenes', and yet without which no publicly visible movement could be possible. Such focus, on what Melucci (1985) calls 'submerged networks' (p. 800), constitutes social movement actors as 'diffuse and decentralized' (Taylor, 2000: 222) and takes account of periods away from the public spotlight.

Therefore, such research reveals insights that are likely to be missed yet are vital to movement life. Moreover, using gender as an analytical lens aids the development of a SMT that explores the 'cultural, emotional and subjective aspects of contention and activism that rationalist or cognitive approaches have not acknowledged' (Holyoak, 2015: 40). Focusing on gender within social movements allows us not only to better explore the cultural and affective dimensions of political engagement, but to contribute to both social movement and feminist theory in original ways.

Research methods

I utilised a combination of participant observation and semi-structured interviews with 30 participants to produce rich, in-depth data about individuals' experiences and meanings of anti-austerity activism. I attended anti-austerity groups' organising meetings, events and protests between 2011 and 2013, including UK Uncut events, the People's Assembly, feminist anti-austerity groups and smaller local campaigns. My extended immersion within the setting enabled me to gain trust among participants and subsequent access to interview participants. While I originally asked for 'activists' to participate, I quickly discovered that the term had ambiguous and complex meanings for individuals. I therefore dropped the word 'activist' from online posts and emails requesting participation and instead recruited individuals who self-identified as having been involved in local anti-austerity activism. Individuals' participation involved organising and attending protests and meetings as well as participating in online petitions, awareness raising and group organisation. There were ten core organisers of UK Uncut and the People's Assembly who are included in my sample. The sample also includes individuals who only attended meetings and/or protests and those who mainly participated online. For reasons of preserving anonymity, I have not identified the roles that individuals fulfilled and use pseudonyms. While a distinction was drawn between the People's Assembly and UK Uncut (which is explored in Chapter 3), most had participated in both as well as other local groups, and it emerged that the 'ideal activist' identity was consistent across groups. Therefore, despite organisational differences, these different groups and campaigns formed part of a wider local anti-austerity activist culture.

The construction of the 'activist' identity became a central theme of the research that emerged from these initial experiences and conversations with individuals involved in local activism. Participant observation therefore helped me to refine my research questions and the topics that I asked about in the interviews. Data gathered from participant observations also contributed to analysing and understanding participants' narratives, providing a wider context to draw on. Data analysis occurred simultaneously alongside data generation, using a thematic analysis approach.

Feminist research practice directly challenges the positivist assertion that research should be 'value-neutral' and objective. It is argued that rather than ignoring the researcher's positionality in a vain attempt to achieve objectivity, by reflexively paying attention to this we can produce better and more rigorous research. This involves both recognising the researcher's position as well as the ways in which we impact on our research sites and how this influences the knowledge we produce. Letherby (2003: 6) notes that the 'research field' metaphor is useful in thinking about the fact that 'when we enter a field we make footprints on the land and are likely to disturb the environment. When we leave we may have mud on our shoes, pollen on our clothes.' Therefore, the research process impacts not only on those who are researched but also the researcher.

While I had an interest in anti-austerity activism, I had not previously been very active in the local scene, and having to participate for research purposes enabled me to become more politically active. After the research ended I continued to be involved in local activism and to build friendships with many of my participants, some of whom are now good friends of mine. I also became more involved in administrating Facebook groups and organising events with other activists and have spoken openly about my research to help strengthen groups. While a positivist approach would consider this bias that negatively affects the research, I contend that, following a feminist approach, such experiences enable me to gain a fuller understanding of local activist culture through sharing activist experiences and being immersed in the research setting. The key is to remain critical and to acknowledge my position. Therefore, further detail about the research project and my positionality is provided in Chapter 3.

Participating in the research also had an impact on participants, demonstrating the two-way impact on researcher and researched. Several key local activists found the interview process therapeutic and emotional – as evidenced by Leonie who at the end of a 90-minute interview was visibly emotional, stating 'I feel all emotional now' and speaking about how good it was to remember. Following this interview and others, participants started to speak to each other about their interview experiences and the thoughts and memories that they brought up, which resulted in them deciding to become active again, organising a march that was better attended than any local event in recent years. It would be arrogant and unrealistic to claim that I was the cause of such organising, something I am keen to avoid doing, but it is clear that participating in the research encouraged individuals to speak to each other about activism and to start making steps to reinvigorate local activities. The interview space can often be a 'welcome space for reflection' (Maddison, 2007: 404), which encourages individuals to reflect upon their experiences more than they otherwise would have done. Such reflection has enabled individuals to discuss problems that occurred during Notts Uncut (which had not previously been addressed as a group), to recognise that many of them experienced the same problems and feelings, and to work on finding solutions for these. It is hoped that this book will further contribute to such conversations and attempts to challenge the problematic features of activist culture.

Chapter outline

This book is organised into four parts. The first part establishes the theoretical and empirical context; the second part explores the enabling and constraining factors of political participation ('doing activism'); the third part discusses the two main activist identity constructions in the local anti-austerity activist culture and the 'dark side' of activist culture that these feed ('being activist'); the fourth and final part provides concluding remarks about the ambivalence of anti-austerity activist culture and the difficulty of resisting such a pervasive force as neoliberal capitalism.

Chapter 2, 'A Critical Review of Social Movement Theory: Gender and Emotion in Activist Cultures', sets up the theoretical context of the book. It begins by establishing the key relevant debates in SMT, including that of new versus old social movements, the influence of new media technologies on social movements and the role of emotions within social movement studies. This chapter identifies the theoretical perspective for studying activist culture, drawing on Bourdieu's (1992) theory of practice. This will serve as the basis for developing an analysis of the affective and cultural dimensions of social movement activism. It is contended that this approach enables the development of in-depth 'thick description' (Geertz, 1973) and an understanding of the interactions between activists as well as between the activist field and the wider social and political context, which is a theme threaded throughout the book.

The chapter highlights feminist critiques of mainstream (or 'malestream') SMT's failure to recognise the importance of gender to theorising social movements. This is contextualised by a wider discussion about the gendered exclusions that exist within the public sphere.

In the next chapter, 'The Empirical and Political Context of Anti-Austerity Activism', an overview of the political context is provided, with a focus on austerity and how this forms part of the wider neoliberal project. The chapter establishes the ways in which austerity is gendered, classed and racialised, themes that will be drawn on throughout the book when exploring resistance to austerity. It moves from setting this wider context to an in-depth description of the specific anti-austerity activist culture that is explored in this book. This involves identifying the key movements and groups in the local context, as well as key features of these movements, such as their positioning as a 'new' form of politics that is outside the system and the centrality of social media to political organising in this context.

In Part II, Chapter 4, 'The Affective, the Normative, and the Everyday: Exploring What Motivates and Sustains Anti-Austerity Activism', explores what motivates and sustains anti-austerity activism within the context of continued austerity. It affirms the centrality of the affective and normative dimensions of political engagement by demonstrating that anti-austerity activism is motivated and sustained by three core elements; emotion, morality and relationship. Individuals are motivated by an emotional response to perceived injustice combined with normative ideals about how society should be and how we should act in relation to others. They utilise notions of humanity and empathy to combat the dehumanising effect of neoliberal capitalism and its focus on individualism and competition. Participants translate such abstract, universal concepts into concrete, particular actions through a focus on everyday activism and individual choices. Rather than an outright rejection of individualism, participants seek to redefine it in ways that move away from the dominant neoliberal understanding and towards reconciling the individual with the wider collective and common good. Here, activism is conceptualised as a moral duty. Participants therefore suggest that everyone and anyone can and should do activism, with small acts making a difference. This chapter begins to unpick the ways in which activists resist, subvert and sometimes unwittingly reinforce neoliberal capitalism, as well as questioning the problematic distinction drawn between 'non-activist' and 'activist'.

Chapter 5, 'Barriers to Doing Activism,' then discusses the costs (financial, physical, psychological and emotional) associated with doing activism. While participants speak about activism in terms of the everyday and suggest that it is something anyone can do, they often do not acknowledge the privilege required to do activism. This chapter draws out the tensions present in the notion that everyone can and should do activism by exploring the barriers and exclusions that prevent individuals from participating politically. This includes the reality that those who are hardest hit by austerity often do not have the resources to protest against it. Therefore, while lived experiences of issues are deemed to be a key and authentic motivation for doing activism (a topic that is explored further in Chapter 6), it becomes clear that those who are most affected by austerity are less able to protest against it because of its effects.

Despite women being disproportionately affected by austerity, this chapter reveals the continuing and heightening gendered barriers that exist in the specific context of austerity and a local anti-austerity activist culture that privileges questions of class over those of gender. It demonstrates how, in response, women are forming their own feminist resistance to austerity, and explores how this is empowering but problematic because it upholds austerity through the provision of unpaid care in the absence of public services.

Part III opens with Chapter 6, 'The Authentic and Ideal Activist Identities: Having the "Right" Motivation and Doing "Enough" of the "Right" Type of Activism'. This chapter explores the ways in which the activist identity is constructed and negotiated within local anti-austerity activist culture. It begins by establishing the shared meanings and context-specific nature of the term before discussing in more detail the two main constructions of the activist identity present in participants' narratives. The first identity is the 'authentic' activist who has the required lived experiences to possess the authority to speak about certain topics. Having explored barriers that prevent individuals and groups from doing activism under the question of who *can* do activism in Chapter 5, this chapter considers the question of who *should* do activism, according to participants.

The second main construction of the activist identity that this chapter explores is the 'ideal activist', which is defined by the type and amount of activism one does. In order to be considered an ideal activist, individuals must do 'enough' of the 'right' type of activism (direct action rather than online activism). This chapter demonstrates that the ideal activist identity is underpinned by the distinction participants draw between talking and doing, which feeds into the construction of direct, offline action as the pinnacle of 'real' activism versus online 'slacktivism'. The final section of this chapter interrogates this artificial dichotomy and reveals the enabling features of online activism, as well as the ways in which both forms of activism interact, rather than conflict.

In Chapter 7, 'The Dark Side of Activist Culture and its Gendered Dimension', I explore what I have called the 'dark side' of activist culture because of its negative effects and the fact that it is hidden from public view. It illustrates the negative aspects, including how the activist identity is maintained and policed by other activists through practices of shaming. It examines the implications of such practices and of the ideal activist identity, focusing on 'activist burnout' and its relation to care (or a lack of it) within activist culture. While the ideal activist is constructed within the local anti-austerity activist culture as an abstract individual, this chapter argues that it is actually the white, able-bodied male, given the criteria that define it. Significantly, this chapter asserts that the implicit gendered nature of the ideal activist identity and its damaging gendered consequences are not recognised, resulting in gendered symbolic violence – with women feeling guilt and blaming themselves for their perceived failure to adequately perform the identity. This chapter thus reveals the complex ways in which spaces of resistance can reinforce dominant gendered power structures, while ostensibly fighting against them.

Finally, in Part IV, Chapter 8, 'Subverting/Reinforcing Neoliberalism: The Complex Ambivalence of Anti-Austerity Activism', concludes the book by discussing the ambivalence and complexity of anti-austerity activist culture and the difficulty of resisting a force that is as pervasive as neoliberal capitalism, raising questions about how this can be more effectively achieved and asserting the importance of paying attention to the messy reality of social movement activism. It suggests that, moving forwards, there is a need for further in-depth 'thick description' of the complex processes of activist cultures that reveal the contradictions, tensions, and advantages of the internal dynamics and how they interact with the wider political context. It reminds us that resistance does not exist within a vacuum and that it is important to consider the multiple facets of political participation, and the implicit power relations that exist, in order to both better understand and change future political intervention. Finally, it considers limitations of the research this book draws on and suggests future directions for research.

Overall, this book presents a critical in-depth analysis of a local anti-austerity activist culture, focusing on the affective and cultural dimensions of political engagement, and utilising a feminist approach to explore the gendered aspects of social movement participation. The book thus firmly re-focuses SMT on the often neglected affective and cultural aspects of political participation and crosses the boundary between social movement and feminist theory, exploring the overlap. In line with feminist research practice, it is hoped that this book will enable local activist groups to reflect on their practices, to begin communicating about ways to improve the negative aspects of activist cultures, as well as to acknowledge and celebrate the positive elements. Therefore, the book utilises the research setting of anti-austerity activism in Nottingham to provide a nuanced, in-depth understanding of the making and practising of activist culture, highlighting both the enabling and constraining factors that impact upon individuals' potential to become politically active during times of crisis. It is important to note that just as it is bounded to a particular location, the research that this book draws on is also a snapshot of a particular historical moment, and as such we must be careful of over-generalisation. Nevertheless, it is argued that this book has wider relevance and implications given what it reveals about gendered experiences of activism, and the ambivalent and complex relationship between neoliberal capitalism and spaces that seek to resist it. The transferability of the research findings has been reinforced by my own and others' experiences and discussions of various forms of activism in different localities.

PART I

Establishing Context

Part I provides both the theoretical and empirical context, beginning in Chapter 2 with an exploration of the key theoretical debates that inform this book and to which it contributes. Chapter 3 provides a more detailed exploration of the research project, the specific political context of austerity and the local context of anti-austerity activism.

2

A Critical Review of Social Movement Theory: Gender and Emotion in Activist Cultures

This chapter provides the theoretical context of the research. It begins by establishing the key relevant debates in SMT, including new versus old social movements, the influence of new media technologies on social movements and the role of emotions within social movement studies. This chapter identifies the theoretical perspective for studying activist cultures, drawing on Bourdieu's (1992) theory of practice. This serves as the basis for developing an analysis of the affective and cultural dimensions of social movements. This approach enables the development of in-depth 'thick description' (Geertz, 1973) and an understanding of the interactions between activists as well as between the activist field and the wider social and political context, which is a theme that is threaded throughout. Critically, this chapter highlights feminist critiques of mainstream (or 'malestream') SMT's failure to recognise the importance of gender to theorising social movements. This is contextualised by a wider discussion about the gendered exclusions that exist within the public sphere.

Social movement theory: old versus new movements

Broadly speaking, mainstream SMT can be categorised in terms of three distinct waves. The first considered social movements as abnormal and irrational, and studied their emergence in order to prevent future movements occurring. This viewpoint has long been abandoned in favour of viewing social movements as 'politics by other means' (Goodwin et al, 2000: 69). However, the earlier positioning of social movements as 'irrational' resulted in a desire to distance SMT from emotions (which are traditionally conceived of in opposition to reason). The second wave was concerned instead with depicting social movements as collectives of rational actors engaged in instrumental action. One of the dominant theories here is resource mobilisation theory (RMT) (McCarthy and Zald, 1977), which focuses on how rational actors make calculated decisions to secure the resources required for mobilisation. Further, second wave theories of collective action were largely grounded in a Marxist tradition, which viewed movements in economic terms as the struggle between the working class (or the proletariat) and the ruling class within an industrial society defined by production. In response to both this Marxist tradition and RMT, the third wave of SMT sought to develop an understanding of the symbolic and cultural features of newly emerging social movements post-1960s, especially in the 1980s and early 1990s. The dominant theory that characterises this third wave is new social movement theory (NSMT). Given its prominence within social movement studies and the questions it raises for a case such as anti-austerity activism and about the role of gender in social movements, I will now discuss NSMT in more detail.

NSMT enables us to consider the cultural and symbolic aspects of collective action, as well as the social processes of political engagement that occur at the micro- and meso-levels, which risk being neglected in favour of focusing on rationality and the macro-, structural level of collective action. Melucci (1996: 9) contends that 'in contemporary societies [...] power operates through the languages and codes which organize the flow of information'. Social movements must therefore interrupt and challenge the dominant codes in order to exercise power. Further, Melucci (1984: 830) stresses the importance of social movement cultures, asserting that collective identity is not merely a strategy to achieve certain ends but a goal in itself: 'since the action is focused on cultural codes, the *form* of the movement is a message, a symbolic challenge to the dominant patterns'.

At the same time, NSMT connects the micro- and meso-levels of analysis to the macro-level by situating social movements within the socio-historical moment from which they emerge and considering the impact of this context. It is here that we see the emergence of two of the key features that distinguish 'new' social movements from 'old' movements; namely, which social problems they are concerned with and who constitutes the movements. It is argued that while 'old' social movements emerged within an industrial context and were thus concerned with material questions of wages, wealth distribution and class relations, 'new' social movements emerged within a post-industrial, post-material age in which a shift has occurred towards post-material values and conflicts about identity, lifestyle and culture. This shift in the socio-economic landscape supposedly resulted in a change in who participates in social movements, with the emergence of a new highly educated middle class usurping the working-class participants and concerns of 'old' movements in the context of a post-industrial society centred around the production of knowledge and information rather than material goods.

Anti-austerity activism problematises the distinction NSMT draws between 'old' and 'new' social movements in terms of the 'what' and 'who' questions. Della Porta (2015: 23) contradicts the notion that contemporary movements are largely constituted by the middle class, noting that within the European context research 'signals the presence of a coalition of various social actors which tend to identify themselves as belonging to the lower classes'. She asserts that it is the people who are directly affected by austerity who participate, reflecting Habermas's (1998: 365) contention that problems should be raised and discussed by 'those who are potentially affected'.

At the same time, Della Porta (2015: 79) draws attention to the populist character of anti-austerity movements; in the vein of Laclau (2005), she defines populism as a 'political logic [...] the naming, the construction of the people as a way of breaking order and reconstructing it'. She demonstrates throughout her research that those protesting against austerity proclaim 'we are normal, common people' (Della Porta, 2015: 100), a claim that is most evident in Occupy's 'we are the 99 per cent' sentiment (though there have been criticisms about the actual make-up of the movement, which I will not go into here). In this respect, Peterson et al (2013: 18) contend that anti-austerity protestors 'take a political power approach to class which saw society divided between two opposing classes: a "them" representing an economic elite and a political elite and an "us" that are the unjust victims'. Therefore, anti-austerity movements challenge NSMT's assertion that a specific target in the form of a privileged class no longer exists within a post-material world. We can interpret protestors' framing of 'us versus them' in terms of Marxist understandings of the working class as those who do not own the means of production in opposition to the elites who do. Furthermore, it could also be a deliberate decision not to differentiate between the working and middle class but to regard these identities as united 'in a common struggle against the "upper" class of "them"' (Peterson et al, 2013: 18).

However, this focus on economic populism is problematic as it relies on 'an essentialised and homogenised construction of "the people" against the "elites", which is hostile to – and seeks to displace – specific racial and gender justice claims' (Bassel and Emejulu, 2018: 26). This results in what Bassel and Emejulu (2018: 26) call 'exclusionary universalism', where a unified (implicitly white and male) working class is the single axis on which resistance to austerity is built. This feature of Left politics has a history that pre-dates austerity; Hall (1988) draws attention to the problem of the 'Socialist Man' who exemplified patriarchal values and the Left's inability to account for pluralism and difference. In this respect, Hall (1988: 194) draws attention to and criticises the traditionalism of the Left, which is deeply embedded in Left movements and the working class, and which, for Hall, explains 'why and where racism and sexism lurk' (Hall, 1988: 194). Yet Bassel and Emejulu (2018) draw attention to the 'dangerous myths' the Left constructs about itself in terms of its movements being open and inclusive for all marginalised groups, which results in racialised and gendered exclusions and an inability to challenge them. Thus, as Coleman and Bassi (2011: 205) contend, by ignoring difference and internal power relations, resistance politics 'may shore up the status quo even as it undermines it'. This is a key criticism of anti-austerity politics, which I will return to in Chapters 5, 6, 7 and 8.

Despite stating that the majority of participants identify as the lower classes, Della Porta (2015: 54) remarks that 'what activists as well as observers stressed the most, was the extraordinary social diversity in the protestors' backgrounds'. As Fuchs (2005: 11) argues, '[C]lass and social movements no longer coincide, movements are made up by people stemming from different social classes, people from classes endowed with high cultural capital are more likely to engage in protest than others'. At first glance, this statement seems contradictory, as traditionally it tends to be the middle class who possess more cultural capital, and thus if those with more cultural capital are more likely to participate, we would expect movements to be largely constituted by the middle class, as NSMT posits. However, in recent years we have witnessed the rise of a class of individuals who are often highly educated (and thus possess high levels of cultural capital) but lack job security or employment opportunities because of the current socio-economic climate, rendering them in a 'precarious' position. Here, we see a clear example of how social class has transformed and become more complex in recent years. Reinforcing Fuchs's (2005) contention that those with higher levels of cultural capital are more likely to participate in movements, there has been increasing participation in anti-austerity movements by this highly educated but insecurely (un)employed class (Della Porta, 2015).

Despite a focus on the questions of who constitutes social movements and what their concerns are, NSMT has paid little attention to the role of gender. Roseneil (1995: 16) remarks that while NSMT explores the impact of economic restructuring and changes in the historical context, 'there is little to no mention of one of the most significant economic changes of the post-war period – women's entry into the labor force'. This significant change impacts on who participates in social movements as well as what their concerns are, as 'old' social movements tended to be made up of working-class men who, unlike women at the time, had access to the labour force. Charles (2000: 32) reinforces that while attention has been paid to how participants of NSM are the new middle class, there has been less notice of the way in which women comprise NSM as 'mothers, sisters and partners, [who] far outnumber men as clients of social services. Their experience thus predisposes them towards action.'

NSMT's neglect of gender reveals its inadequacies at explaining feminist social movements. NSMT's suggestion that social movements are now oriented towards civil society rather than the state is inappropriate for women's movements of the 1970s and 1980s where politics and the state, as well as cultural innovation, were central. Furthermore, Smith (1988) contends that NSMT's argument that material production has been replaced by the production of signs is gendered (and classed), with men of the non-labouring classes being able to abstract themselves from the material production of daily life, something that is not so easy for women and the labouring classes. It appears that women's movements are problematic for NSMT precisely because they straddle both so-called 'old' and 'new' movement concerns. This is recognised by Touraine (1985) and Habermas (1981), who seek to solve the problem by not considering such movements as (new) social movements at all, though this solution is clearly inadequate (and, as with most theory that invokes 'newness', NSMT has been criticised for potentially over-emphasising the split between so-called 'old' and 'new' movements).

We arrive at the question of whether anti-austerity movements fit satisfactorily within this category of 'new' social movement. Most obviously, anti-austerity movements have emerged within a post-material and post-industrial socio-economic context and utilise strategies outside mainstream political institutions, which align them with new social movements. However, in terms of the movements' participants, despite evoking populism, Della Porta (2015) demonstrates that participants within anti-austerity movements tend to identify as the 'lower classes' and are those who are affected by austerity. This distinguishes anti-austerity movements from 'new' movements that are perceived to be constituted mainly by the middle classes. Furthermore, despite not relating to class relations in traditional terms, as was the case in 'old' social movements, anti-austerity politics *is* concerned with material questions of redistribution and welfare, implying that when it comes to the types of topics addressed, anti-austerity movements fit within the 'old' movement category. Yet, as we shall see in Chapter 4, the movements' concerns are wider than this and constitute what has been termed 'post-materialist' values, such as morality and humanism.

Given the complexity of who takes part and what topics the movement is concerned with (in other words, the answers to the original 'who' and 'what' questions posed at the beginning of this section), it is clear that anti-austerity activism, like women's movements, does not fall into either the 'new' or 'old' category of social movements. Reflecting this, Giugni and Grasso (2015: 12) suggest that anti-austerity movements are 'new old social movements' that share a number of characteristics with 'old' social movements in terms of addressing inequality, struggling for social justice and socio-economic rights, but do so in a 'new form determined by the contemporary post-industrial, neoliberal context'. We arrive at a point, then, where NSMT's division of so-called 'old' and 'new' movement concerns reveals the theory's inadequacies for understanding movements such as women's movements and anti-austerity movements. It is here that Fraser's (2013) discussion of the politics of redistribution and recognition, and its specific relevance for considering questions of gender in social movements, is useful.

Fraser (2013) critiques the shift in feminist politics away from structural quasi-Marxist understandings of gender towards identity-based conceptions of gender. She highlights the very real risk of undoing the economic and political gains made by earlier feminist movements through replacing their focus on distribution of material resources with a focus on recognition and difference. Furthermore, she contends that this shift towards cultural struggles 'dovetailed all too neatly with a hegemonic neoliberalism that wants nothing more than to repress socialist memory' (Fraser, 2013: 160). In this respect, Fraser touches upon the ways in which neoliberalism infiltrates and influences spaces of resistance, a key theme that this book will pick up in Chapters 5, 6, 7, and 8.

Critically, Fraser (2013) asserts that we need to undo and overcome the false distinction that has been drawn between the politics of redistribution and recognition. She uses the example of gender as a 'two-dimensional concept' to demonstrate this. Rather than viewing gender through either the lens of distribution, as a political economic category, or through the lens of recognition, as an identity and status, we need to view gender 'bifocally – simultaneously through two lenses' (Fraser, 2013: 162). Doing so enables us to conceive of gender as a two-dimensional category concerned with both politics of redistribution and recognition, and to thus make claims for both. She recognises that these categories exist independently of each other, and that the question may arise about which is more important (though this is not her focus); but, crucially, she asserts that the two types of politics (or, in NSMT's language, 'old' and 'new' concerns of movements) are not antithetical. Fraser's (2013) theory thus offers us a useful way of understanding the concerns of movements such as the women's liberation movement and anti-austerity movements.

Networked social movements

In response to movements such as the Arab Spring (2010–12), which combined the use of communication technologies and public spaces for political protest, Castells (2012: 15) has argued that we are witnessing the emergence of 'a new species of social movement', which he calls 'networked movements'. Such movements tend to be leaderless, organised online, with no official membership but a 'network' of connected individuals that may be dispersed geographically. Though we should be careful when asserting the newness of movements (as demonstrated above), networked movements appear to share distinctive features that were not previously prominent. The most obvious of these is that they harness the power of online networks for political mobilisation, raising questions about the role and use of the internet, and particularly social media, within contemporary movements. The term 'networked movements' emphasises their rhizomatic character with multiple connections and roots, reflecting the way such movements tend to be organised horizontally rather than vertically. This reflects a shift from traditional hierarchically structured organisations and indicates how the internet provides people with new communicative possibilities.

However, it is important not to lose sight of the ways in which online and offline arenas of political action interact. Indeed, while Castells (2012) acknowledges the role that new media technologies played in connecting individuals and sparking dissent, he argues that the Egyptian revolution of 2011 would not have been possible without public spaces. The role of public space in contemporary movements characterised by online networks is especially pressing in the context of neoliberalism, which seeks to privatise public spaces.

Yet, despite evidence of the interaction between online and offline spaces of political engagement, critics of online activism worry that individuals will substitute traditional offline forms of political action with online forms that are ineffective. Here, so-called 'slacktivism' (emphasising the lack of effort involved) is perceived to be easy and to alleviate the guilt that individuals feel for not participating politically. There are several key assumptions underlying this substitution theory that need to be interrogated and explored empirically. First, it is assumed that people who engage with online activism do so as a replacement for offline activism, in which they would otherwise be taking part. However, it could be the case that online activism is an additional layer of participation. Loader and Mercea (2012) demonstrate that people who are the most likely to become involved online are those who are highly active offline. Furthermore, a key problem is how online activism is narrowly defined and understood. Critics in particular tend to refer either to email tactics and e-petitions or 'clicktivism', where one 'likes' a Facebook page or changes one's Facebook profile picture to demonstrate support for a cause. This is problematic as it neglects the ways in which online activism encompasses a wide range of activities, including discussions, (offline) event organising, publicity, group formation, spreading information and raising awareness, among others. Therefore, throughout this book I will be referring to online activism as another form of activism that involves a diverse range of activities.

Contrary to critics' beliefs, online activism 'entails the *symbolic construction of a sense of togetherness*' (Gerbaudo, 2012: 14). Papacharissi (2015: 7) explores how affect is produced within networks on Twitter, examining 'what these mediated feelings of connectedness do for politics and publics networked together through the storytelling infrastructures of a digital age'. In the same way, Castells (2012: 173) highlights how Occupy utilised the 'power of personal narrative' by using Tumblr so people could tell their stories online. He suggests that this process 'humanizes' the movement and, like Papacharissi (2015) and Gerbaudo (2012), Castells (2012: 225) contends that 'horizontal multimodal networks, both on the Internet and in the urban space, create togetherness'. Such networked movements create and sustain collective identities and solidarity within the context of an increasingly fragmented and heterogeneous society, often mobilising emotions. We start to see here the centrality of everyday experiences, ideas of humanity and emotions – themes that are central to this book.

On the one hand, new media technologies such as the internet are extolled as holding the potential to transform political participation due to their ability to encourage citizens to become active. On the other hand, it is argued that these claims are overly optimistic and that new media technologies actually contribute to the fragmentation of the public sphere, producing radical enclaves that speak to themselves. It is important to distinguish between recognising technology's potential uses and reifying it to a position of power in and of itself. While there is much debate about whether the internet constitutes a virtual public sphere, I am primarily concerned with the interaction between online and offline political participation in this book. I will therefore be exploring how online and offline spaces for political action are constructed by activists in relation to one another. A key question that emerges is the extent to which the internet overcomes or heightens traditional exclusions and barriers to political participation in the public sphere. It is important to keep in mind that the subject of and related literature about new media technologies is constantly evolving, in line with technological advances and how people utilise them. Therefore, conclusions drawn about the internet are transient and situated within a particular time and place.

Taking into account the ways in which UK Uncut is organised through the internet and how it combines this with public spaces for political action, along with its horizontal structure, we can refer to UK Uncut as a networked movement. However, the other key anti-austerity movement that will be explored in this book – the People's Assembly Against Austerity – is structured in a more vertical manner, reflecting traditional organisational structures, and places less emphasis on the role of networks and social media. Therefore, this movement does not fit Castells' (2012) definition of networked movements. Moreover, I will be exploring a diverse range of anti-austerity activism outside and overlapping with these two key groups. Given the heterogeneity of the research setting and the lack of an over-arching clearly defined 'movement' (which is why I have referred to anti-austerity movements in the plural), combined with the epistemological decision to avoid conceiving of social movements as externally existing fixed and unitary objects, I will instead be referring to 'anti-austerity activism' throughout. Of course, there are issues concerning how 'activism' is defined and understood, and this is a key topic that this book will explore. For now, I am using a wide definition of activism that incorporates participation in protests, direct action, online petitions and campaigns, and community groups that are focused on resisting austerity. However, it is noted that the term is fluid and that this definition is open to revision.

This section has been concerned with outlining the relevant theoretical debates within social movement studies and identifying key gaps in the theory, beginning with an overview of the three waves of SMT. As I noted at the outset, the second wave was concerned with distancing itself from theories of movements that perceived actors to be irrational and thus neglected the role of emotions. Here, the influence of the traditional binary construction of reason versus emotion persists, thereby tying emotion to irrationality, meaning that any concern with rationality presupposes the irrelevance of emotion. Notably, this binary construction is tied to other binaries including public/private and male/female, where the former is valued as superior and the latter is perceived to be inferior. Indeed, Goodwin et al (2001: 15) remark that emotions have 'regularly fallen on the 'bad' side of a number of prominent dichotomies in Western thought'. Further, Ahmed (2014: 3) notes that 'feminist philosophers have shown us how the subordination of emotions also works to subordinate the feminine and the body'. We start to see the connections between gender and emotion, two dimensions that require further theorising within social movement studies; I will explore them further in this chapter and seek to make them visible throughout this book. While we have seen that Castells (2012) brings emotions into his theory of networked movements, I contend that his study of the processes of emotional mobilisation, its connection to morality and the role of emotions more generally within political engagement is underdeveloped. Further, Castells (2012), like many other social movement theorists, neglects to consider the role of gender in the emergence, organisation and continuing of social movements. It is here that this book will make a contribution, by providing a cultural, affective and feminist exploration of anti-austerity activism.

Social movements and emotions

We have seen that since the 1960s there has been a focus in social movement studies on explanations of collective action that assume individuals are rational, calculating social actors concerned with the costs and benefits of political participation. Alongside this there has also been a focus on the macro-, structural level of social movements. In response, we witnessed a cultural turn in social movement research beginning in the 1980s with theories of framing and New Social Movements and continuing in the 1990s with a focus on narratives and discourse. However, this cultural turn has its limitations, and has tended to focus on the cognitive aspects of movement activities rather than the emotional. Benford (1997: 419) notes that:

> Those operating within the framing/constructivist perspective have not fared much better than their structuralist predecessors in elaborating the role of emotions in collective action. Instead, we continue to write as though our movement actors (when we actually acknowledge humans in our texts) are Spock-like beings, devoid of passion and other human emotions.

Over a decade and a half later, Della Porta (2013) affirms that despite the growing prominence of cultural approaches to social movement studies, researchers remain reluctant to focus on emotions. The cognitive bias reveals an underlying assumption that emotion and thinking are two separate functions. Williams's structures of feeling (1977: 132) sidesteps the harsh opposition often constructed between thinking and feeling: 'not feeling against thought, but thought as felt and feeling as thought'. Likewise, Alexander (2006: 53) draws attention to the role of feeling as well as thinking in political engagement and argues for an analysis of 'the critical role of solidarity'. Durkheim (2002 [1925]: 85) emphasises the social aspect of morality as a key factor that strengthens groups internally and suggests that the social and the moral always go together. Crucially, such a focus does not remove rationality but transcends the archaic dichotomy of reason versus emotion and instead puts forwards the notion that 'emotions underpin rather than contradict the rationality of action and that emotions are an integrated and sometimes explicit part of social movement activities' (Wettergren, 2009: 1).

A key question concerns what motivates people to participate in politics. While a rational consensus model may be appealing, Habermas's seminal model of the public sphere neglects to adequately explain *why* we should want to act rationally. When approaching this question, I argue that we need to pay attention to the affective dimension of political participation. Whereas the deliberative model of the public sphere encourages the putting aside of passions in order to render rational consensus possible, Mouffe (2005) argues that it is precisely those passions that require mobilising in order to produce democracy. However, Mouffe's (2005) theory overly focuses on conflict within the public sphere and, as Alexander (2006: 43) asserts, 'it is not only difference that sustains democracy, but solidarity and commonality'. Yet Alexander (2006: 53) notes that there is a silence 'about the sphere of fellow feelings, the we-ness that makes society into society [...] and the processes that fragment it'. I intend to break this silence by exploring the processes of how solidarity and collective identities are created, as well as how they are threatened, within the context of anti-austerity activism. Such an investigation challenges the recent shift away from the study of collective identities within sociology that we have witnessed with the rise in theories of reflexive modernisation that emphasise individualism above collectivism.

In order to develop an understanding of the processes of solidarity and collective identity, it is necessary to pay close attention to the lived experiences of individuals' day-to-day lives, investigating how such processes occur within a particular setting. Despite writing over a decade ago, Alexander's (2006: 115) assertion that 'we need to develop a model of democratic societies that pays more attention to solidarity and social values – to what and how people speak, think and feel about politics than most social science theories do today'. This involves recognising the construction of symbolic codes that are drawn upon by groups and form the basis of the narratives that communities construct. A central part of translating traditionally abstract, normative concepts is to look at the concrete, everyday experiences of citizens and the symbolic codes that they invoke. Alexander (2006: 551) asserts that 'rather than an abstract deduction of philosophers, the normative stipulations of civil society turn out to be the language of the street'. This book investigates the significance of the normative in mobilising and sustaining political participation and the ways in which movements articulate such normative values in everyday language and acts.

Focusing on the everyday lived experiences of political engagement reminds us of the need to consider not only the initial engagement phase of movement participation, but also how participation is sustained. Yet social movement literature has tended to focus on how individuals become mobilised and are recruited to movements, which is the main place where emotions are mentioned. This reveals a further criticism of traditional rationalistic approaches to social movements, namely their focus on strategy and effectiveness. Here a concern is with 'how' social actors become mobilised, rather than 'why' they do, where the affective dimension plays a central role. A key question that emerges, then, is the role of the affective not only in motivating but also in sustaining political engagement. In order to answer this, I contend that we need to explore wider activist cultures that are 'submerged and woven into the fabric of daily life' (Melucci, 1989: 95).

Activist cultures

Activist cultures are not a fixed reified 'thing' but active and continual processes of interaction. In attempting to conceptualise and understand this notion, Calhoun and Sennett's (2007) analysis of culture as practised is a useful departure point. They remark that (2007: 5) 'Too often the sociology of culture takes on the static character of a sociology of cultural products. It is a study of paintings not painting [...] culture is practice: embodied, engaged, interactive, creative and contested.'

Likewise, Thompson (1963: 9) stresses the *making* of the English working class. Emphasising the active process and effort involved, he uses the word *making* because 'it is a study in an active process, which owes as much to agency as to conditioning. The working class did not rise like the sun at an appointed time. It was present at its own making'. Thompson's (1963: 9) approach emphasises both relationships and the active processes involved in the making of cultures, as well as the need to pay attention to particular settings: 'I do not see class as a "structure", nor even as a "category", but as something which in fact happens (and can be shown to have happened) in human relationships [...] [t]his relationship must always be embodied in real people and in a real context.'

However, Thompson arguably neglects structure in his focus on agency and the relational aspects of class. Instead, Bourdieu's (1992) theory of practice reconciles agency and structure by combining the interconnection of individuals' dispositions (habitus), their position within a field (capital), and the state of play within a particular social arena (field). This is a simplified overview of the key elements of his theory, represented by the equation *(habitus) (capital) + field = practice* (Bourdieu, 1984: 101). Crossley (2002: 171) condenses Bourdieu's theory of practice by arguing that 'Social practices are generated through the interaction of agents, who are both differently disposed and unequally resourced, within the bounds of specific networks which have a game-like structure and which impose definite restraints upon them.'

Crucially, Bourdieu offers 'a theory of structure as both *structured (opus operatum*, and thus open to objectification) and *structuring (modus operandi*, and thus generative of thought and action)' (Grenfell, 2008: 45). Bourdieu (1984; 1992) thus provides a theory that can aid our understanding of how specific activist cultures are constituted and their dynamics, or, in other words, the processes of 'making' and 'practising' activist cultures. I will now expand upon the key concepts of Bourdieu's (1992) theory of practice to demonstrate their usefulness for exploring activist cultures.

The complex notion of habitus acts as 'a hinge between agency and structure' by explaining the ways in which individuals act in situations according to their pre-existing dispositions, schemas and attitudes, which in turn are influenced by social structures (Crossley, 2002: 177). It entails the 'embodied competence or know-how' that provides individuals with a 'feel for the game' (Crossley, 2002: 176). There is a sense, then, that habitus forms and acts at an un- or subconscious level and is carried within one's body. Demonstrating the way in which habitus connects agency and structure, Crossley (2002: 172) remarks that 'we make ourselves in particular ways, in response to the conditions we find ourselves in'. Intimately linked to habitus is doxa, which comprises the taken-for-granted practices that we perceive to be natural within a particular context. Both of these terms relate to the specific 'field', or social space, within which an individual participates. In order to understand interactions, we need to understand the social space within which they occur.

We can therefore conceive of an activist field with shared discourses, rules, beliefs and understandings, or activist habitus and doxa, to use Bourdieu's terminology (1992). Fields are structured spaces organised around different types of capital that individuals struggle to control. Portwood-Stacer's (2013) study of anarchist activist culture demonstrates that symbolic (status and reputation) and social (connections that can be used to the individual's advantage) capital are at stake in the activist field. Portwood-Stacer (2013: 21) suggests that 'subcultural capital' is awarded to those who abide by anarchist norms, which is defined by the extent to which an individual deviates from mainstream norms.

It is necessary for boundaries to be constructed that define the activist field and, in the process, determine 'insiders' and 'outsiders'. The negotiation of these boundaries and identities results in internal hierarchies that are enforced by how 'individuals discipline themselves and their peers in line with accepted lifestyle norms' (Portwood-Stacer 2013: 5). Radical movements thus constitute their own hegemonic spheres, or 'an alternative hegemony' with rules that members are encouraged to adhere to (Denning, 1996: 63).

Bourdieu's (1992) theory of practice enables an exploration of both the interactions between activists, including the power dynamics at play, and the wider space within which activist practices occur and from which protest emerges. It therefore draws our attention to the cultural dimension of political engagement without neglecting wider structural forces and context. Indeed, cultural fields do not exist in isolation but have porous boundaries, permeating and being permeated by other fields, with boundary construction (and policing) being a further area of struggle. In particular, the issue of who is to be included within particular fields, and ergo who is to be excluded, is fought over, opening space for discussion about how individual and collective identities within activist fields are established and maintained, or achieved.

Therefore, questions are raised about how a common political identity is constructed within the context of anti-austerity activist cultures, given how the movements' participants frame themselves as 'ordinary people', and the '99 per cent', which problematises where the boundaries are constructed and what it means to be an activist within this context. Furthermore, the context of heterogeneous, loose, networked movements adds another layer to this, as again it is unclear where (or whether) boundaries exist, which provokes enquiry into the extent to which solidarity can be fostered and maintained.

Studies have increasingly demonstrated the important role played by collective and individual identities in sustaining social movement participation (Melucci, 1989; Gamson, 1992). Exploring the intersection between emotion and identity, Goodwin et al (2001: 9) remark that 'the "strength" of an identity, even a cognitively vague one, comes from its emotional side'. Taylor (1999) explores this relationship between emotions and identity in her study of women's self-help movements, demonstrating how negative emotions can be translated into more positive understandings of self and collective identity that invoke solidarity and a shared understanding.

Contrastingly, studies of the activist identity reveal how its typical construction as an extraordinary individual (Bobel, 2007; Portwood-Stacer, 2013; Stuart, 2013; Cortese, 2015) often functions as an unreachable standard that results in individuals feeling unworthy of the title. As Brown and Pickerill (2009) identify, this has a negative emotional effect on individuals. Similarly, Jacobsson and Lindblom (2012) recognise that expectations within activist communities result in feelings of guilt when individuals perceive themselves to underperform (though they contend that guilt can function positively as a motivation to do more). While studies identify the negative emotional effects of the extraordinary activist construct, the majority do not recognise the gendered dimension of this. By utilising a feminist approach to explore how the ideal activist identity is constructed within a local anti-austerity activist culture, this book reveals how the construct and its negative emotional effects are implicitly gendered.

Bourdieu's (2001) study of 'masculine domination' is a starting point for understanding how gendered power relations are reproduced in these spaces and how they go unnoticed. He explains the 'paradox of doxa', which is how we respect the order of the world and take it for granted as a given while it is continually constructed and reproduced by our own actions and despite its sometimes negative effects. Crucially, he contends that 'the strength of the masculine order is seen in the fact that it dispenses with justification: the androcentric vision imposes itself as neutral and has no need to spell itself out in discourses aimed at legitimating it' (Bourdieu, 2001: 9). Similarly, feminist theorists have remarked on the ways in which the category of 'universal abstract individual', conceptualised in theories of citizenship, masks the dominance of white middle-class males, a point that I will return to in the next section. Bourdieu's (2001) analysis of masculine domination provides a potential explanation for the absence of gender in mainstream SMT, as such gendered experiences and effects are masked by the wider doxa of society that naturalises masculine domination, conceiving it as neutral.

I now turn to explore questions of gender and political participation in more detail, beginning with a discussion of traditional gendered exclusions from the public sphere. Building on this I will discuss the relationship between gender and political participation more generally, before focusing on the specific context of anti-austerity activism that I will detail in preparation for the coming analysis.

Gender and the public sphere

I have identified the problematic distinction drawn between the public and private spheres and its relation to other binary constructions including reason/emotion and male/female, all of which have influenced the development of mainstream SMT. In order to better understand these constructions and the related absence of gender from SMT, as well as to break down these divides, it is important to consider their theoretical and historical context. While such binary constructions have long existed, Habermas's (1989) theory of the public sphere is a key starting point for exploring questions of women's political participation because of its theoretical influence. Habermas's *Structural Transformation of the Public Sphere* (1989) laid the foundations for the theory of a deliberative public sphere that engaged in rational, critical debate about issues of public concern and the 'common good'. For the purposes of this book I will focus on gendered critiques of the exclusionary nature of Habermas's conceptualisation of the public sphere, using this as a foundation to discuss gender and activism.

In his historical-sociological account, Habermas (1989) attempts both to outline the history of the bourgeois public sphere and to identify its kernel of emancipatory potential. He contends that the emergent bourgeois public sphere challenged the principle of traditional feudal rule and created a new basis for authority: the consensus formed by the rational, critical debate of private persons coming together as a reasoning public. Although limited to property-owning, male citizens in practice, Habermas argues that the bourgeois public sphere held within it the emancipatory potential for universal inclusion (1989: 34). Indeed, Habermas (1989: 34) argues that the bourgeois public sphere rested on the normative ideal that people should be able to participate on an equal footing, with inequalities of status and difference being 'bracketed' so that it is the content of the argument that matters rather than the speaker.

However, Fraser (1992: 113) argues that the 'official' public sphere both rested on and was 'importantly constituted by a number of significant exclusions'. In contrast to Habermas, she presents a darker view of the bourgeois public sphere as ideologically masculine and highlights its many exclusions, including women, working-class men and ethnic minorities. From this perspective, deliberation serves as a 'mask for domination' where 'such bracketing usually works to the advantage of dominant groups in society and to the disadvantage of subordinates' (Fraser, 1992: 113). Fraser (1992: 119) draws attention to the ways in which 'informal impediments' exist that prevent individuals from participating fully and equally, regardless of whether differences are successfully bracketed. Fraser (1992: 126) also remarks that 'participation means being able to speak in one's own voice', which is not possible when classed and gendered modes of communication are discredited or ignored.

Moreover, rather than bracketing and ignoring inequalities, Fraser (1992) contends that it is precisely these differences and inequalities that should be addressed and challenged within the public sphere. Fraser (1992: 124) argues for the existence of conflicting counter-publics, asserting that when they 'emerge in response to exclusions within dominant publics, they help expand discursive space'. Thus, Fraser (1992) illustrates that civil society is a dynamic space where tensions constantly play out between different interest groups, resulting in the pushing of issues previously deemed 'private' into the public domain (for example, domestic violence and abortion rights). It emerges, then, that there are two central forms of exclusion within the public sphere, *who* can enter the debate and *what* issues are addressed, both of which are fundamentally gendered.

We may now begin to trace the ways in which the gendered division between the public and private spheres produces exclusions from political participation. While the bourgeois public sphere is an historical example, Beard (2014) demonstrates the current influence of the public/private boundary, noting that women's voices are still ignored or that, when heard, women are punished for speaking out. Beard (2014: 13) asserts that 'this is not the peculiar ideology of some distant culture. Distant in time it may be. But this is the tradition of gendered speaking – and the theorising of gendered speaking – of which we are still, directly or more often indirectly, the heirs.' Further, women's difficulty in entering the public sphere is reflected by their disproportionate representation within parliament, with only 32 per cent of MPs being women. Not only are women considerably under-represented at higher levels of political power, but when women do occupy political roles they are judged more harshly than their male counterparts, often in relation to their image. The democratic deficit combined with the treatment of women politicians clearly demonstrates the persistence of patriarchal and gendered norms about the role and character of women. Indeed, Einwohner et al (2000: 693) assert that 'Women have traditionally been ignored as political actors because femininity is associated with emotionality and passivity – characteristics that are thought to be at odds with the "masculine" traits of toughness, aggression and objectivity believed necessary for political involvement.' We are reminded of the role of emotions in political engagement, and particularly the persistent influence of and the relationship between the traditional binary categories of public/private, reason/emotion and male/female, where the latter is perceived to be inferior; thus problematising women's contemporary participation in (or exclusion from) the political sphere.

Gender and activism

Research has demonstrated that gendered barriers to participating in activism exist, with studies in the 1960s and 1970s revealing that women were less likely than men to participate in protest. Such studies focused on the recruitment stage of social movements, and discovered that women faced significant structural availability barriers that prevented them from participating in protests. These were tied to the gendered division of reproductive labour, with women tending to be the main caregivers in a household and having the responsibility of maintaining the home, as outlined in the traditional breadwinner/homemaker model.

However, this gendered gap in political participation is supposedly disappearing, and women's participation in social movements is increasing. It has been suggested that in the wider context of an individualised and insecure society, traditional structures such as gender have become less relevant, resulting in the 'detraditionalisation' of society (Beck et al, 1994). The influence of this detraditionalisation thesis is evident within post-feminism, understood here as a 'sensibility' in which a selectively defined feminism is both 'taken into account and repudiated' (Gill and Scharff, 2011: 4). Neoliberalism and post-feminism go hand in hand, with their emphasis on the autonomous woman or girl who makes individual choices without restriction and who excels within the current context.

However, this gendered 'ideal neoliberal subject' is limited to a small section of young, educated and usually middle-class girls, with most women's accessibility to equal opportunities under neoliberalism being restricted. Brown (2015) highlights the gendered contradictions of neoliberal logic. The neoliberal individual is portrayed as an independent, genderless individual who is expected to both care for and invest in themselves. However, this depiction ignores the way in which the 'neoliberal figure is dependent on invisible practices and unnamed others' to be able to fulfil an economic role (Brown, 2015: 104). Overwhelmingly, this invisible infrastructure is constituted by the reproductive labour of women.

The neoliberal subject, then, is not as independent as it first appears; moreover, it is portrayed from a masculinist bourgeois viewpoint and 'nourished by [gendered] sources and qualities themselves not featured in the story' (Brown, 2015: 193). Therefore, gender subordination is both intensified and fundamentally altered in the neoliberal context, where the work and cost of providing eliminated public services is returned disproportionately to women.

The Fawcett Society (2012) draws attention to how women are subject to 'triple jeopardy' within the context of austerity, losing not only their services and jobs providing these services, but also by being expected to fill the newly created service gap, unpaid. Such an expectation reflects traditional gendered notions of caring being women's work, and reinforces the traditional boundaries between the public and private spheres, where women are tied to the domestic, private sphere and men are associated with the public and political spheres. There is a risk that in the context of austerity, previously public concerns are being quietly subsumed, once again, into the private and assumed to be women's domain.

This contradicts the detraditionalisation thesis and instead supports the 'retraditionalisation' thesis proposed by feminists in response to theories about the disappearance of gender structures. Here, traditional gender norms and roles are reinforced under neoliberalism, resulting in the restriction of women's opportunities to participate politically. Yet, problematically, neoliberalist discourses conceive of women as more free, autonomous and capable than ever before. Indeed, women, and young women in particular, are perceived to be 'the ideal neoliberal subject' (Gill and Scharff, 2011). Clearly, there are tensions here that need to be explored further within an empirical context, provoking exploration into the role of gender, gendered barriers to political participation and the effects of neoliberalism on women's lives.

While the gender gap in political participation appears to be closing, individuals' experiences within movements demonstrate the continued influence of wider gender norms and roles. Dodson (2015: 379) notes that 'aggregate gender ideology (widely shared attitudes about gender roles) discourages women from participating in confrontational activism'. He draws attention to how the division of labour within social movements is gendered, with women often being assigned the mundane organisational tasks, which Thorne (1975: 181) termed 'shitwork'. Despite studying a distinctly male-oriented movement in a US context (the draft resistance) during the 1960s, Thorne's (1975) findings have been reinforced over the years (McAdam, 1992; Culley, 2003). McAdam (1992: 1226–7) notes that 'it was not simply that the female volunteers did different jobs than the males, but that the jobs typically assigned to them were seen as less important than those the men did'. In fact, Thorne (1975: 188) contends that 'even when they took the same actions, women and men often met with differential response'. Hence, men are more visible in social movements and given more prestige while women's contributions are not clearly or publicly recognised. Indeed, the environmental group that

Cable (1992: 42) studied emerged from a meeting between two men; what is less known is the fact that it was their wives who encouraged and initiated this meeting. It appears that there are deeply engrained gendered and sexist attitudes towards women participating in politics that result in women's contributions being undervalued or ignored. Culley (2003: 452) reinforces this, identifying ways in which women's gender was used against them, including not being taken seriously by men in meetings, with participants referring to men as 'very condescending'. Such attitudes act as gendered barriers to activism, discouraging women from participating politically.

Moreover, female participants report many instances of sexism and racism within anti-austerity activist spaces (Emejulu and Bassel, 2015; Maiguascha et al, 2016), demonstrating that such spaces often uphold the dominant structural oppressions that they supposedly aim to bring down. While the increased conversation about such occurrences might signal a heightened awareness of sexism and a strengthened feminist consciousness, the lack of serious attention being paid to structural issues of gender oppression within anti-austerity groups' ideological visions and documentation, combined with women's narratives of their experiences in these groups, casts serious doubt on Maiguashca et al's (2016) optimistic claims of a 'feminist turn' within the overarching anti-austerity movement.

Instead, it appears that women and issues of gender (and racial) oppression have been excluded from this wider movement. Where feminist anti-austerity activism occurs it tends to be isolated from these main groups and organised by women for women, as Chapter 5 will show. Emejulu (2017) demonstrates that minority women activists were often excluded from anti-austerity movements when they attempted to raise gendered and racialised critiques of austerity, and attributes this to the incompatibility of difference with a populist movement where 'There could be no space for analyses and actions that centred race and gender since these supposedly "controversial issues" could potentially fracture the unified "people"' (Emejulu, 2017: 64). A gendered analysis of anti-austerity activism is especially important within the theoretical context of the supposed detraditionalisation of gendered roles and norms, and an empirical context where women are being disproportionately affected by austerity. Questions are raised about the extent to which we are actually witnessing a 'retraditionalisation' of gender.

It becomes clear that we need to study individuals' experiences within social movements, including the differences between experiences, and pay attention to the gendered dimension of these. McAdam (1992: 1212) observes that in the literature activists are seen as distinguishable from non-activists (though within the context of anti-austerity activism we have seen that this may not be the case), and makes the point that activists are not an homogeneous population. Therefore, we need to pay more attention to the differences between activists within the same movement.

From a feminist standpoint, women's experiences differ structurally from men's because of the type of work that they do, with 'women's work' of reproduction being a 'labour of love' (Rose, 1983: 83–4). Moreover, women's dual marginal and central position in current social relations affords them a privileged viewpoint, as Tanesini (1999: 142) states: 'from their [women's] position, relations which are invisible from dominant positions become visible'. It has been suggested that women not only have different experiences but different cognitive ways of understanding and knowing the world, with women's caring labour endowing them 'with an affective way of knowing' (Tanesini, 1999: 143; see also Rose, 1983; Culley, 2003). Such views assume the existence of a female essence that is common among all women, leading to the criticism that this approach is essentialist and ignores differences between women in order to focus on differences between men and women. It risks reinforcing traditional sex differences, along with the supposed biological basis of women's oppression. Clearly this is problematic, and while I do not have space to explore this theory further here, it is something that I will return to in Chapters 5, 6, and 7. For now, it is worth noting that a key merit of feminist standpoint theory is its emphasis on using women's lives as a starting point for developing theory, with lived experiences being central.

This chapter has identified the key theoretical debates to which this book contributes, including those of new versus old social movements, the influence of new media technologies on contemporary movements, the need to consider emotions in social movement studies and the need for an exploration of the gendered experiences of social movement participation. I have drawn on feminist literature to demonstrate the importance of considering the role of gender when exploring social movements and used this to highlight the absence of gender in mainstream SMT. Overall, I have argued for the development of a cultural, affective and feminist approach to explore the making and practising of anti-austerity activist culture within a specific local setting, thus contributing to a feminist theory of social movements. The following chapters will demonstrate such an approach, build on the existing theoretical debates and introduce new areas of literature as they arise in relation to the research findings. The theoretical context having been outlined here, Chapter 3 explores the empirical and political contexts, providing an in-depth analysis of austerity, situating it within its wider neoliberal capitalist context and detailing the specifics of the research context this book draws on.

3

The Empirical and Political Context of Anti-Austerity Activism

This book draws on research into anti-austerity activism in a specific local context that was conducted between 2011 and 2013. The aim of this chapter is to present background information about this specific case in order to provide context for the analysis and to give the reader a sense of the research that this book draws on. To begin with, I provide an overview of austerity, its relationship to the wider neoliberal capitalist context and the ways in which it is gendered, classed and racialised. This is followed by detailing the research project which this book draws on, providing demographic information about participants and an explanation of the methodological approach and methods used to produce the data, in order to provide the reader with sufficient detail in order to situate participants' narratives in the following chapters. Alongside this, I provide information about myself in order to enable researcher positionality, in line with a feminist approach to research. I then provide an in-depth description of the specific anti-austerity activist culture where the original ethnographic research took place. This involves identifying the key movements and groups in the local context as well as key features of these movements, such as their positioning as a new form of politics that is outside the system and the centrality of social media to political organising in this context. In order to understand anti-austerity movements, we need to look at the particular socio-economic, cultural and political context out of which these movements develop. I therefore begin by providing an overview of neoliberalism, the wider political context out of and against which anti-austerity activism is situated.

Neoliberalism: a brief history

Most simply understood, neoliberalism is a political ideology and its associated policies, which assert the importance of free markets as the guiding principle of society and the most efficient distribution of resources. Neoliberalism proposes that through market-based economic practices individual freedoms are fostered. The state, and particularly the welfare state, are seen to hamper such freedoms and thus need to be minimised. The state guarantees the quality and integrity of money, secures private property rights and guarantees the proper functioning of markets but other than this, according to neoliberal logic, state intervention should not exist, resulting in the deregulation of markets, privatisation and the withdrawal of the state from social provision.

The first phase of neoliberalism began in 1979 with Margaret Thatcher in the UK and Ronald Reagan in the US. Thatcher rolled back state interference and consolidated free market mechanisms, deregulating the labour market. Welfare and full employment were condemned by her as obstacles to economic growth; she proclaimed in 1980 that 'the relentless growth of the public sector has put a crushing burden on the private wealth-creating sector' (Thatcher, 1980). Thatcher proposed a vision of a society where class did not matter, created by the free market and competition rather than co-operation, thereby destroying collective forms of organisation such as trade unions.

The second phase of neoliberalism began in the 1990s with the New Labour government and Tony Blair. It continued this notion of the 'classless' society, with a famous remark being made by the Deputy Prime Minister, John Prescott, in 1997: 'we're all middle class now'. This second phase continued the privatisation of previously public services through the rolling out of new policies that reinforced this. Britain was becoming an increasingly unequal society, with the poorest 10 per cent of the population getting poorer while a tiny elite concentrated greater amounts of wealth in its hands. Rather than eradicate this inequality, New Labour sought to ameliorate poverty, focusing on discourses about the 'underclass' that perpetuated a 'culture of worklessness' and demanded 'rights without responsibilities' (Todd, 2014: 339).

Such moral discourses, which began with Thatcher's claim to transform people's 'souls' through economic practices and strengthened in the days of New Labour, have continued to gain currency in the current, third, phase of neoliberalism. The 2010 Coalition government blamed unemployment on workers, and reaffirmed the discourse of shirkers versus workers or skivers versus strivers. In 2012, the Chancellor of the Exchequer, George Osborne, denounced those who spent their days 'sleeping off a life on benefits' (Osborne, 2012). The growing presence and influence of these discourses is reflected by the rise in the use of the word 'scrounger' in British tabloid papers from 46 times in 2007 to 240 times in 2011 (Todd, 2014: 350). A key part of neoliberalism's success is its use of common moral discourses and traditional values such as individual freedom, work ethic and fairness (Harvey, 2007); the last of which has been invoked in the fight against austerity to turn the focus back onto the growing inequality between the rich and the poor and the injustice of this.

Critically, neoliberalism is not just a set of policies or ideologies but a strategy of governance for the global world that pervades all areas of social life. The neoliberal value of competitiveness permeates all areas of society and human activity from households to the world economy. Crucially, this includes areas of social life that are not supposed to be economic, with neoliberalism configuring all human beings as market actors, always and only, and transforming them from *homo politicus* into *homo oeconomicus* (Brown, 2015). Thus, neoliberalism erodes democracy as rule by the people for the people, as well as the human capacities for ethical and political freedom, creativity and any activity that is non-economic. At the same time, it encourages the 'economisation' of all arenas of social life, meaning that individuals no longer start from a position of equality as humans because the value of competition is grounded in inequality between individuals. As Brown (2015: 44) asserts, then, 'neoliberalism is the rationality through which capitalism finally swallows humanity'.

Significantly, neoliberalism's transformation of government into governance involves 'soft power' that is 'termitelike [...] boring in capillary fashion into the trunks and branches of workplaces, schools, public agencies, social and political discourse, and above all, the subject' (Brown, 2015: 35–6). However, it is not merely destructive but also creates new subjects and relations, centred around the economic rationality of competitiveness. By operating in this manner, neoliberalism infiltrates all areas of life but does so quietly, becoming the hegemonic mode of discourse to the extent that it is viewed as 'common-sense' and the only way, through which individuals interpret, live in and understand the world (Harvey, 2007).

It is here that austerity enters, as a key element of the latest phase of neoliberalism. While such a lengthy explanation of the historical roots of neoliberalism may seem superfluous, it is vital to situate the current period within this history and to set out key features of neoliberalism at the outset, as these re-emerge throughout. Neoliberalism provides the backdrop to anti-austerity movements; moreover, it is within a neoliberal context that such movements operate, and I will demonstrate in Chapters 4, 5, 6, 7 and 8 how activists both internalise and subvert neoliberal ideologies, as well as the subtle ways in which neoliberalism and its discourses infiltrate and impact on activist culture.

While the current period represents the continuation of the neoliberal project that began in 1979, the use of austerity as a guise for this project is distinct and significant as, largely, the British public have accepted austerity as necessary. Austerity therefore acts as a Trojan horse that enables the rapid dismantling of the welfare state and the increasing privatisation and financialisation of society to occur with little resistance. Reflecting the historical roots of this neoliberal project, in 2013, David Cameron echoed Margaret Thatcher, announcing resolutely that 'there is no alternative [to austerity]' (Cameron, 2013).

Neoliberal capitalism

Throughout this book I refer to 'neoliberal capitalism' in order to remind the reader of the specific political and socio-economic context that anti-austerity activism emerged from and seeks to resist. While 'neoliberalism' refers to the political ideology, 'capitalism' is concerned with economic conditions, and the two combine to produce a form of economic and political liberalism that emphasises free markets, individualism and the role of the private sector above the public, which produces the dehumanising attitude of 'profit above people'. When focusing on the cultural dimension of movements, it is important to situate this within the wider socio-economic context. Thus, as Della Porta (2015) asserts, we must bring capitalism back into the analysis of social movements and remember that the current political ideology of neoliberalism is linked to and perpetuates a particular form of capitalism. It is argued that neoliberal capitalism is immoral, 'with cynical refusal of values of social protection and solidarity, to which movements responded through appeals to re-establish the social order they perceived to be broken' (Della Porta, 2015: 23). In this respect, neoliberal capitalism's challenge is not only material but also normative, with humanist concerns about dignity forming a moral and political resistance to this challenge, as Chapter 4 will demonstrate. Having outlined the wider socio-economic context, I now turn to unpick the dominant narratives associated with austerity that are produced by and perpetuate neoliberal capitalism.

Austerity's dominant narratives

When the UK government's programme of austerity was announced in 2010, the official narrative was that, in the wake of the financial crisis, cuts to public spending were both necessary and inevitable. It was argued that the Coalition government was cleaning up the mess left by the previous Labour government, using the only method possible — austerity. Therefore, austerity was used to transform the crisis from a financial to a fiscal one. Clarke and Newman (2012: 300) describe the development of the austerity discourse:

> It [austerity] has been reworked, at least in the UK, from an economic problem (how to 'rescue' the banks and restore market stability) to a political problem (how to allocate blame and responsibility for the crisis): a reworking that has focused on the unwieldly and expensive welfare state and public sector, rather than high risk strategies of banks, as the root cause of the crisis.

They draw our attention to a key feature of the government's austerity discourses, namely the allocation of blame and responsibility that is underlined by moral and political ideologies.

One of the central underlying moral discourses is that of 'strivers versus skivers', a repackaging of the nineteenth century's 'deserving' and 'undeserving' poor discourse. Here, those who work hard (producing capital) are conceived of as 'good' and deserving individuals who are pitted against the lazy, workshy, 'skivers' and 'benefit scroungers' who do not deserve any 'benefit'. This narrative plays on what is deemed fair and moral within a society where rewards are expected to be preceded by hard work and, most crucially, where individuals are perceived to be responsible for their own situation. The consequence of this is that structural factors are erased and individuals are blamed for their predicaments, with any failure being perceived to be a personal failing. It is therefore no longer the role of the state to support people who are to blame for the situation they find themselves in. This emphasis on responsibility is highlighted by David Cameron (2009) in his 'Age of Austerity' speech, where he asserts that 'the age of irresponsibility is giving way to the age of austerity'. Thus, austerity is seen as a solution to this moral deficit. As the New Economics Foundation (2013) states, 'Well-framed, well-crafted and often repeated, the austerity story is the dominant political narrative in Britain today [...] [the government] have developed a clear plot, with heroes and villains, and use simple, emotional language to make their point clear.'

The use of the word 'story' draws our attention to the fact that austerity is a narrative that has been constructed by those in power, and that it is not the only solution to the financial crisis; nor is it 'inevitable', as has been portrayed to the British public. UK Uncut attempt to draw attention to this in their statement that austerity is an ideology, not a necessity. However, these narratives become taken for granted as truths within the context of what De Certeau (2011: 186) refers to as 'the recited society', which is 'defined by stories (*recits*), the fables constituted by our advertising and informational media, by citations of stories and by the interminable recitation of stories'. As Forkert (2018) explains, these narratives become truths through their constant repetition and their synergy with pre-existing narratives.

Moreover, such narratives often frame the undeserving in gendered terms, such as 'the single mother who has had too many children in order to claim welfare benefits, reflecting value judgements about "the right kind of motherhood"' (Anderson, 2013: 4). This gendered framing extends to the nation state, where the government is accused by the tabloids as a 'soft touch' for undeserving immigrants or benefit claimants, using language that is associated with a 'feminised and disabled body' (Tyler, 2013: 88). In response, the government must 'get tough' and prove its hardness in the face of such accusations of 'softness' (Forkert, 2018).

Yet it has become clear that austerity does not work, with British government debt going up from 52.3 per cent of gross domestic product in 2009 to 85.6 per cent in 2018 (*The Guardian*, 2018). In practice, austerity policies do not stabilise economies or promote growth, as is argued by their proponents (Blyth, 2013) but instead result in economic stagnation. Austerity has led to a dramatic increase in inequality, with changes to tax and welfare resulting in the poorest 10 per cent of the population seeing a 38 per cent drop in their income while the richest 10 per cent only lost 5 per cent (Horton and Reed, 2010: 22). Moreover, austerity has disproportionately affected those who already face structural oppression, hitting the most disadvantaged the hardest.

'We're all in it together'?

One of the dominant narratives of austerity is that 'we're all in it together', harking back to wartime discourses of austerity as a necessary sacrifice for the common good. This sentiment of people pulling together for the sake of the nation is echoed in Theresa May's 2018 Conservative Party Conference speech (May, 2018), where, contrary to the facts and figures of the 2018 budget that clearly demonstrate austerity is very much not over, she proclaimed that:

> The British people need to know that the end is in sight and our message to them must be this, 'We get it', we're not just

a party to clean up a mess, we're a party to steer a course to a better future. Sound finances are essential but they're not the limit of our ambition. Because you made sacrifices, there are better days ahead [...] Because, a decade after the financial crash, people need to know that the austerity it led to is over and that their hard work has paid off.

This speech suggests that austerity has impacted everyone in equal measure, despite evidence to show that women and ethnic minorities have been disproportionately impacted by public spending cuts, as they are more likely to be in low-paid work in the public sector and in receipt of income benefits (Runnymede Trust, 2015; Trades Union Congress 2015). Women suffer 75 per cent of the tax and benefit cuts with, on average, one fifth of women's income being made up of welfare payments compared to one tenth of men's (Fawcett Society, 2012). Further, women are subject to 'triple jeopardy', losing not only public services and jobs, but being left to fill the newly created service gap, unpaid (Fawcett Society, 2012). Thus, austerity reverses feminist gains, including women's access to the public sphere and paid work, which provided financial autonomy, and entrenches care work as unpaid 'women's work'. In response, the Women's Budget Group (2016) has called the austerity measures 'regressive'.

By 2020, low income black and Asian women will have lost nearly double the amount of money that poor white men have (Goodfellow, 2016). The disproportionate impact of austerity reflects how the economy is already gendered and racialised, as well as its intersection with class. Yet minority women's voices are seldom heard in debates around austerity and its resistance; this was regretfully mirrored in the research context that this book draws on, where there was a distinct lack of black and minority ethnic (BME) activists and concern with the impact of austerity on minority women, although wider issues of racism were prominent. However, Emejulu and Bassel (2015) reveal that minority women are not only disproportionately affected by the public spending cuts but also undermined by the discourses around austerity and its resistance that cast these women as either victims or enterprising actors. Furthermore, Forkert (2018) explores how austerity has coincided with an increase in anti-immigration sentiment and rhetoric, and the ways in which the context of austerity has heightened fears around 'the other', as well as further demonising those in poverty.

People with disabilities have been especially impacted by the introduction of the 'bedroom tax' between 2011 and 2013, which involved cutting housing benefits for those with supposed 'extra rooms' by between 14 and 25 per cent (Shelter, 2018). Additionally, highly stringent and invasive disability assessments carried out by private companies have resulted in people with significant disabilities and terminal illnesses being declared fit to work and having to undergo repeated, distressing and often dehumanising tests. At the same time, an increase in benefit sanctions and a move towards universal credit, a new single payment system designed to 'incentivise work' (Department for Work and Pensions, 2015) has left many of the poorest in society without an income and/or drastically reduced payments (Shelter, 2018).

It is clear from the figures, lived experiences and academic analyses that we are not 'all in it together' but that austerity, aside from being ineffective, disproportionately impacts negatively on those in society who already face significant structural oppression and disadvantages. It is therefore important to develop studies that listen to the voices of those who are often ignored by mainstream politics and media, and to explore the lived and felt realities of austerity and its resistance. Having briefly outlined the wider political context of austerity, the next section provides some information about the research study this book draws on.

The research project

The research used a combination of qualitative research methods including participant observation and semi-structured interviews. It invoked a feminist approach that is threaded throughout, and emphasises the importance of subjective experience. Rather than attempting to fulfil a researcher position that is detached from the social world that it studies, and seeks to excavate pre-existing facts, it is recognised that knowledge is relational and produced intersubjectively, and that the researcher's relationship with participants influences the subsequent knowledge produced. Oakley (1981: 49) reinforces this:

> A feminist methodology [...] requires [...] that the mythology of 'hygienic' research with its accompanying mystification of the researcher and the researched as objective instruments of data production be replaced by the recognition that personal involvement is more than dangerous bias – it is the condition under which people come to know each other and to admit others into their lives.

It is therefore important to foster good relationships with participants, something that I achieved through participating in anti-austerity events, protests and meetings for two-and-a-half years between 2011 and 2013. It is especially important to develop trusting relationships when researching activism because of the 'security culture' that exists, with activists being wary of outsiders. This is particularly the case in Nottingham given the high-profile case of Mark Kennedy, which broke in 2011: he was an undercover policeman who infiltrated Nottingham environmental movements for years, even having a relationship with one of the activists involved. Therefore, understandably, individuals are wary of newcomers when this betrayal of trust is still at the forefront of their memories, particularly as some of my participants knew Mark.

My extended immersion within the local anti-austerity activist scene enabled me to gain trust among participants and access to interview participants. Earlier participants helped to recruit subsequent participants by spreading the word that I could be trusted (for which I am very grateful). I interviewed 30 local individuals who self-identified as having been involved in local anti-austerity activism. The interviews lasted, on average, for 90 minutes and were recorded and transcribed. While I used a minimalist structure, allowing participants to speak openly about topics, the artificial nature of the interview setting remained evident. Several participants made comments about how they should have 'done research' or 'extra reading' before the interview to be knowledgeable enough (in their eyes) for the occasion (regardless of how often I stressed that it was just a conversation about their experiences). Although many participants eased into the interview after realising that it was not as formal or intimidating as they had anticipated, there was still the sense that once the Dictaphone was switched off participants relaxed. Conversations were often continued long after recording had stopped because participants felt more comfortable and wanted to continue chatting.

Participants were also eager to know what others had said and whether their views matched those of their peers, perhaps to see whether they had 'toed the line' in terms of group narrative, but also out of a human curiosity. Obviously, owing to confidentiality, I was unable to reveal information about other participants (though they often discussed the interviews among themselves). Amusingly, several male participants demonstrated performance anxiety, asking whether their interview had lasted longer than other males whom they knew had participated. Moreover, there were some advantages to the interview being a constructed occasion, with participants feeling more able to speak openly with someone in this setting than if it had been an informal conversation between friends. Adrian remarked that though he only agreed to speak to me because of our mutual friends (meaning he could trust me), he found it easier to talk with strangers than people he was close to.

The interview situation produces narratives through which participants attempt to make sense of their experiences. It is important to recognise that these narratives are fluid and constantly reshaped by participants during the telling. Furthermore, narratives do not speak for themselves, and thus they need to be interpreted. While research participants' voices were central to the research project and form a key element of this book, it is nevertheless important to remember that the product of research is always 'our story of their story' (Oakley, 2015: 14). I have provided extended quotations throughout, so that the reader can judge my interpretations and make their own. By combining document analysis, participant observation and interviews, I was able to compare my own analysis with participants and establish a strong body of data using triangulation. Ethical approval was granted by the institution and the research adhered to the British Sociological Association's (2017 [then 2002]) statement of ethical practice. It is important to note that engaging with ethical concerns was an ongoing process which occurred throughout the research.

I will now provide some demographic information about the participants of the research before outlining my own positionality as a researcher. However, in order to preserve anonymity, I attribute quotations to pseudonyms and offer minimal information about participants' characteristics.

Participant demographics

The sample included 17 males and 13 females, seven of whom were mothers, including two single mothers. Eighteen participants were in their 20s, nine in their 30s, two in their 40s and one in her 50s. Just over half of the participants were university educated. Several worked in the public sector. Fifteen participants identified as working class, seven as middle class and the remaining eight had an ambivalent relationship with class, having been raised in working-class families but now considering themselves to be middle class through education, occupation or marriage. The majority were white, with one British Pakistani, one Black British, one Chinese and one white first-generation Eastern European migrant. Participants noted the visible absence of BME anti-austerity activists and had tried, unsuccessfully, to address this. However, in the post-Brexit political context there are signs that anti-austerity campaigns are attempting to address issues of racism and anti-immigration. The local People's Assembly has held several anti-racism protests, but whether this will reflect an increase in BME participants remains to be seen.

Unlike positivist objective research, a feminist approach actively acknowledges and reflects on the power imbalances that exist between researcher and researched. A key part of this is recognising the researcher's 'positionality' and how this influences the research process. I will therefore briefly provide some details about myself before expanding upon the specific groups that make up the local anti-austerity activist culture.

I am a white woman who was in her mid-20s at the time of research and is highly educated. Like my participants, I find class to be a difficult category to negotiate. Although I am highly educated, at the time of the research I was in a precarious position in terms of employment, working part time in a bookshop alongside other jobs to support myself. My parents both come from working-class backgrounds; my granny on my mum's side worked in a factory and my mum's father worked on steam trains for the National Coal Board in the Welsh valleys. My great-grandparents on my dad's side had a market stall in the local market. My dad was the first in his family to go to university and trained to become a civil engineer. My mum left school at 15 and has worked as a typist in various contexts since then. I assumed that my parents would now identify as middle class, but when I spoke to my mum she revealed similar tensions as my participants about how class is defined and understood. I therefore relate to participants' ambiguous relationship with class, but because I have a fairly nondescript accent and am in academia I expected to be read by participants as being middle class, which could have created a boundary between myself and participants who strongly identify as working class. Getting to know my participants over time prevented (or broke down) such boundaries that might have been formed on first impressions. Despite this, I remain aware of the privilege that I have as a white and highly educated person.

I am a feminist and a woman. Therefore, I start from the position that we live in an unequal, patriarchal society that oppresses and disadvantages women. This gives me the motivation and understanding to research gendered experiences utilising a feminist approach, demonstrating how researchers' politics impact on their methodological choices. I am politically left wing and am not a member of any political party. I therefore chose to research anti-austerity activism as I am sympathetic to the movement's cause but wanted to critically explore the cultural and affective dimensions of political engagement, applying a feminist approach. I subscribe to an intersectional feminism that acknowledges the need to consider how different oppressions and experiences such as gender, race, class, disability and sexuality interact. Therefore, I have tried to consider in this case how class and gender intersect to produce various experiences and am aware of the absence of other intersections, owing to the practical constraints of conducting a project such as this.

While attempts were made to collect as much demographic information as possible, I did not request participants to fill out a questionnaire about their personal demographic information, as I felt that this would compromise my ability to gain participants and valuable data, given that individuals were keen to be as anonymous as possible. Therefore, it is highly probable that more participants identify as having a disability or being lesbian, gay, bisexual or transgender (LGBT) than I have identified, but I have only provided information that was self-disclosed. Similarly, while I could provide extensive details about my own demographics, I have chosen to focus here on gender and class not only because they are the most prominent throughout this book but also because this is what I am comfortable disclosing (though, as mentioned, I found the topic of class difficult to articulate clearly). Indeed, while a feminist approach emphasises positionality and the importance of lived experience, there is a delicate balancing act to maintain between providing enough information to add depth to participants, with the aims of asserting that they are real human beings rather than detached subjects and contextualising their narratives, and providing a list of characteristics or structural oppressions that reduces their lived experience to a checklist and risks their anonymity.

While I can only assume how my participants viewed me, from our interactions there seemed to be varying perceptions of my identity. I entered the field as a researcher and thus this is how participants were first introduced to me. Though I became friends with many participants over time, they were still aware of my researcher role, which would surface in the form of jokes about whether I was 'analysing' conversations for my research. Further, because of my position as researcher, some participants considered me to be an 'expert', seeking advice and reassurance from me about the amount and type of activism they do (as will be demonstrated in Chapter 6 and 7). While I was mostly positively received, and considered to be an activist by many participants who spoke of 'us' activists and included me within this, there were some individuals who were more hostile to my position, suggesting that I was not a 'real' activist. I therefore experienced some of the judgements that participants spoke about at first hand, enabling me to develop a better understanding of their impact. As Hesse–Biber and Piatelli (2007: 498–9) assert, 'not only do we researchers attempt to define our role; how others see us is also in flux [...] researchers can only come to understand themselves as subject/ object, insider/outsider by reflexively examining the continuously shifting nature of one's role in the field'. Therefore, '[r]esearchers are never fully insiders or outsiders'.

The local context: Nottingham

Nottingham is the largest city in the East Midlands, built on a history of heavy industry that includes coal mining, manufacturing and engineering. Between 2010 and 2014, the City Council faced cuts of £123 million. As Nottingham City Council (2015) states, 'we're facing budget pressures like never before'. Since the austerity programme was initially announced in 2010, there was an emergence of anti-austerity groups and campaigns across the city. At the height of anti-austerity activism in Nottingham in 2010–13, there were several specific campaigns against the cuts that protested on a weekly basis, forming a vibrant and dynamic local activist scene. These included groups that campaigned against specific cuts, such as Notts Save Our Services (which has since disbanded), feminist activism and groups operating from the Women's Centre, such as Nottingham Women Campaign for Change, and local branches of wider national movements, such as UK Uncut and the People's Assembly Against Austerity. These two movements have been the most popular and visible, protesting against the cuts since 2010 with a variety of direct action tactics combined with petitions and public meetings.

Somewhat apt, and drawn upon by anti-austerity groups, is Nottingham's legend of Robin Hood, the heroic outlaw who robbed from the rich to give to the poor. Nottingham has a long history of resistance politics, including the Luddite uprisings and the riots of 1832 when Nottingham Castle was burnt down (one of many other local riots at that time). More recently, there was the Miners' Strike of the 1980s, which is still prominent in local memory and history. This history is reflected in the contemporary local scene, with Nottingham being home to one of only five radical bookshops in the UK (a shop that has roots in another local radical bookshop from the 1970s), the presence of an activist and community centre – The Sumac (established in 1985) – and the Nottingham Women's Centre, which has existed for 40 years. Much of the feminist anti-austerity activism is organised out of this centre, and there has been a surge in local feminism, evidenced by the quickly growing popularity of a local feminism Facebook group and a rise in local feminist events. Participants reflect this general atmosphere of progressive politics and resistance, referring to Nottingham as a 'Left city' that is 'alternative' and has a 'buzz', and where there is an 'underground' activist scene where 'a lot's going on'.

The aim of this chapter is to provide a detailed descriptive account of the specific local setting where the research took place. It is important to remember, as participant Beth states, that 'austerity is a thread that runs through many campaigns'. Therefore, participants have been involved in various groups and campaigns that resist austerity, with anti-austerity activism being a broad area. However, given the prominence of the two movements UK Uncut and the People's Assembly, and the ways in which participants define the two in relation to one another, I will be focusing mainly on these, exploring some key features of the movements that participants referred to, namely those of organisational structure and the relationship between activism and party politics.

UK Uncut

UK Uncut is a grassroots movement that formed in October 2010 to protest against tax avoidance by large corporations and banks. Describing itself as 'taking action to highlight the alternatives to the government's spending cuts', UK Uncut (2010) argues that the cuts are 'based on ideology, not necessity' and seeks to highlight this perceived injustice by taking direct action against tax-avoiding corporations such as Starbucks, Vodafone, NatWest, Lloyds TSB and Boots, the last of which has local significance having been founded in Nottingham. UK Uncut has been successful in creating a link in the public imagination between tax avoidance and public spending cuts, utilising the popular discourse of 'fairness' that is also used to legitimise austerity. We start to see how dominant ideologies can be reinterpreted and turned against themselves. In this respect, anti-austerity activism employs a 'hermeneutic of faith' (Ricoeur, 1981), which is 'an attempt to restore meaning to a narrative and its different voices and silences' (Levitas, 2012: 332). At the same time, such movements read austerity discourses through a 'hermeneutics of suspicion', which involves 'an attempt at unmasking disguised meanings and practical implications' (Levitas, 2012: 332). Thus we see the complexities and dialectics present in anti-austerity activism. Similarly to how it draws on the 'common sense' of fairness, UK Uncut does not question the need to reduce the deficit, which is a point that has largely been accepted by the public, but instead argues that it should be reduced in a way that does not hit the most vulnerable the hardest. Given that tax avoidance is legal, UK Uncut has to find an alternative grounding for its argument, which it finds in the frame of morality.

According to its website, the first mention of UK Uncut was on 27 October 2010 in the Twitter hashtag #UKUncut. This was the date of UK Uncut's first direct action, when approximately 70 people formed a sit-in at Vodafone's flagship London store to protest against austerity measures that had been announced one week earlier. From the outset, then, it is clear that social media played a central role in the organising and constitution of UK Uncut. After this single action group in London, Uncut quickly spread to 55 locations across the UK with a diverse range of participants; the movement (UK Uncut, 2010) states that 'everyone from pensioners to teenagers, veterans to newbies have already joined our actions in towns from Aberdeen to Aberystwyth'.

There is no official membership; people join UK Uncut by organising or attending an action near them (UK Uncut, 2010). Uncut claims to be leaderless, having been formed on and organised through the internet and has a strong virtual presence. Most participants discovered UK Uncut online. The UK Uncut Facebook page currently has more than 160,000 supporters who have subscribed to its posts (a number that has doubled in two years and is growing every day). The Notts Uncut Facebook page has almost 2000 likes. Reflecting Castells's (2012) notion of 'networked social movements', some participants contend that social media is a central feature of newer horizontal forms of activism. In fact, social media is perceived by participants to have changed the political landscape. Research participant Harry states that 'a smartphone in the right hands is the nuclear bomb of the activist', emphasising the potential impact that social media can have as well as its accessibility. At the same time, UK Uncut remains concerned with the use of public spaces for protest, reflecting Castells' (2012) contention that networked movements combine online and offline spaces for activism.

Despite its claims to leaderlessness, within Nottingham there was a core group of around eight to ten activists who managed the Notts Uncut social media and organised many of their actions. This core group is included within my sample, as are others who had more casual links to the movement. While UK Uncut is still active, in Nottingham the movement peaked between 2010 and 2012; there are occasionally plans to revive it, and participants describe it as currently 'sleeping'.

The People's Assembly

The main anti-austerity group currently active in Nottingham is the People's Assembly, which is part of the national People's Assembly Against Austerity that acts as a platform for anti-austerity protests and events, and has attracted several celebrity supporters such as Owen Jones and Russell Brand. It was formed in 2013 and states '[t]here is no need for ANY cuts to public spending; no need to decimate public services; no need for unemployment or pay and pension cuts; no need for Austerity and privatisation. There IS an alternative' (People's Assembly, n.d.), demonstrating a similar message to UK Uncut. Whereas Notts Uncut was more horizontal and used consensus decision-making methods, the People's Assembly is a more vertically structured group that is mainly organised by one local activist (who is also part of my sample). This is a point of contention for some participants who choose not to be involved with the movement because of this.

Reflecting their more organised approach, the People's Assembly support 'The People's Manifesto', a list of policies that the movement proposes to create a fairer society. The People's Assembly national Facebook page has just over 77,000 likes and the local Nottingham page has over 5000. Similarly to UK Uncut, though the People's Assembly does not claim to be mainly constituted online, participant Mary notes that 'we have started doing a lot of our stuff [People's Assembly], events that we organise we set up Facebook events and that sort of thing and you get very quick shares of things and you get an impact quite quickly'.

Although participants were involved in a range of anti-austerity activism, including UK Uncut and the People's Assembly, those who were solely involved with the People's Assembly did not speak about it in detail. In contrast, those who had been involved with UK Uncut spoke extensively about the movement, suggesting that there was a strong collective identity and loyalty to the group among participants. Several participants had attempted to be involved with the People's Assembly but had had negative experiences, and many others who had been central to Notts Uncut refused to associate with the People's Assembly because of its organisational structure and perceived corruption. It was clear from the outset that participants constructed the People's Assembly as the antithesis of UK Uncut, with the former representing the negative aspects of political organising and the latter the positive. Therefore, the People's Assembly functioned as the undesirable 'other' to UK Uncut, and was used to construct and position Uncut as the more ideal form of anti-austerity activism for many participants. This does not mean that participants were uncritical of Uncut, as reflexivity was a key quality emphasised by participants; however, it does mean that where particular groups and organisations were spoken about, UK Uncut was the main subject, with the People's Assembly acting as its foil. Therefore, the following discussion reflects this focus.

Working within or outside the system: hierarchical versus horizontal movements

There was a clear distinction made by participants between working 'within the system' by belonging to or working alongside political parties and working 'outside the system'. This distinction tended to correlate to whether a group's organisational structure was perceived to be horizontal or hierarchical. While not all participants fit neatly on one side of these distinctions, it tended to be the case that those who supported horizontal forms of activism defined this in opposition to more hierarchically organised campaigns, and that this organisational structure was seen as a defining feature.

UK Uncut is spoken about by participants as a clear example of this non-hierarchical, horizontal form of activism and is contrasted with the People's Assembly, which represents a more hierarchical, structured organisation that is perceived to be rife with internal politics:

> Whereas the core people of UK Uncut, there was no hierarchy, for the other people at Uncut the issue was the most important thing, I would say. The issue was the thing, I couldn't give a crap about the internal politics, and I don't think they did, I think they were just happy to have other people around them doing the cause. Whereas, People's Assembly, I think UK Uncut, everyone was welcome, as well, and I don't think that's the case with People's Assembly. UK Uncut definitely everyone was welcome, the more the merrier, and it was very focused on that whereas there's so much other bollocks with People's Assembly. (Tony)

Here we not only see how UK Uncut and the People's Assembly are constructed in opposition to one another, but also the emphasis placed on issue-based politics, where 'it is about the issue, not the brand' (Morris). In this respect, participants claim that UK Uncut 'just happens to be the UK brand name that was effective in getting people out there and protesting' (Morris). Participants suggest that there are similarities and movement between different groups:

> I don't know where UK Uncut starts and where UK Uncut finishes. 'Cause, it doesn't have a constitution, or membership, things like this, so I guess Occupy, Anonymous [...] they're very similar, things, trying to achieve very similar things and just different names have been given to it. (Tony)

James suggests that the name UK Uncut was 'only really there to provide this sort of unitary idea for which people can go behind'. Tony reinforces this:

Maybe that's why I'd give a leaflet out [for Uncut], 'cause I think it's for the actual cause, and maybe that's why I wouldn't give a leaflet out for the People's Assembly because I feel that I'm just promoting something for someone else to try and jump around and move around and that and all their political manoeuvrings. So, yeah, it's more about the issue. I think for that it makes me feel like it's purer. When I say it's purer, I think that's what I mean.

We see how participants construct Uncut as a natural, spontaneously occurring event that is not tainted by internal politics or power dynamics, implying that horizontality and issue-based politics are more authentic. However, despite this emphasis on the issue over the organisation and the fluidity of the movement's boundaries, we will see in Chapter 4 that the brand Notts Uncut was held in high regard by participants and fiercely protected. Nevertheless, for participants, a key advantage of such issue-based politics is that they overcome the 'petty factionalism' and 'fragmentation' that characterises the Left (Morris; Helen). Given that the focus is on the issue, not the organisation, there is opportunity for groups to unite and work together.

Unlike other fragmented and hierarchical Left groups, UK Uncut is perceived to be inclusive and welcoming (as demonstrated by Tony's comment above). Here, the permeable boundaries of the movement resulted in Uncut having a diverse range of participants. Leonie remarks:

There wasn't a typical kind of person. I mean within our group in Nottingham we were really really wide ranging. I mean we had … students […] actual proper political anarchists rather than the type that the press like to paint the picture of […] trade unionists, we had pensioners. I mean I was a fairly typical, kind of, married, two kids, mortgage, civil service job, you know, not the sort of person you would necessarily expect to get involved in that kind of direct action, but I think that was the beauty of it, because within the actions that Uncut took there was a role for everybody.

Crucially, participants assert that those who were involved with Notts Uncut were not just 'the usual suspects'. Helen says:

You would also find people coming along who hadn't been to previous protests. So you would find people turning up saying 'I read about it online, I heard about it, I was interested so I came' which you don't often get in a lot of kind of Left organisations.

Again we see the centrality of social media to UK Uncut's organising, as well as the ways in which participants position Uncut as different from and better than other Left organisations. However, rather than claiming that Uncut's participants were totally atypical, Helen suggests that 'there's kind of a solid core who are the people who have been involved in everything forever' but that 'what UK Uncut started to do was bring other groups into that'. It seems that participants were eager to stress the populist character of the movement by emphasising the 'ordinariness' of its participants rather than focusing on core individuals' extensive histories of activism.

UK Uncut: a 'new' politics?

Participants construct UK Uncut as a unique, new form of politics in order to detach it from negative connotations of 'the Left' and party politics. Tony states that 'Uncut *seems* to have come out of nowhere and it doesn't have that connection with, it doesn't seem to have the baggage of … 'the Left', to go along with it'. The seemingly spontaneous emergence of Uncut is significant as the movement has no history or Left roots, allowing participants to feel that Uncut really is a different and new form of politics. Participants achieve this erasure of history and subsequent positioning of Uncut as unique through the shared origin myth, where the movement spontaneously emerged via social media and developed from there:

> The way I *perceive* it is, I do perceive it as a lot less hierarchical and it is genuinely based from this kind of like, from Twitter and from Facebook, social media movement that a few people have, come online and … shared a, interest, passion, about the issues and it's kind of gone from there and snowballed from there. (Tony)

Likewise, James states 'We didn't have a framework […] we are not an ideological group with a solid thing, it was always how people came together that produced Uncut.' Here emphasis is placed on relationships, as well as the horizontal, non-hierarchical organisation of the movement. Uncut is largely perceived to be less restrictive and more inclusive than other Left movements, especially the People's Assembly, because of its lack of strict and rigid organisational structures. Participants refer to this horizontality as the 'Uncut model' and contend that it reflects a 'true democracy' where individuals can participate fully and decisions are made collectively. For many this lack of hierarchy and authority is central to Uncut's appeal. Will states: 'I didn't want someone telling me what to do'. Tony asserts that: 'They [Left organisations] had no control over Uncut. You know the hierarchy of these little things, they didn't have the control over Uncut. Well no one had control over Uncut, it was a natural, pure thing.'

This spontaneity affords authenticity to the movement by distancing it from any negative associations and instead constructing UK Uncut as 'natural' and 'organic'. Participants speak of how the movement 'grew' and 'evolved', as well as referring to its 'birth' and 'death' and describing Notts Uncut as currently 'sleeping'. James notes how the local Uncut groups 'all set up organically, they fell, they grew again, completely independent'. Participants also use natural imagery when describing the wider activist scene, speaking about 'waves' of activity, 'ebbs and flows', 'peaks', 'troughs' and 'lulls' in activism, implying that this is the natural order of things. There is a sense that such processes are external to the individuals involved, with the movement taking on a life of its own. Demonstrating this, Leonie speaks of how Uncut 'just turned into this massive behemoth of a project' invoking ideas of a large beast with a mind of its own. Likewise, participants speak about 'energy' and 'momentum' as something external to, and independent of, the individuals involved; it is conceived of as a general mood or atmosphere: 'during the initial couple of months there was a lot of momentum, we weren't trying to do things, they were happening and we just sort of went with it' (James). Significantly, participants equate 'natural' with good, with the implication being that the movement is thus untainted or marred by human intervention or 'baggage'.

Yet, at the same time, participants speak about 'building' momentum and pushing the movement forwards, recognising individuals' conscious efforts to create and sustain momentum. There is a tension between this organic, spontaneous process that participants speak of and accounts of the work involved in activism. Furthermore, though it is not openly spoken about, participants are aware of Uncut's alternative 'origin' story that contradicts this spontaneous emergence. In this alternative mythscape, Uncut was formed by a group of 20-something Oxbridge graduates in a London pub in response to the *Private Eye* article revealing Vodafone's tax avoidance. The existence of different accounts concerning Uncut's beginnings is not inconsequential. Such origin stories are deliberately constructed to convey movements as spontaneous and contagious; what

THE EMPIRICAL AND POLITICAL CONTEXT

matters is not the 'trueness' of the account but the stories that are told and their effects (Polletta, 2006). Participants perhaps distance themselves from the alternative origin myth because it implies a level of organisation and type of activist that is oppositional to their own conception of activism, which we will see in Chapter 6.

'New' activist politics versus 'old' party politics

Participants not only construct UK Uncut in ways that distance it from other Left organisations such as the People's Assembly, but also in ways that separate it from party politics. This is reflected by how some participants reject the 'political' in 'political activist' because of its connotations. Further, some participants suggest that UK Uncut is not 'politics', Will demonstrates this view:

> We just said anyone could turn up, we were apolitical, we didn't say we support this political party or this, we just said we're not supporting any of that. And we always had the rule that you can't bring any banners that had a party name, so the Socialist Party couldn't turn up with Socialist Party banners because we didn't want it to be, it wasn't a political event. We weren't there saying oh, we're this party and this is our view, we're there saying we're all individuals from, doesn't matter where we're from (laughs), we're all here for a common purpose.

Similarly, Leonie contends that 'I think you have got to get away from the politics and focus on what your actual issues are'. We are again reminded of issue-based politics (for want of a better word) and how this is perceived to be a radical break from traditional Left activism.

It becomes clear that in rejecting 'the political' participants mainly mean party politics, representing a deep and widespread disillusionment with the mainstream political system. There is a sense that party politics has failed individuals, with participants declaring political parties 'all the same', referring to the broken promises of the Coalition government and the trust lost because of this: 'you can't trust any of them, they all say the same and then they do something different'. Reflecting Della Porta's (2015: 119) claim that we are witnessing a 'crisis of responsibility', participants do not feel that there is a party that represents them, describing most politicians as being out of touch with the lived experiences of citizens.

Within this environment of disillusionment and distrust, participants construct direct action as a 'more active form of activism', which is dynamic and disruptive, in opposition to the traditional politics of the ballot box, which is portrayed as stagnant and irrelevant. This contrast is demonstrated by several participants, with activism being perceived to be a more participatory and 'real' politics, compared to voting, which is pointless and ineffective. Will states:

> Well going to the ballot box, because there's so many people in the country all with different views, you need to get a lot of them to say no to something, for it to make any difference. And that's very hard to do. But with an action you kind of speak to the people just at street level, you're almost having a chat, a lot of people when we were doing actions would come up and have a chat with us and that's kind of, that kind of worked really.

Participants therefore define political action in alternative ways, outside mainstream political institutions. Morris demonstrates this, speaking of 'the protest movement', which he defines as people who are 'questioning the way that things are being done through other means than the ballot box'.

So far we have seen that participants construct UK Uncut in ways that distinguish it as a unique, positive and new form of politics that overcomes the disadvantages of traditional Left organisations and party politics. Central to this are the movement's focus on issues rather than the organisation and its horizontal structure. The People's Assembly serves as the representation of the negative features of politics, or 'the other', which Uncut challenges and is perceived to overcome. However, while many participants are enthusiastic about this new issue-based horizontal model of politics, some are more critical, raising key problems with how such organisational structures function. Morris criticises issue-based politics for attending to the symptom rather than the cause of social issues, while acknowledging that '[b]y not having an underlying political philosophy, by just being an issue-based protest it allowed a solidarity between those people that if you were to debate political philosophy [with], it would soon become petty factionalism, and it would break up'.

He goes on to say:

> But again, it's limited. Because you solve this issue... and what's next? It's another issue and another issue, and another issue, and another issue ... it's almost, to use a medical analogy, it's like, I don't know, if you bang your head on the wall every

morning, your issue is you've got a headache. Your issue-based protest is that you take aspirin. Your political based protest is that you stop banging your head on the wall because that's your problem.

Furthermore, the way such movements tend to come together and dissipate quickly is a potential flaw of the model. For, although issue-based politics may help to temporarily unite a fragmented Left, their short lifespan may prevent the development of solidarity between individuals and loyalty to the movement. Yet, despite claims that the issue matters and the brand does not, participants have strong ties to Notts Uncut. Indeed, participants are fiercely protective of the brand, expressing anger when other groups encroached upon or 'infiltrated' Uncut actions. Morris states 'we owned the Notts Uncut brand' and explains that the group's banner is a symbol of collective identity: '[the banner's] fundamental, this is an Uncut protest so that's who we are, we are Uncut'.

Moreover, Jack questions how non-hierarchical the movement really is, arguing that there need to be visible democratic structures in place. For Jack, a key drawback of Uncut is its lack of organisation and accountable leaders; thus he prefers to be involved with the People's Assembly. Phillips (1991: 133) demonstrates this view, drawing on Freeman's *The Tyranny of Structurelessness* to argue that 'all organisations have their procedures for making decisions, and that when a group claims to be without them, it is evading the crucially democratic task of keeping such procedures under control'. Therefore, the biggest threat to democracy within such movements is their supposed non-hierarchical organisation, which often conceals hidden power structures. Given that 'it does not look like power [...] it is therefore rarely brought to account', whereas, '[p]ower that is acknowledged can be subjected to mechanisms of democratic control' (Phillips, 1991: 134). Morris raises concerns about the emergence of 'de facto leaders' and notes how, in practice, such a model falls apart. Amin agrees that a clearer organisational structure is needed but is reluctant to make such a comment, remarking 'I'm going to hate myself for saying this'. Clearly, there are tensions between the ideal and the reality and, like some other participants, Amin feels that the horizontal model is an ideal that does not work in practice. Further, his comment suggests that he is aware that this view is not the common narrative within Notts Uncut, and his reluctance to question this narrative may reflect concern about being disloyal to the group and its values, again demonstrating the strong group identity. We will see in Chapters 4, 5, 6 and 7 both the positive, enabling aspects of this identity as well as its negative and more constraining elements.

This chapter has established the wider political context of neoliberalism and how it is interlinked to austerity. It has provided an overview of the dominant narratives of austerity in mainstream politics, such as 'there is no alternative' and 'we're all in it together', and challenged these by demonstrating the unequal impact of austerity on groups that are already in disadvantaged positions. Following this, it has provided more detail about the research project and context for the data used in this book, and demonstrated the ways in which participants construct anti-austerity activism as a 'new' distinct form of political engagement. This has involved highlighting some of the tensions that exist between key players within the local anti-austerity activist culture, though it is important not to over-emphasise these differences. Having situated the research within both its theoretical and empirical contexts, Part II of this book explores the enabling and constraining factors of doing activism.

PART II

Doing Activism: Enabling and Constraining Factors

Having outlined the theoretical and empirical context of the research that this book draws on in Part I, Part II draws on the data produced from interviews and participant observation to explore what motivates and sustains anti-austerity activism, as well as the barriers and exclusions that prevent individuals from becoming politically active. It reveals that these are often gendered and explores possibilities for overcoming them.

4

The Affective, the Normative and the Everyday: Exploring What Motivates and Sustains Anti-Austerity Activism

We have seen that emotions have been sidelined in social movement studies because of their traditional association with irrationality and researchers' desire to distance themselves from this. I have unpicked this association and its related binary constructions of male/female and public/ private, which will recur throughout Chapters 4, 5, 6, 7 and 8, asserting that there is a need to develop an in-depth understanding of the emotional and cultural dimensions of political engagement. Further, while the focus of research tends to be on the initial engagement phase of participation, I contend that it is vital to pay attention to the latent phases of movements in order to better understand individuals' everyday experiences of political engagement and how this engagement is sustained over time. It is here that the affective dimension plays a central role in answering the question of 'why' individuals become and remain mobilised for political action.

This chapter explores what motivates and sustains anti-austerity activism within the context of continued austerity. It affirms the centrality of the affective and normative dimensions of political engagement by demonstrating that anti-austerity activism is motivated and sustained by three core elements; emotion, morality and relationship. Individuals are motivated by an emotional response to perceived injustice combined with normative ideals about how society should be and how we should act in relation to others. They utilise notions of humanity and empathy to combat the dehumanising effect of neoliberal capitalism and its focus on individualism and competition. Participants translate such abstract, universal concepts into concrete, particular actions through a focus on everyday activism and individual choices. Rather than rejecting individualism outright, participants seek to redefine it in ways that move away from the dominant neoliberal understanding and towards reconciling the individual with the wider collective and common good. Here, activism is conceptualised as a moral duty. Participants therefore suggest that everyone and anyone can and should do activism, with small acts making a difference.

However, this notion clashes with the distinction often drawn between 'activist' and 'non-activist', which this chapter begins to interrogate. Furthermore, this chapter begins to unpick the ways in which activists resist, subvert and sometimes unwittingly reinforce neoliberal capitalism. It reveals that while empathy and putting others above oneself are seen as key motivations for doing activism, there is also an element of self-interest that motivates and sustains individuals' political activities. Nevertheless, it is argued that this is distinct from the neoliberal capitalist selfish individualism that participants criticise, as a concern for others and the collective still remains. It concludes by exploring the ways in which the social dimension of fun and relationships sustains individuals' activities, alongside the important emotion of hope.

Overall, this chapter demonstrates the multilayered affective and normative motivating and sustaining forces behind anti-austerity activism, revealing that it is about much more than simply trying to impact policy. Therefore, anti-austerity activism is not solely concerned with reversing austerity or defending social protections of the past such as state welfare, it is also about imagining a potential better future and what it means to be human, and enacting this in the present. It is therefore important to pay close attention to activist culture and listen to the ways in which individuals speak about their political engagement in order to develop a more nuanced, realistic explanation and understanding of what motivates and sustains activism. In a similar manner, E.P. Thompson's (1971) analysis of the eighteenth-century food riots reveals the need to avoid economic reductionism when investigating political action that on the surface appears to be solely about material conditions. Doing so reveals underlying moral values, normative assumptions about social obligations and the ways in which these combine to inform political action.

Notably, unlike Chapters 5, 6, 7 and 8 that highlight the gendered differences in experiences of local anti-austerity activism, this chapter reveals the common motivating and sustaining factors for activism that cross gender differences, with women and men providing largely similar explanations and justifications for their participation in local anti-austerity activism. As we will see in Chapter 5, the key exception to this is how women with children construct their activism as being part of their duty as mothers. However, this is linked to the relationship between private caring roles and activism, and constitutes a response to the gendered barriers and exclusions that women face in participating politically; therefore it will be discussed in this context in Chapter 5. To begin with, I turn to the question of what motivates and sustains anti-austerity activism.

The affective and normative as motivations for activism

Participants' sustained political engagement is motivated by a combination of emotions and normative ideals. Joe speaks about the 'unfairness' of austerity, arguing that society is currently 'wrong' and that 'we need to pull together to change it'. Owain questions 'the way society is run' and Lily contends that 'society shouldn't be this way'. Significantly it is an emotional response to this perceived injustice that motivates participants to do activism, signifying that emotions and morals combine to produce action.

The initial emotion drawn upon by participants is anger. Owain states that he 'hates injustice' and is moved to act because of his anger at the current situation. Likewise, Beth says 'I'm quite political in that I get very irate [...] always angry and wanting to do something about it'. Martin says 'I think there is a lot of anger that is still there, kind of bubbling under the surface', suggesting that this needs to be tapped into by activists to galvanise support. Similarly, Charlotte suggests that 'we should be more angry, I think we should be protesting more, we should be demonstrating more', implying that anger incites political action. Adrian suggests that channelling his anger into activism is 'therapeutic … 'cause it's like, yeah, my anger can't go at the world 'cause the world doesn't owe fucking anyone anything but it can go at the injustices'. Here, protest is a healthy outlet for anger.

In contrast, some participants suggest that anger is actually detrimental to activism. Joe says: 'people tend to think that being angry about everything is a positive, can be a positive trait, whereas I don't agree'. Martin suggests that while anger can be a motivation for action, it needs to be translated into a longer lasting, positive movement: 'so I think there is anger there and there is energy, but doing that all the time – getting people on the streets all the time won't work unless people think that it is leading to something positive'. Similarly, Solnit (2005: 28) contends that the nature of 'adversarial activism' leads to an obsession with the enemy that can hinder movements' progress. A key question that emerges is whether a movement that is 'anti' in name and goals is capable of being anything but adversarial and defined by this opposition. For some theorists, this antagonism need not be a negative thing, as Mouffe (2005: 30) contends:

> A well-functioning democracy calls for a clash of legitimate democratic political positions [...] such confrontations should provide collective forms of identification strong enough to mobilise political passions. If this adversarial configuration is missing, passions cannot be given a democratic outlet and the antagonistic dynamics of pluralism are hindered.

For Mouffe, the development of an 'us versus them' approach is central to democracy in that it mobilises individuals through their feelings of belonging to a particular group and helps to maintain the pluralistic nature of the public sphere. Mouffe (2005: 25) recognises the role of the affective dimension in political engagement, arguing that it is passions that motivate people to engage with politics.

Participants' narratives reveal a widening of emotional responses and motivations beyond anger. Adrian suggests that activism involves 'channelling emotions full-stop, not just anger'; Martin asserts that he gets involved with issues 'that I feel'; Amanda speaks of how austerity 'breaks my heart'; and Charlotte remarks 'I am sad about how things are going'. There is clearly a strong emotional dimension to participants' motivations for doing activism that is combined with concerns about the normative and morality. Jasper's (2011: 291) notion of 'moral batteries' draws our attention to the combination and interaction of positive and negative emotions, where anger at injustice is combined with hope for change, and this combination of negative and positive emotions (as in a battery) energises action. Indeed, Jasper (2014: 38) asserts that 'emotions provide the motivational thrust of morality'.

Empathy: the moral emotion that motivates and sustains activism

Empathy emerged as a central motivating and sustaining emotion for activism. Charlotte comments that her reasons for becoming politically active were 'just sort of an empathy'. Empathy is a relatively recent Western word that draws on the traditional meanings of the Greek word 'sympathy', which means to feel or suffer with somebody. It connects thought and feeling by translating an idea into a feeling through the use of the imagination. Though the word itself is relatively new, this idea of 'feeling with another person' has a long history that can be traced throughout religious and philosophical traditions. Its contemporary use more accurately reflects the traditional use of 'sympathy', however, empathy is possibly used instead by participants because the popular understanding of 'sympathy' evokes ideas of pity, which imply a paternalism and condescension on the part of the empathiser.

Participants use empathy and compassion interchangeably, with Amanda describing her activism as 'active compassion'. In the same way, Lampert (2005: 20) speaks of 'radical compassion' that drives individuals to action and Berlant (2004: 5) refers to compassion as an 'emotion in operation' that can enable individuals to understand and thus try to change structural conditions of injustice. Emphasis is placed on being moved to act by empathy; we must not view empathy as an end in itself but as a spur to social activism.

Many participants suggest that while they may personally be in a comfortable position, they are motivated to act out of empathy for the plight of other people. Dermot remarks that despite the fact that 'I don't need to change anything, necessarily' his motivation for doing activism is 'because I have empathy'. This reinforces Slote's (2007) suggestion that action is inherent to empathy as the capacity to feel like another and to imagine their situation is enough to spur an individual to action. Jasper (2014: 31) remarks that 'we must observe the emotions involved in the imagination: empathy and sympathy for the imagined others, which can lead to indignation on their behalf'. This element of 'imagined' loyalty and connection is significant, as participants do not necessarily know those whom they empathise with and often draw on a common humanity, rather than a tangible relationship with others, as a motivation for doing activism. In a similar way, Castells (2012) stresses the importance of empathy in networked social movements that span large geographical areas and where individuals are connected via communication technologies.

Empathy is not simply considered to be one affective response among many, but it is seen to have ethical legitimation in a way that other emotions do not. Todd (2004: 339) remarks that 'empathy is thought to embody both moral force and political possibility'. Hume contends that the motivation for justice originates in sympathy that is not only a source of information about the other's experience, but also a 'force of morality' (Agosta, 2011: 9). Therefore, sympathy takes on the content of benevolence and is grounded in an interest in furthering humanity; Agosta (2011: 7) asserts that 'Hume establishes sympathy as the glue that affectively binds others to oneself and, by implication, binds a community of ethical individuals together'. Mary demonstrates this by suggesting that 'We have to fight for everybody. I could just go oh well I'm all right, but that doesn't help society generally and I think it is unjust and I think our society is becoming very unbalanced in terms of wealth'. Here, Mary links caring for others to the material dimension of economic inequality and suggests that the common good needs to be placed above individual interests.

Adrian perceives acting out compassion as a moral duty grounded in care for 'the other'. He notes how his activism involves 'usually questioning for someone else and not for myself', and that even though he may feel uncomfortable he stands up for others 'because this is important for this person that I do this'. Similarly, Joe suggests that he is motivated to do activism by his 'social conscience'. Slote (2010: 13) contends that empathy is the basis for an ethics of caring about those who are not kin, and thus the ability to empathise provides the 'cement of the moral universe'. Similarly, Kohut (1977) uses the metaphor of empathy being the oxygen that breathes life into the relationship between the individual and the other.

Moreover, participants perceive neoliberal capitalism to perpetuate values that are not only in opposition to empathy and caring for the collective but that also actively erode such moral values. Holloway (2010: 9) asserts that 'humanity (in all its senses) jars increasingly with capitalism' and ties the rejection of capitalist values to 'becoming fully human' (Holloway, 2010: 7). Empathy is thus utilised by participants as a way of redefining and reasserting what it means to be human in the face of neoliberal capitalism. Alex states that 'having the capacity for empathy' means 'to be human in that sense'. Similarly, Lampert (2005: 175) considers the possibility of 'understanding compassion as an empiric, day-to-day, universal human phenomenon' and Rifkin (2009: 84) suggests that empathy is part of human nature: 'we are wired for empathy – it is our nature and what makes us social beings'.

Rifkin identifies a potential biological basis for empathy, exploring the scientific discovery of 'mirror neurons' that 'allow humans – and other animals – to grasp the minds of others "as if" their thoughts and behaviours were their own' (2009: 83). This notion of empathy being an innate characteristic is demonstrated by Adrian, who speaks about feeling empathy for others, even from childhood: 'I mean one of the earliest incidents I remember as a kid was my cousin throwing stones at another kid and me being upset about that'. Rifkin (2009: 83) suggests that this process is produced 'by feeling, not by thinking', emphasising the emotional roots of empathy, though this statement reinforces the problematic separation made between thinking and feeling.

While Rifkin contends that empathy is part of human nature, he also suggests that particular conditions are more likely to encourage its development, and that competitive, individualistic capitalism hinders it. Participants demonstrate this attitude in the way they perceive neoliberal capitalism, and how they construct empathy and caring for others as being in opposition to dominant values. Joe contends that 'it's that kind of attitude that I just can't make any sense of, you know, it's giving to people in need, in desperate need, is wrong but spending it on luxuries for yourself is fine … it's that kind of self-centred thinking that I want to get away from'. Amanda demonstrates how this selfish attitude is part of Conservative (neoliberal) ideology and announces caring for others as its opposite: 'I'm not a Tory bastard, that I'm not just out for myself, that I do want to create a caring sharing world'. Likewise, Charlotte, Alex and Mel speak of the 'greed' and 'selfishness' of 'Tory ideology', contrasting the focus on individual wealth and profit with caring for others and community values.

In response to the dominant neoliberal capitalist values of individualism and selfishness, participants attempt to reverse the status quo by emphasising caring and putting others before themselves. Mel contends that 'any campaign and particularly the anti-austerity [movement is about] starting to care about people again'. Participants therefore construct their activism in terms of care, referring to 'caring', 'empathy' and 'helping' other people. This care involves both caring about austerity and its impacts, as well as caring about the people affected by austerity. Sevenhuijsen (2000: 12) asserts the value of using a broad definition of care as a point of departure for a 'political vision on the place of care in society'. In this vein, feminist theorists have explored an 'ethic of care', where private and public care are rooted in a commitment to human interdependence that is contrasted to the dominant emphasis of citizenship on independence (which tends to be associated with maleness) (Bubeck, 1995; Lister, 2008). An ethic of care is a way of combining such feelings of empathy for the other with the moral duty to act, resulting in the practical act of providing care for others. However, the gendered nature of care work, with women tending to provide unpaid care, poses problems concerning the burden of responsibility to care being placed on women's shoulders. This is especially pressing in the context of austerity, where in the absence of service provision women are expected to fill the gap by providing services that were previously provided by the state. This provokes debate about the gendered impact of austerity and its resistance, which I will turn to in Chapter 5.

Significantly, participants frame their case against austerity and for activism in terms of a shared humanity rather than social class. This appears to be a strategic decision in response to both the wider hegemonic context of neoliberalism and the more specific context of anti-austerity activism. Participants suggest that to frame austerity resistance in solely class terms would not appeal to the wider public in the current context. Harry contends that although 'austerity just seems to be the latest way, the most palatable way of ... England retreating back into a Victorian based obvious class ridden system [...] austerity is to create re-establishment of an obvious class system', neoliberal politics has deliberately obscured social class in order to convince individuals that it does not matter. He says: 'there's the proverb that 'the devil's greatest trick was to convince everyone that he didn't exist''. This undermines the potential for and power of class-based movements to develop and gain popular appeal, thereby eliminating the threat of resistance to those in power.

However, traditional social movements concerned with working-class politics tended to focus on and be constituted by white working-class men, who had access to the labour market – unlike women at the time. Class therefore dominated both movement concerns and discourses as well as SMT's analysis of such movements, which has traditionally ignored the relationship between class and gender (Charles, 2000). This neglect appears to still be present in anti-austerity activism, with concerns about gender and race often being ignored in both local contexts and the wider movements (Emejulu and Bassel, 2015; Maiguashca et al, 2016). In tackling this bias, it makes sense that participants tend to focus on issues of gender above class (though of course the two intersect along with race and other dimensions). The dominance of white working-class men in anti-austerity activism and the resulting gendered barriers and exclusions to political engagement will be explored in Chapter 5.

Participants therefore seek to ground their reasoning for doing activism in universalist discourses about shared humanity, reflecting Harvey's (2007: 178) assertion that as dispossession is fragmented it is difficult to fight without recourse to universal principles. Della Porta (2013: 15) speaks of activists' indignation, remarking that 'indignant is a definition of the self which manifests the outrage at the disrespect for the right of a human being, which then resonates with a widespread claim: humanity'. Reflecting this, Hazel argues that everyone having enough food to live is 'a basic human principle'. In the context of neoliberal capitalism, participants reinforce Touraine's (2014: 57) argument that morality can function as a unifying force: 'If we are to successfully resist the threat of destruction, we need to identify a principle strong enough to mobilize us against the omnipotence of profit: only a principle which is moral as well as social can stand up to the power of money.'

Similarly, Jared argues that we need to respect people's inherent worth as fellow human-beings, rather than attaching a value to individuals based on their productivity or monetary worth.

However, assumptions of a core human nature and shared humanity rest on the problematic notion that a universal 'core' of humanity exists once all other layers are stripped away. This is problematic because the stripping away of such layers results in the ignoring of differences that prevent people from being treated the same. This casts doubt on our ability to build understanding on ideas of a universal humanity and raises questions about the tension between universalism and difference, which will be explored in Chapters 4, 5 and 6. Furthermore, while such universalist discourses may have a wide appeal, there is the risk that their abstract nature may result in the concepts becoming empty and lacking a real-world application. Participants overcome this by translating abstract universal concepts of empathy and humanity into concrete, particular actions in the everyday context. Here, participants are not only motivated by wider normative concepts and abstract ideas of a common humanity but also by witnessing the effects of austerity on those around them. Henry says that he is motivated to do activism against austerity because of seeing the effects that policies such as the bedroom tax have on his mother and others he knows. Several participants speak of being motivated by witnessing the effects of austerity on those they work with. Dana says: 'when you work in the public sector in the NHS, you see how bad things are for people'. Similarly, Mary speaks of 'seeing it as it is in those situations' through working at a school and seeing children who have not eaten and do not have adequate clothing. Their response to these injustices is therefore rooted in the everyday.

Making a (small) difference and the everyday

Participants demonstrate activism as care by helping individuals and creating change in the local community. Dermot asserts: 'just because I might not ever change the system, you can help individuals. Which is worth doing.' He reinforces this by giving the example of a recent local protest against an individual being evicted from their property: 'I haven't stopped people being thrown out of their houses but for now we've stopped Tom from being thrown out of his house.' Maeckelbergh (2013: 109) observes how in the aftermath of the crisis, across the world, 'informal networks of solidarity' functioned as 'mechanisms for survival', providing much-needed material support to individuals and groups in localities. This understanding of solidarity as physical acts emphasises how emotion 'does' things (Ahmed, 2014), and links together the material and symbolic dimensions of protest. Similarly, Alison says:

> I can help a person that day, so I think that's important and I think you can fight back in your everyday life like, I don't know, I really sort of believe in the stuff that Gramsci wrote about the everyday, like the battleground of common sense.

Mel reinforces that politics is an everyday lived phenomenon rather than an abstract concept that is out of individuals' control: 'Because everyone has a little thing they can do, the problem is the way the propaganda machine works for politics is "oh politics is this huge serious thing that happens in the Houses of Parliament" – bollocks it does!' Participants affirm Horton and Kraftl's (2009) suggestion that we need to widen the definition of activism to include everyday 'implicit activism', such as caring for others and working in community projects. Charlotte speaks about her partner's work as a mental health nurse: 'he helps people, like individual people, and he does things for people, very quietly, so I think that is a way of being active, you know, changing things.' Other participants who work in women's and social services suggest that, like Charlotte's partner, their work constitutes a form of activism.

Participants' narratives further reveal the creative, subtle ways in which they resist the dominance of neoliberal capitalism in their everyday lives. These range from using their workplace's time and resources for printing protest materials to deliberately provoking shops. Participants clearly derived pleasure from doing and recounting private acts of resistance as secret, personal victories against 'the system'. Helen (an active participant in Notts Uncut during its peak) notes that 'I used to occasionally stop outside of a Vodafone shop just when I was walking to see if they started pulling down the blinds (laughs)'. Such acts seem to be a way for participants to exercise autonomy and feel empowered, demonstrating the importance of listening closely to experiences of quiet, quotidian resistance.

Participants suggest that small acts add up and connect to wider change: 'let's really make a difference, let's have everybody make tiny small differences and have a bigger society that really works' (Mel). Similarly, Beth speaks of 'the butterfly effect' in terms of the potential for small actions to have significant effects. Adrian suggests that minor subversions in his everyday life can empower people to challenge authority:

> I do sort of like poking at figures of authority with words often. Even just minimal things like sitting on the Council House steps and just sitting there and just telling the PCSOs [Police Community Support Officers] where to go really when they try and move you along. Just minor things like that because I

think people feed off that as well, just like questioning someone
in the street doing something horrible.

He asserts that 'I think you put yourself in a position that you know is risky
but may have the fallout that other people see that and go "oh, that person
did it and it's fine, I'm going to do it"'. The perceived costs and benefits
of protest change when we see others taking a stand, and this increases
the likelihood of mass mobilisation. Adrian suggests that there is a level of
fear among people about 'crossing the line' into activism, and that people
need to realise that the consequences of doing so are not as bad as feared.
Again, Adrian suggests that challenging dominant narratives can lead to
a more widespread dissent and effect: 'if it's just a few people pick up on
that and start questioning it then that can have an effect'. Similarly, Beth
says: 'I think that there's a definite correlation there that means that if you
can disrupt something kind of in the everyday [...] who's to say that won't
make [people] think differently?' Here, raising consciousness and changing
the way people think forms part of doing activism.

Participants' narratives further reveal how discourse and language
constitute action. For Harry, this is a key part of what being an activist
means:

> It [being an activist] means using every single opportunity by
> every means necessary to instigate, to agitate, to change, and
> to educate. From anything, from just somebody makes a casual
> racist remark in the street and you make it obvious you don't
> like it, someone drops some litter in the street and you make a
> point of picking it up, so literally from just everyday interaction
> to like, making sure that the language you use doesn't entail
> any kind of patriarchal hegemony in it.

Here we see a level of ultra- or perhaps hyper- activism, with 'every
single opportunity' being used for activism, raising questions about
how much individuals are expected to do in order to be considered
activists, a pertinent question that will be explored in Chapter 6. Dermot,
Jared and Adrian speak of challenging people in their daily lives if they
encounter someone using sexist or racist language and educating them to
do otherwise. Jared says: 'I think I do things through day-to-day sort of
challenging. Sometimes I'll challenge if I hear people saying racial slurs
or sexist slurs or transphobic things.' We see this notion of 'educating'
non-activists, with the implication being that activists have special access
to a particular type or level of knowledge that needs to be spread, giving
the impression of activism as evangelism.

In a similar way, Mel speaks about conversations with members of the public that aim to 'educate and empower' people to boycott unethical companies and to take up a more environmentally sustainable approach. Mel suggests that making individual choices is a relatively easy way to start making a difference and to empower individuals. The notion of individual responsibility and being able to make a difference through our choices is attractive in how it shifts away from the notion of individuals as powerless victims, instead giving them agency that can lead to mobilisation and political change.

However, neoliberal capitalism draws on and utilises people's desire to be ethically responsible, accumulating money by doing so. As Brown (2015: 27) asserts, 'caring' has become 'a market niche', with 'social responsibility' representing little more than 'the public face and market strategy of many firms today'. Often, ethical consumption choices require money as well as knowledge. While Mel attempts to help with the latter, the former is rarely recognised by participants, hinting at the ways in which privilege goes unnoticed in some respects, forming invisible barriers to becoming politically active and revealing that individuals are not equal. Indeed, neoliberal capitalism relies on individuals being unequal, creating competition between them.

Therefore, while actively fighting against neoliberal values, activists also problematically reinforce them, revealing the tensions present here and the difficult reality of resisting such a pervasive force as neoliberal capitalism, which we are all complicit in upholding. Kennelly (2014: 250) asserts how 'even within activist subcultures contesting neoliberalism, we see the cultural effects of neoliberalism at play, in particular via the belief that young people might "choose" to "change the world" through their individual actions'. In this respect, McGuigan (2016: 23) describes neoliberalism as a 'structure of feeling', drawing on Raymond Williams: 'it is inscribed into habitual modes of conduct and routine practices governing everyday life in largely unexamined and unconscious manner [sic]'.

While it may not be possible to always and completely resist neoliberalism, attempts can be made to utilise and subvert its dominant discourses in ways that create an alternative, emancipatory meaning.

Activism as (individual) responsibility to the collective

Participants draw on the neoliberal responsibilisation discourse but reinvent it in ways that both appeal to the public and undermine the dominant narrative, demonstrating both a hermeneutics of faith and suspicion (Levitas, 2012). Amanda states that the neoliberal narrative says 'you should stand up for yourself, take responsibility' and counters this, saying 'we're not saying people shouldn't take responsibility, for me that [doing activism] is taking responsibility'. Amanda's use of 'we' suggests a collective identity and an activist community that is opposed to neoliberal ideology. This discourse of responsibility is transformed to mean having a duty to stand up for others and against injustice. Joe notes how, for him, activism is a responsibility to others less fortunate than him and speaks of it as 'serving society'. Similarly, Hazel quotes Alice Walker, saying: 'activism is the rent I pay for living on the planet'. There is a sense of 'giving something back', which Mel draws on to raise the questions 'What is my gift? What can I give back?'

Walker's emphasis on 'the planet' reflects many participants' concern with the environment and animals, which several participants believe should be included within empathetic concerns. Rifkin (2009) reinforces this, arguing that the development of an 'empathic consciousness' that includes the environment is vital to create sustainable economies and ensure the planet's future. Several activists commit to veganism because of their empathy for animals and the environment, which acts as a key motivation for their activism. However, this is a point of contention for some participants, who feel that human beings should be given priority, a viewpoint that vegan activists disparage as 'speciesism' and that, we will see, causes tension within the activist community. Despite this, for some participants, concerns about the environment and humans come together to form a more 'holistic' activism. Mel speaks of how her activism is concerned with 'always looking for where is the hole in the whole'. Likewise, Adrian and Dermot speak of how their activism connects different issues, rooted in concerns for animal welfare and criticisms of capitalism.

Participants suggest that individuals have a responsibility to make choices that alleviate suffering, as Alex says 'to reduce harm', and that this is rooted in morals, ethics and empathy. In this respect, activism is a moral duty and something that everyone should and can do. Mel asserts 'it's about doing what you can, where you can', Lydia contends that 'you can't just do everything straight away, but activism is something that you can do'. Though participants acknowledge that attempts to change things may be futile, they contend that 'there is no excuse for not doing so' (Dermot). Here, 'doing something is better than doing nothing'. Dana says 'Unless I try I can't say I've tried ... so I might be whistling in the wind but I'll just keep whistling'. We start to see how participants place significance in the process of doing activism, regardless of its outcomes;

Jasper (1997: 82) acknowledges that 'bearing witness and "doing what's right" are satisfying in and of themselves, lending dignity to one's life even when stated goals are elusive'. Reinforcing this, Alison notes 'but you have got to fight the fight, haven't you? Even if you know that you're going to lose'. While this seems negative, Alison makes the point that 'although it might feel like you are arguing with people and it seems pointless I kind of think that it is important to have those arguments and to raise awareness and that by doing that you are changing things'. Similarly, Amanda speaks of her work rehabilitating male domestic abusers and says how:

> With that job I sometimes think oh [sighs], you know, I might work with 200 women, I might only actually properly help maybe 1 or 2 but rather that than none at all. So it's a bit like that, I'd rather do something than nothing. I'd rather go on a march where at least someone I talk to might think 'oh right yeah, I understand now the way that they exploit people' and that kind of stuff rather than like, you know, save the world kind of thing.

Amanda highlights the importance of making a difference, however small that may be and often in the face of perceived 'failure'. Furthermore, she contrasts small acts of consciousness-raising with larger 'save the world kind of thing[s]', alluding to different types and levels of action but also recognising, as Alison and others do, that interactions with non-activists count as action. We see here the distinction drawn by participants between activists and non-activists, raising questions about the differences between the two groups as well as the implications of drawing this boundary.

For Mel, it appears to be a simple case of making the choice to assert control over one's life. She states that 'throwing your hands up and wailing and saying you can't do anything is like oh please, get a life, you know? It's, well, get your own life.' Yet, if empowering oneself and doing activism was as easy as Mel implies, then the question remains of why more people are not involved in activism. Furthermore, the emphasis that participants place on educating and empowering others in order to encourage them to do activism reveals the effort required to persuade people to become politically active. This suggests that there needs to be an external influence that helps to change people's perspectives and actions, and therefore that doing activism is perhaps not an isolated individual choice that people come to by themselves. Again, we return to questions about the differences between those who are already activists and those who are not, and the distinction between 'activist' and 'non-activist' is reaffirmed.

'Activist' and/or 'non-activist'?

While Anna contends that everyone *should* do activism, she acknowledges that not many people do. Therefore she suggests that the term 'activist' is required as a way of distinguishing between those who do activism and those who do not:

> I said to myself it's [activism] what good people do. Good people stand up against injustice. And activist sounds like 'cause you've ... I don't know, you're kind of special I guess. But I think, now that I've lived long enough on this earth, I've come to realise that most people don't do anything and I guess you do need a label to differentiate between the people who do and the people who don't. However sad that is. Yeah. Yeah so I guess now I would consider myself an activist, in that respect.

Likewise, Harry says that activism 'is what everybody should be doing, by nature', and yet distinguishes himself as an 'activist' and says he sees 'it as the definition of my identity'. Unlike Harry, Anna highlights the notion that activist sounds like 'you're kind of special' and seems reluctant to claim the title because of this. Like Anna and others, Alex says: 'I'm kind of uneasy with the idea of it [the 'activist' label] because ... like for a number of reasons, like I think it can sound arrogant to think of yourself as an activist'. Similarly, Bobel's (2007: 153) participants remark that 'there was some connotation of better than thou or arrogance attached to activist'. Perhaps in rejection of this arrogance, participants displayed what I began to call 'activist modesty', where even those who are incredibly active say 'I don't do much' and 'I'm doing little bits'. Bobel (2007: 150) suggests that 'the conception of activist is anchored in key values of humility', which may explain participants' reluctance to appear arrogant by calling themselves activists and flouting these values. However, this 'activist modesty' may also signify that participants do not feel that they do 'enough' activism to legitimately claim the activist label, a topic I will return to when exploring the 'activist' identity in Chapter 6.

Critically, Anna and other participants contradict the notion that anyone can be an activist by suggesting that activists are a particular type of person, thus implying that to be an activist requires innate qualities that cannot be earned. Anna demonstrates this by comparing herself to her partner whom she does not identify as an activist, and wonders: 'what makes me such an individual and not him?'. We are reminded of comments previously made by Adrian about how he has always felt the need to stand up against injustice, even from childhood, again suggesting that this attitude is innate. Similarly, Charlotte suggests that activists tend to be caring people:

> I think you have to look after yourself because you can just see, I think if you really care, you're a really caring person, I think a lot of activists are, you can just see the world as a complete mess and that it's your job to fix it all and you're never going to do that. And that can leave people very sort of overwhelmed.

Charlotte constructs activism as a vocation and draws attention to the strains and risks of activism, which I will explore in Chapter 7. She also highlights the notion that activists are more caring, more sensitive and more likely to be hurt; as Mel suggests, those who are 'choosing to think bigger and around things are more sensitive, tend to be empathics, will get hurt'. Therefore, though participants claim that empathy is a universal human quality, there is the implication here that activists are naturally more empathetic than others, reinforcing the notion that an 'activist' is a particular type of person.

At the same time, however, participants speak about activism as a journey, suggesting that people become activists by learning and being critical and reflexive about theory and their own experiences. In this respect, 'activist' is an identity to work towards and which shifts over time according to the activities an individual is involved in. Here, the idea emerges that the type and amount of activism that one does impact upon who is considered to be an activist. Clearly, this is problematic as it suggests that those who are unable to do much action, or certain types of action, cannot be activists. Furthermore, this shifting of the identity over time contradicts the notion that being an activist is linked to an innate quality or essence that exists within some people and not within others. We start to see the ways in which the distinction drawn between activist and non-activist is problematic and contradictory.

So far, this chapter has highlighted how activism is motivated and sustained by emotions, especially the moral emotion of empathy, and normative ideals about how society should be and what it means to be human. Emphasis is placed on caring for others and placing the common good or the collective above the individual and their interests. These motivations are thus constructed in direct opposition to neoliberal capitalist values of selfishness and individualism. However, it would be disingenuous to suggest that there is no element of self-interest or personal reward that motivates and sustains individuals' activism. To do so would remove a key layer of the experiences and meanings of anti-austerity activist culture, and risk presenting participants as more than (or perhaps less than) human. In unpicking the complexities of the affective dimension of political engagement, it is important to explore all aspects, including those that on the surface might appear to reinforce the dominant neoliberal capitalist values that activists resist. The next section explores how self-interest motivates anti-austerity activism, demonstrating the continual balancing act that participants perform between the individual and the collective. Moreover, it reveals the third key motivating and sustaining force behind anti-austerity activism – relationships and the social element of doing activism.

The personal as motivation

> First they came for the socialists, and I did not speak out—
>   Because I was not a socialist.
> Then they came for the trade unionists, and I did not speak out—
>   Because I was not a trade unionist.
> Then they came for the Jews, and I did not speak out—
>   Because I was not a Jew.
> Then they came for me—and there was no one left to speak
>   for me.
>
> Martin Niemöller (n.d.)

While participants emphasise the need to speak out and stand up for others out of empathy, it appears that this is combined with self-interest, though participants do not openly admit this, as it reinforces the selfish individualist attitude they associate with neoliberal capitalism and to which they seek to construct an alternative. Anna speaks of a poster of Niemöller's poem that we had previously seen together:

> The poem that I live my life by is outside, the one that [says] 'and then they came for me'. So that was the first thing that I was taught as a child, it's, by the time they come for you it's too late, you have to speak out when they come for everyone else already.

She stresses the notion that 'an injury to one is an injury to all', but also demonstrates a concern with the potential (dangerous) consequences of remaining silent – namely, that your turn to be persecuted will come and there will be no one there to protect you. Similarly, Mary and Lily speak of the importance of speaking out and taking a stand because of the dire consequences if they do not:

[my mother] talked about having to have the money on top of the fridge in the jam jar for the doctor and all that sort of stuff, she was in that era pre-NHS, so you are just aware that if you don't do something then you potentially could go back to those sorts of things. (Mary)

People are taught nowadays to be neutral and to not have an opinion but I do, I have an opinion on racism because it affects me, I have an opinion on disabled policies because it will affect me and if you can't have an opinion on something that directly hurts you, it would lead to a really really dangerous situation where you just become silent and let things take over. (Lily)

Lily refers to the idea that people get involved in issues that personally affect them and links this to the need to speak out. Similarly, participants suggest that being personally affected by austerity is a motivation for doing activism. Dermot asserts that those who are the most affected by austerity (women, ethnic minorities and people with disabilities) 'are the most active' as they have a bigger stake in trying to change things, and Owain claims that 'people are far more likely to take an interest when they have a personal stake in it'.

In fact, Hazel contends that 'necessity drives a lot of activism'. She suggests that there are two types of motivation for activism:

Some people are very altruistic and they come into it from very privileged backgrounds and they feel that they want to make things better for people who don't have the same privilege, which is nice, sometimes it's nice but misguided, because they don't necessarily understand the issues they're fighting about. But other people come into it because they're literally skint and they see that they're skint and they see that it's not fair, and they want it to be more fair. And also they just want the truth to be known about the reality of living in poverty, you know?

Here, economic concerns about money are combined with normative ideas about justice and how things should be. Significantly, lived experiences of austerity and poverty are crucial for understanding these issues. Mel suggests that she understands austerity because of her personal experiences growing up in the context of austerity, and Anna asserts that having everyday lived experiences of an issue is different from having an abstract understanding. Moreover, Hazel suggests that the two types of motivation for activism do not link up:

> I don't think there's this level of thought in a lot of activism because the two sides don't link, you've got people who are in activism for basic need and they're just angry and they need stuff and they want to get stuff done, and that's kind of where I'm coming at it from. But then you have other people who maybe have ideas, about language and protest and movements, and their ideas may be very valid but they don't have the empathy to connect with the other people.

It appears, then, that empathy can act as a bridge between those without lived experiences and those who are personally affected by the issues. Beth talks about the importance of being able to 'put yourself in the shoes of' others in order to feel compassion and understanding, suggesting the importance of lived experiences. In a similar way, Alex says 'I've definitely been in really shit disempowered kind of positions and so I can, not only empathise, but I've actually lived that life.' While empathy is central to Alex (he describes activism as 'actively wanting to reduce harm' and his reasons for doing so being rooted in 'empathy' and 'ethics') there is again a sense that lived experience is somehow a more valid form of identifying with people's suffering that gives him the legitimacy to speak about and act on such issues. This raises questions about issues of representation; who can speak about particular topics, as well as who can legitimately claim the label of 'activist', which I will explore in Chapter 6.

While participants speak about the individual benefits they receive from helping others, this forms part of a wider emotional and social motivation for doing activism. Amanda speaks about the individual rewards she receives from doing activism in terms of how it makes her feel: 'If I can create a caring sharing world just in my little part of the planet then, and support people, support women I work with, support colleagues I work with, then I get a lot back from that.' Similarly, Mel acknowledges that 'if someone helps you, quite often you're helping them, even if it's just helping boost their self-esteem on a bad day'. Therefore, there is an individual benefit from helping others that is recognised by participants. As Dermot describes, referring to trade unions: 'of course a union is about protecting *your* job if you get in trouble, otherwise what's the point? But you also need to be in there to protect everybody else's jobs.' Significantly, there is still a focus on helping other people and on drawing together as a collective to protect the individuals within it; self-interest is not presented as the primary motivation for doing activism. Participants enact such values of community and solidarity within their activist culture, demonstrating the emotional and personal benefits of caring for others through their relationships with one another.

The sustaining force of the social and affective dimensions of activism

Participants' narratives reveal the varied ways in which social relations and emotion motivate and sustain activism. A key element of this is the strong sense of solidarity and community between activists that developed through their shared emotion and activities:

> It felt and to look around and see all these people, wow, actually this is something that people care about and people think this is wrong. And it makes you feel, sometimes you feel like you are on your own, you are the only one who has noticed this or who is bothered about this, and it makes you feel actually it is not just me. (Leonie)

> I just don't feel like anyone was taking these issues serious and it was just reassuring to see that there was loads of other people out there that not only had your views but were passionate about them to ... go and do something about it. I guess that's why they [Uncut] were really appealing ... it wasn't just me out there thinking 'oh my god, I can't believe all of this crap is happening'. (Tony)

For some participants, their first introduction to activism was through activist friends. Lily got involved 'mainly through personal relationships' and says 'because I knew them it made it very easy to join'. Jared explains 'I've become more active due to the people I've got involved with over the last couple of years'. Friends who are existing members of a movement act as a gateway for non-activists' involvement and help to lower the costs of participation. Lydia demonstrates this, explaining that relationships were a key sustaining factor that helped her to overcome personal difficulties and attend protests.

Moreover, participants made new friends and developed strong relationships with activists they met through their political involvement. Joe remarks that 'most of the friends that I've made have been through those same activities'. Leonie notes '[w]e met through political action really' and Tony states 'the only reason we knew each other was because of UK Uncut'.

Adrian suggests that meeting new people 'who are exciting and speak their mind' can reinvigorate his participation when he is feeling disillusioned or fed up: 'it [meeting new activists] sort of ignited a flame again'. Forming these relationships through activism enriched participants' lives; Mary says 'I just meet loads of people. I have developed so many friends in a whole sphere of places over the years that I have been active and I would miss all of that. If I hadn't engaged in it I wouldn't have all of those links really.'

Those who were involved with UK Uncut spoke of the formation and existence of a 'core group' of activists who were particularly active and who formed close and enduring bonds through their experiences. There is a strong sense of collective identity among the core group, with participants speaking as 'we', 'us' and talking about '*our* feelings'. Amin speaks about how he 'felt part of a wider community'. Will even notes '*we* had three arrests in all', despite not personally being arrested or even present at the event. What is particularly striking is how strong and enduring these group bonds were. Participants reinforce Corrigall-Brown's (2012: 12) interviewee who remarked that: 'it's like you served in the trenches of a war and you have these war buddies. You have a common experience that is so intense'. Joe explains that sharing political beliefs and joint experiences of activism is 'quite intimate' and helps friendships to develop. Similarly, Amanda speaks of the special bonds she shares with other activists as a 'deeper thing', and Alex asserts that such bonds are 'empowering and inspiring'. In fact, Adrian recalls meeting Alex as 'almost something spiritual ... it was just an understanding that came without words' and describes them as 'almost like brothers'. Likewise, Leonie speaks about a particularly difficult time for her:

> That year was a horrible, horrible year for me and, probably one of the worst years that I have had [...] and the people that were there for me and kept me going and were like my family, were the people that I met through Uncut. Whereas longer standing friends didn't really get it so much. They [Uncut people] were the people who bolstered me when I was really at my lowest point.

Here, we see the importance of caring for other activists as well as the issues and those who are affected by them, with these new relationships that develop through shared emotion and morality helping to sustain ongoing activism in the face of perceived failure to impact policy.

Alongside this emotional support and significant relationships, participants speak about another sustaining force of the social side that provided individuals with personal rewards – 'fun':

> And we made it fun, you know, nobody does anything because it is entirely altruistic. There was a personal gain element in it as well. You know some of those planning sessions were actually me spending weekends with people that I loved very very much and having a jolly good laugh (laughs). (Leonie)

Mary speaks of enjoying activism: 'I get really bored if I am not, I just do enjoy doing it. I would do stuff, there is political stuff I don't really enjoy, but I do it because it is the right thing to do, but I do really enjoy the stuff I do'. For Mary, making political events social is important as she does not have many opportunities to socialise outside activism. She claims that this is particularly important for women, given the extra time pressures that they have, which I will explore in Chapter 5. As demonstrated by Leonie's comment, Brown and Pickerill (2009: 27) contend that 'it is important not to underestimate the pleasurable dimensions of collective action. If activism was all hard work and drudgery, few people would sustain their involvement in movements for very long, no matter how strongly they supported a given cause'. Likewise, Wettergren (2009: 1) contends that 'fun and laughter are also key ingredients' of protest, which provide activists with instant rewards and attract others to get involved.

Wettergren (2009: 1) recognises that fun is also a key ingredient of late capitalism, but contends that activists 'reject the fun of consumption and offer their own definition of a kind of fun which is real and authentic'. In this respect, fun in protest is perceived to be qualitatively different from consumer 'false fun', and 'reclaiming control over the means of providing pleasure becomes a critical point of resistance' (2009: 5). Indeed, Morris asserts that protest is a legitimate source of fun and should be encouraged in society. He calls himself a 'protest-hobbyist, we went out protesting because we enjoyed it' and says protest 'is a good usage of time and a healthy, good thing to do'. Furthermore, Lasn (1999: 130) contends that 'realizing the full potential of human nature means realizing its natural creativity and propensity to *enjoy* freedom and autonomy'. It could be said, then, that the fun of protest represents a central feature of what it means to be human by harnessing the creative aspect of human experience. Harry emphasises the importance of creativity, contending that it is a central feature of protest because:

> When you create a dogmatic power structure that doesn't allow people to express themselves or be creative and then traps that human spirit, it becomes pointless. And if you don't have that democratic free participation right from the beginning, and that spontaneity and that ability to be spontaneous and creative

90

right from the off then you're inevitably going to create a locked in power structure, if you give up on democracy right from the very beginning, you're not going to come out with democracy at the end. And surely, surely, being spontaneous is the only thing that you can do in a true democracy.

Here, Harry links creativity to ideas of what it means to be human and to the ideal of democracy, suggesting that spontaneity is a way to resist constraining power structures.

Gadamer (1982) speaks about the centrality of play for human development, referring to it as an engrossing activity within which we can 'lose ourselves' and, significantly, become part of the collective. Therefore, play reinforces solidarity and a sense of community as well as providing the opportunity for individuals to transcend both their selves and mundane, daily life. Such ideas are reflected by Bakhtin's (1984) analysis of the carnival where the social order is inverted for a day and a sense of possibility is embodied by the spirit of rebellion, festival and fun of the carnivalesque. Furthermore, Rifkin (2009) refers to play as central in developing empathy and social behaviour as it encourages interaction between individuals and the ability to imagine the other's position. He (2009: 96) asserts that 'play, then, is far from a trivial pursuit. It is where we stretch our empathic consciousness and learn to become truly human.' Such activities challenge neoliberal capitalism's attack on humanity.

Therefore, while there is an element of self-interest that motivates and sustains activism, this is distinct from the individualistic capitalist values that participants reject as it is rooted in relationship with others, and 'an ethos of concern for others remains' (Brown and Pickerill, 2009: 32). Moreover, shifting the focus to the process rather than the outcome breaks with the instrumental reasoning of capitalism, where everything has to be justified as a means to an end. As Holloway (2010: 33) asserts, just doing something for its own sake can be a 'crack' in capitalism. Solnit (2005: 117) states:

> If your activism is already democratic, peaceful, creative, then in one small corner of the world these things have triumphed. Activism, in this model, is not only a toolbox to change things but a home in which to take up residence and live according to your beliefs, even if it's a temporary and local place, this paradise of participating, this vale where souls get made.

For some participants, activism is a way of living which has value in itself, regardless of the outcomes. Participants reinforce Solnit's claim that 'resistance is first of all a matter of principle and a way to live, to make yourself one small republic of unconquered spirit' (2005: 12). Lily refers to activism as her 'purpose in life' and Harry says it is 'a defining part of my identity'. Alison says: 'I guess that [activism] motivates me in my life and for some other people that's money. They will probably get a bit further than I do, but that is what motivates, that is what gets me up in the morning, I suppose.' Alison contrasts activism with neoliberal, capitalist values reflecting the construction of a selfish individualistic attitude versus caring about the collective, though she appears to have internalised part of this narrative: that progress is related to monetary gain.

For many participants, doing activism is in part about how they wish to perceive themselves and how they wish to be perceived by others. As Jasper (1997: 136) asserts, 'doing the right thing is a way of communicating, to ourselves, as well as others, what kind of people we are'. To not do activism is seen to be a negative reflection on an individual's character; Owain states: 'I can't not fight, I wouldn't be able to look myself in the mirror if I didn't.' Participants refer to doing activism as a 'moral imperative', emphasising its vital importance. This is different from the notion of activism being a moral duty that everyone should do, as it forms a key part of participants' identity. Anti-austerity activism, then, becomes a way of being for participants who attempt to forge spaces of resistance to the wider neoliberal society, where the collective is privileged over the individual and humanist values are enacted. This reflects what Kiwan (2017: 123) refers to as 'understandings of social change as a "way of living"', where it is the 'activity of activism' that is important, conceiving social change 'not as a vocation but as a way of life'.

Notably, despite the difficulties that participants face, a sense of possibility is evident throughout their narratives. Uncertainty is translated by participants into possibility; as Harry states, 'if you keep on demanding the impossible, you might just get it'. Participants demonstrate Solnit's (2005: 29) contention that 'uncertainty and instability thereby become grounds for hope'. Mel quotes a Chinese proverb: 'Keep a green tree in your heart and maybe the singing bird will come'. Crucially, she emphasises the importance of 'maybe': 'it *might* happen, but it also may not. However, wouldn't you feel better at the end of your life having done something? You've got to at least try.' Again, we see individuals' self-identity and morality being a motivation for doing activism as well as the high value given to activism, with doing it being something to judge your life's worthiness by. As Solnit (2005: 31) contends, 'activism itself can generate hope *because it already constitutes an alternative* and turns away from the corruption at the centre to face the wild possibilities and the heroes at the edges or at your side' (my emphasis). We see the value of the process, rather than a focus on the outcome, with participants forging spaces in the present where they enact normative ideals of justice, equality, empathy and a shared humanity. However, Solnit's comment portrays the activist as an extraordinary person, or a 'hero', which both valorises activists and distinguishes them from non-activists, a distinction that needs to be interrogated and will be explored further in Chapters 6 and 7.

It becomes clear that anti-austerity politics is about more than merely preserving social protections of the past and influencing social policy. It is also about reconfiguring democracy, challenging neoliberalism and raising normative and moral questions about how society should function and how human beings should act. In fact, Haiven and Khasnabish (2014: 3) contend that anti-austerity politics encapsulates the 'radical imagination' that imagines society in ways it might be, considering possible, positive, futures and finding a way to 'bring these back' to '*work* on the present, to inspire action and new forms of solidarity today'. In this sense, it involves a prefigurative political approach, acting in ways that constitute better alternatives to the current situation. The radical imagination builds upon this to aid feelings of empathy for others and produces solidarity. Crucially, the radical imagination is 'not a thing that individuals *possess* in greater or lesser quantities but [...] a collective *process*, something that groups *do* and do together' (Haiven and Khasnabish, 2014: 4). Here, the active, intersubjective and affective dimensions of movements are emphasised.

Rather than conceiving of social movements as 'things' but 'as products of the collective labour and imagination of those who actually constitute them' (Haiven and Khasnabish, 2014: 479), exploring the everyday processes of lived and felt experiences of political participation, reveals that activists are concerned with spreading wider moral and normative ideals of equality, justice, empathy, community and humanity. Further, these normative ideals are not merely rational values but are *felt* by individuals as an emotional response to the current context of neoliberal capitalism, demonstrating the intertwining of thinking and feeling, and challenging the traditional emotion/reason dichotomy. The combination of such moral ideals and strong emotions sustains anti-austerity activism over a long period of time because it is about more than achieving the instrumental goal of ending austerity.

Furthermore, sharing such emotions and morality with others forms the foundations for enduring social bonds and new relationships that bolster individuals and sustain their activism despite the apparent failure to impact policy. The continued existence of anti-austerity activism, then, encourages us to widen the definition and our understanding of political engagement and to refocus attention on the process rather than the ends, reflecting the approach taken by the movements themselves.

In this respect, we move towards an understanding of movements as 'living spaces of encounter, possibility, contestation, and conflict' (Haiven and Khasnabish, 2014: 479), where what matters is 'the formation and continuation of new social relationships, new subjectivities, and a new-found dignity' (Sitrin, 2012: 14). It is important to recognise such processes and their impacts given the ways in which they help to sustain activism and combine individualism and collectivism in a neoliberal capitalist context that pitches the two in opposition to each other.

This chapter has explored how anti-austerity activism is motivated and sustained by a combination of the affective and the normative, with a focus on the moral emotion of empathy, normative ideals about how society should be and how individuals should act towards one another. It has demonstrated that such abstract, universal ideals and discourses about empathy for a shared humanity are translated into concrete, particular actions through how participants enact activism as a form of care in the everyday. Here, participants emphasise 'doing something rather than nothing' and suggest that small acts can make a significant difference. Furthermore, this chapter has explored the centrality of the social element of activist culture and how its emotional effects sustain political action. While focusing on these enabling features, this chapter has also touched upon the ways participants resist, reinvent and sometimes reinforce neoliberal capitalism. Chapter 5 explores the constraining factors to doing activism.

5

Barriers to Doing Activism

We saw in Chapter 4 that participants speak about activism as both a responsibility and rooted in the everyday. A key part of this is the idea that everyone can and should do activism; participants stress 'doing what you can'. However, this chapter will demonstrate that not everyone *can* do activism, highlighting that it requires a certain privilege that is not always recognised by participants. Having explored the enabling and positive features of anti-austerity activism, this chapter unpacks the constraining factors that prevent individuals from becoming politically involved. It begins by exploring the concept of privilege, which is threaded throughout this and Chapters 6 and 7. It considers how the financial, temporal and physical costs of doing activism can prevent those who are the most disadvantaged and affected by austerity from becoming politically active.

Although women are disproportionately impacted by the public spending cuts, it emerges that there are gendered barriers and exclusions to doing activism that in turn reinforce the dominant oppressive structures that anti-austerity activism seeks to resist. This chapter elucidates this gendered dimension and provides a discussion of the ways women have responded to such barriers and exclusions by forming women-only groups that provide practical support for other women affected by the cuts. While this empowers women and enables them to become politically active in a way that subverts the gendered barriers and exclusions they face in the wider local anti-austerity movement, it problematically places an additional, unpaid, caring burden on women's shoulders and, in doing so, reinforces austerity, as well as the increasing divide between the public and private spheres that is associated with the traditional male/female dichotomy. This chapter thus continues to explore the tensions and contradictions involved in resisting the pervasive and dominant wider political context of neoliberal capitalism, demonstrating the way in which activist cultures interact with and are influenced by the context within and out of which they emerge.

(Not) checking your privilege

Participants' emphasis on activism as an everyday activity that anyone and everyone can and should do neglects to consider the privilege required to do activism. A key example of this is the way in which Harry, Dermot, Jared and Adrian speak about challenging people's language and actions in their daily lives as a form of activism, highlighted in Chapter 4. However, Amanda, Lily and Lydia muse that they do not feel confident or comfortable making such challenges. Beth says that she would rather tweet Blackwell's about a sexist display in order to be given distance and anonymity that is not present in face-to-face interactions, for fear that the man working in the shop may react badly and 'punch me in the face or something'. Though she laughs when giving this example there is a serious point here – that not all individuals are willing or able to take the risk of challenging people face to face. It is notable that there is a gendered divide between those who feel comfortable challenging strangers in their everyday interactions and those who do not, and that this gendered dimension is implicit, a topic that I will explore in Chapter 6. Moreover, there is an issue here of privilege in terms of the position that an individual comes from and how this may be advantaged in comparison to others.

Privilege is frequently spoken about by activists, with the common phrase 'check your privilege' being used by activists to alert others to the need to be self-reflexive about how their position may influence their thoughts, behaviour, and entitlements. Such sentiments are reminiscent of third wave feminists' necessary criticisms of second wave feminists' neglect of race and class (hooks, 2000), and the ways in which these intersect with each other and with gender to produce different experiences of oppression. However, it becomes clear that despite constant references to challenging and acknowledging one's privilege, many activists are not aware of some of their own privileges when it comes to doing activism (as demonstrated above). Moreover, it appears that such third wave feminist ideas have been misappropriated and mutated within activist communities into something that is not only removed from its theoretical and practical ancestry but is actively damaging. Lamon (2016), in a recent blog post that was turned into an article for *The Independent*, refers to such practices of activists policing one another by telling them to 'check your privilege' as part of the 'toxic culture of the Left' that silences dissenting opinions. She highlights the judgemental and policing aspects of activist cultures that underlie such concerns about 'checking your privilege' and that serve to repel not only non-activists, but those within the activist community who dare to disagree with this dominant view. These are central themes that

I will be returning to throughout Chapters 6 and 7, particularly when I explore the 'dark side' of activist culture.

However, in her attempt to denounce this 'toxic culture of the Left', which she associates with certain activists' focus on language and abstract theory, Lamon rejects other more positive features of activism, such as attempts to make spaces safer, and adopts a harsh approach that risks dismissing emotions and vulnerability entirely. Lamon's criticisms of the (perceived to be) overly sensitive jar with her call for complete freedom of speech by shutting down possibilities for emotion, reflecting a traditionally masculine attitude of 'quit whining and get on with it'. Yet, as we will see throughout Chapters 6 and 7, it is traditional masculine attitudes and behaviours, as well as male activists, that tend to produce much of the toxicity found within the activist community. First, this chapter will consider in more detail the question of who can do activism and the relationship between 'non-activists' and 'activists'.

Who can do activism?

Participants speak about lived experiences as a key motivation for doing activism but also acknowledge that being personally affected by austerity acts as a significant barrier to doing activism. Many participants remark that people are so focused on the daily struggle of survival that they do not have the time or energy to engage with activism. As Jared says, 'we're sort of crushed and inhibited by our need to live'. Hazel says, 'the most marginalised people don't have time or the energy 'cause you're literally struggling how to pay your rent or how to do this that and the other. And a lot of your focus is going on that.' Beth reinforces this, saying that while she was always taught empathy growing up (which we have seen is considered to be a key motivation for activism), her parents did not translate their experiences of poverty into 'being politically active' because 'they were so busy trying to survive, to raise me … I don't think they had the energy or time'. Similarly, Mary says:

> For some of the families, just getting by day to day is all they can think about so where they are going to get their next money from to put in the electric meter, that is their priority and they don't really engage at any level with what is happening and why the government are doing what they are doing, so for them I think they just see it as being a further attack on them and the things that they have to achieve with very limited resources becomes harder day by day.

Here we see the notion of austerity being an attack on the poorest, as well as the idea that the most affected are not in a position to engage politically. Hazel states:

> So while people can't pay rent, or buy food, that [money] will be their primary concern. So it's in the interests of privileged people and the government to reduce benefits and put a cap on it and have people living in a constant state of fear 'cause they're less likely to engage with activism and try to change the system. 'Cause they're too busy focusing on keeping a roof over their heads and buying food for themselves and the children. Once people have that basic level of need sorted, then they can go on to further things ... Maslow's hierarchy of needs, you know? And this is it, you have shelter, food, and further up you're going to get to things like fulfilment and people who are struggling at the bottom are never going to get to be self-fulfilled and learning for learning's sake or furthering their own souls, because they're constantly fighting for the money and the housing and the food.

Hazel's comment about fear draws our attention to the way that austerity and the threat of it are affectively lived by individuals. Visceral experiences, including the anxiety of struggling to find money for food or receiving a sanction letter that cuts your benefits, 'make austerity affectively present as they [experiences] become expressed through the feelings and actions of living beings. Bodies, therefore, are an important medium through which austerity erupts from "background noise" into the fore' (Hitchen, 2016: 104).

Moreover, austerity is often felt as a presence of absence – absence of money, of services, of confidence (Hitchen, 2016: 113). Notably, the responsibility to budget is often placed on women, reflecting another gendered dimension of austerity (Coleman, 2016).

Like Hazel, several participants refer to 'the hierarchy of needs', including Alison, who says:

> I don't know if those people [who are affected by austerity] always will organise because they are too busy worrying about what they are going to eat and it is all that Maslow's hierarchy of needs isn't it? If you are like me and you are kind of comfortable, knowing where you are going to get your food from next week, then you have got time to think about other things, but if you are a single mum on benefits and they

keep on cutting you all the time, more and more sanctions all the time, then you are generally worried about how you are going to pay the bills. You are not going to be out there organising against it, are you [...] Because they have got more immediate concerns and they are not politicised a lot of the time and they are not educated a lot of the time so they don't look at things in the same way.

Alison suggests that while those who are most affected by austerity are too busy focusing on survival, there is an additional problem in that they are not political. She explains: 'I guess that the people that I work with in terms of service users are not very political at all, but they are hugely affected by austerity. But they probably wouldn't even think about it'.

In contrast, Hazel argues that 'need is political', and draws on the idea that politics is rooted in everyday life. Helen makes the point that individuals affected by austerity have been protesting against it, but that changes in individuals' circumstances make it difficult to sustain this resistance:

The people that they're attacking are the same people that are fighting back against them so you might have been involved in 2010 but since then you might have had care or transport withdrawn from your kid with autism, you might be under the risk of redundancy at work so putting in extra time there, all sorts of things have changed in the way that those particular people have been attacked which then means that they're less likely to have the confidence and the security and the time and the energy to be involved.

Indeed, Hitchen (2016: 113) remarks that:

The affective presence of austerity in everyday life can generate subtle differences in the body, or 'micro-cracks' that mark a threshold of lower resistance [...] as the affective presence of austerity becomes greater and a more intrusive part of individuals' lives, these 'micro-cracks' in the body accumulate; eventually, they can accumulate so much that they surpass bodily thresholds and transform capabilities to act.

Thus, the multiple and continual affective experiences of austerity 'can change the body's disposition to austerity, and may make individuals less willing to contest, and instead accept austerity itself' (Hitchen, 2016: 117). Those who are the most affected by austerity are often so fatigued by these 'micro-cracks' that they are paralysed from acting against austerity, 'meaning that individuals' everyday lives become consumed with trying to stay afloat' (Hitchen, 2016: 117). In this way, austerity's effects are 'affectively disempowering' (Hitchen, 2016: 117).

Several participants suggest that this daily grind wears people down, forcing them to become accepting of the current situation and resulting in them feeling powerless. Hazel says: 'So, it is easy to become ground down, and just think oh well, this is the way life is.' Likewise, Alison laments that everyone has accepted things as they are, and Martin notes that 'there is not a great deal of hope that things can get better in the short or the medium term I don't think'. Participants reinforce the suggestion that the cumulative effect of austerity in everyday life makes individuals less likely to resist it and more likely to accept it (Coleman, 2016; Hitchen, 2016). Significantly, for participants, such feelings of hopelessness and powerlessness are perceived to be the main causes of apathy. Thus, it is not that people do not care about the issues or are unaware of them, but that they feel powerless and that there is no point in resisting austerity. Indeed, participants remark that the general feeling is 'what difference can I make?'. Mel notes that a common response she faces at actions is 'I see what you mean, but I just don't know what I could do'.

In response, Martin draws on the idea of doing what you can, acknowledging that while people's focus 'rightly is on the day to day getting by, making sure that they have got enough money, enough food, the rent is paid, the kids are clean and fed and off to school', at the same time it is important to develop 'a dialogue' with people affected by austerity, otherwise 'you can't achieve very much'. He suggests that there needs to be a great number of people involved in activism against austerity, including those who are most affected, but that this should be done according to what each individual is capable of doing:

> And people can take part to a lesser and greater extent, there might be people who you know could only spare an hour a week or half an hour a week doing something, but I think if enough people thought 'here is something that I could get involved with' and felt a part of it, whether they were actively doing a great deal towards it or not then that in a sense would be enough, because their thinking would have changed, not necessarily what they practically and actively do and it might take just one thing.

Martin draws our attention back to the affective dimension by suggesting that it is important for people to feel that they belong to a movement. He also highlights the importance of consciousness-raising, suggesting that activism is about changing not only people's actions but their thinking too, as I showed in Chapter 4. This not only problematises how we define and understand activism, but raises questions about the role activists and social movements play in relation to 'non-activists' and those who are affected by the issues that are being protested about.

Participants' narratives reveal an underlying assumption that activists have special access to the 'truth', which others do not, and that the role of social movements is therefore to bring this truth to the public. In a similar way, Alexander (2006) and Melucci (1996: 1) contend that social movements are key vehicles of social change, which 'force power out into the open and give it a shape and a face'. This is because 'power operates through the languages and codes which organize the flow of information; therefore, social movements must interrupt these dominant languages to exercise power' (Melucci, 1996: 9). Tony reinforces this, contending that UK Uncut are 'representing these issues that are going untold and that no one's doing anything about', saying Uncut 'breaks society's narrative' by highlighting injustices and revealing the 'truth'. This underlying assumption that UK Uncut has access to 'the right information', and has the responsibility to spread this, draws on evangelism discourses and invokes images of removing the scales from the eyes of the masses, implying that activists are more 'enlightened' than others. Participants speak about the need to educate 'ordinary people' about the ideological nature of the public spending cuts, unmasking the government's 'blatant lie' by bringing the issue 'out into the open' and into the 'public consciousness'. Leonie states:

> But the whole point of it really, right at the very heart of it I couldn't actually give two hoots whether or not Vodafone pay their tax, that is kind of irrelevant to me, the whole point of it was to say look, we are being told that these cuts are necessary, but actually they are not ... that these are totally ideological cuts.

Similarly, Tony argues that:

> If people don't have this understanding or the ability to understand this or... or are not getting told the right information to be able to make these decisions then, they're the people you're fighting for the most, I think. Who is representing these people and telling their story? No one. So, I think that's where UK Uncut comes in.

Tony raises issues of representation regarding who can and who should speak for disadvantaged groups in society, which I will return to in Chapter 6, as well as the fact that these groups do not have a voice in the public sphere. Therefore, Tony perceives social movements to act as a bridge between those who are disenfranchised, the public, and those in power. Similarly, Scott (2012: 20) contends that radical social movements are 'the transmission belt between an unruly public and rule-making elites'. However, by positioning themselves as more knowledgeable than 'ordinary people', a clear distinction is made between 'activist' and 'non-activist', with the former being in a privileged position. Joe suggests, though, that he can use his privilege to push oppressed groups' desires and needs into the public sphere and thus help to empower those who currently lack a voice in politics:

> As I speak from a position of privilege I don't really have the right to dictate how people from less privileged backgrounds should live. But I want to... I want to extend the power to, in order for them to speak out, in order for them to have a say, where, given that that right is currently concentrated in the upper echelons of society.

We return, then, to the issue of privilege and the question of who can do activism. There appears to be a tension between the need for activism to be focused on and led by those who are the most affected and the daily reality of living with the effects of austerity preventing people from getting involved in activism. Participants often speak of the 'time' and 'energy' involved in doing activism, suggesting that such costs act as a barrier to activism. Problematically, it is usually the most vulnerable and disadvantaged who cannot afford such costs and who are therefore excluded from doing activism.

Costs of activism

Hazel notes that the financial costs of doing activism prevent working-class people from being involved; when speaking about the national Women's Assembly meeting, she comments, 'it was expensive, it was in London. So, same situation really, even people who are on the Left and supposedly against austerity and speaking for working class people exclude working class people by their choice of location and their price.' Similarly, Lydia and Lily speak of practicalities that prevent them from doing activism, describing 'the issue of travelling'. Accessibility is reduced because many individuals do not have a car and cannot afford to travel to protests, Tony acknowledges this: '[the cost] does obviously limit the people, you might not afford £10 to go to London to go on a demo. I used to spend an absolute fortune going to London and back … no way could people do that!'

Alongside financial costs, there are time costs that can prevent individuals from becoming politically active. Activism requires time; As Oscar Wilde reportedly exclaimed, 'the trouble with socialism is that it takes too many evenings'. Indeed, Walzer (1970) observes that if individuals were truly 'active citizens', there would be little time left in their lives for much else. Many participants speak about how other commitments prevented them from being more active. Adrian says 'the daily rigmarole gets in the way', Martin and Dana contend that 'people are busy!' and Mary suggests that 'the difficulty always is that the people that are doing those sorts of things [activism] are generally very busy people'. Likewise, James recognises the time costs of activism, which not all individuals can afford: 'Sunday afternoon for me or one of the others, that's a Sunday afternoon, it is not really anything. But to a lot of people that might be their only day off, their only chance to relax, they might be working, you know?' Beth remarks: 'I'm in a different position to Georgie or Hazel [other activists] because I work full time, and I'm also trying to finish a PhD so I'm not allowed to take an afternoon off on a Thursday to go and attend these meetings.' Here we start to see how individuals compare their own activity to others, a central theme that will return in Chapters 6 and 7.

Participants with disabilities and health conditions highlight additional barriers to attending protests and meetings. Both Lily and Lydia struggle with crowds because of their health conditions, and they find attending protests challenging. Lydia notes how she can only go 'if I am feeling well enough, up to it, and if I'm able to do it'. Similarly, Adrian remarks that 'I find it very tough to go to places where there's people' and Martin speaks of how his partner's health condition means 'she gets very tired a lot of the time, so she is physically not able to do a great deal'. Likewise, Mel is unable to attend events without spending money on an accessible taxi and the use of a rollator (a mobility walker), thus increasing the costs of activism and making many protests inaccessible.

When making the decision to attend events (if they are accessible), these participants have to consider the recovery time needed afterwards and the impact of activism on their health. Mel draws on 'spoon theory' to illustrate this, describing how when one has a chronic health condition it is like having a finite number of spoons each day, where spoons represent a person's energy. Therefore, individuals have to carefully consider how to use their spoons and what actions are likely to require time for recovery afterwards. Lily remarks that 'a lot of disabled students find it difficult, either because of their illness or because there are accessibility issues to do the kinds of things that activism expects you to do'. We begin to see the notion that activism requires (or 'expects') certain activities, implying that if an individual cannot do these they cannot be an activist. I will explore the distinction made between different types of activism, how they are organised hierarchically and the implications of this for vulnerable and disadvantaged groups in Chapters 6 and 7. The key point here is that the typical types of protests and meetings that anti-austerity activism involves are often inaccessible to those with health conditions and disabilities, which is especially problematic given that these groups are disproportionately affected by the public spending cuts.

Moreover, the experience of participants with disabilities alerts us to the problem that those who are the most affected also face bigger costs and risks when it comes to doing activism. Being personally affected by an issue makes it impossible to escape or take an (often needed) break from it, meaning activism becomes all encompassing. Anna demonstrates this:

> It's pricier. So I think it takes a greater toll on your well-being because you can't remove yourself from it. If you feel disillusioned, you feel disillusioned with yourself and the possibility for your life to be a better life. You can't just say 'oh let them deal with their issues, I'll just take a break for now'.

Similarly, Lily notes 'it just gets like, it's all around, you know? It's really hard to turn off to.' Indeed, Anna suggests that people with disabilities are active in fighting austerity 'because it's about themselves' but acknowledges that this personal attachment makes it a 'painful fight'. It appears then that the costs of activism are felt more acutely by those who are the most affected by the issues.

Activism as a luxury?

So far we have seen that the financial, temporal and energy costs of activism prevent people who are less privileged in these areas from doing activism. Because of the privilege that participants have, they have the opportunity to channel their frustrations and desire for change into more socially acceptable actions. In this respect, participants possess the cultural, symbolic and social capital that enables them to engage politically in a more socially acceptable way (Bourdieu, 1986). Participants demonstrate this by drawing comparisons between Uncut and the 2011 riots, arguing that both arose from the same emotions and concerns but that these frustrations were channelled differently. James notes how 'they were both born out of a similar thing which is awareness that things aren't right'. He elaborates:

> Speaking to people on the night [of the riots] you definitely got the sense that even if it was very gruff, very guttural and ill-educated understanding of how things stand that they [the rioters] knew what was going on, that they knew what they were doing and there was an awareness of it, they just weren't sort of channelling it into the accepted ways.

Helen says:

> I think that's interesting in terms of the riots, that the people who finally took that sort of action were people who were genuinely disenfranchised, as in genuinely had very little to lose. I might think that it's fine to destroy property in order to get a political gain, but I also think that my work in education is really important and if I throw a brick through a window, that then means that I am not a teacher any more, almost certainly. And so, there's levels of involvement in society, I think you have to reach quite an extreme point for people who are assimilated into the society to be able to take actions that put themselves at risk.

She goes on to say that:

> It is at huge times of disruption, so, in revolutions, or in the riots in London, or whatever, you do get the people who are actually oppressed involved in fighting it. I think what happens with more regular activism is it's people who have the levels of social awareness and the levels of consciousness to be able to become involved. The key group, I suppose, is people who work with people who are disadvantaged.

It could be argued then that 'regular' activism is a luxury that only the privileged, in terms of cultural and symbolic capital, can afford, given its financial and temporal costs and required social [under]standing. At the same time, more confrontational action is a risk that 'regular' activists cannot afford to take precisely because of their position in society. Several participants felt constrained by the risk of losing their jobs because of participating in activism, with those who work in the public sector (and the most affected by public spending cuts) being particularly aware of this risk. Beth speaks about the structural constraints of being an activist and working within an institutional setting, referring to herself as a 'tempered radical'. Such fears about losing one's job were related to the real risk of police control and arrest at direct actions. Dermot acknowledges that direct action often involves the danger of 'putting yourself on the line'. Participants also speak of the less physical but nonetheless daunting risk of public humiliation, with Harry remarking 'if you stand up like a nail, you'll be knocked down'. Although men spoke about the risks involved in activism, women seemed especially susceptible to the risks of direct action, with mothers having concerns about the safety of their children at protests: 'so in that sense I think it is harder for women [...] I think you don't take as many risks with kids probably'. Furthermore, women were more likely to work in the public sector than men, thus meaning that concerns about losing one's job were also gendered.

This chapter has so far demonstrated that despite participants' claim that everyone and anyone can and should do activism, because of the costs involved not everyone *can* do activism. Problematically, it is those who are the most affected by austerity who are the least likely to be able to participate, raising questions about issues of representation, which will be explored in Chapter 6. Furthermore, while the costs of activism are felt by many individuals, it becomes apparent that there are perhaps bigger costs and barriers to becoming politically active for women, and especially working-class women and women with disabilities.

Gendered barriers and exclusions to doing activism

In contrast to claims that gendered structural availability barriers are disappearing, participants contend that women's particular 'time burden' impacts on their ability to participate politically. Beth summarises, remarking 'women are busy, they're so busy [...] women's time is precious, more so than men's, because they still have to take on this burden of like, housework, or childcare, other care'. Beth draws our attention to the widespread notion that 'women have more pressures on their time' because of their 'caring burden', and Mary explains that 'there is still an expectation that women are the people who look after the kids [...] caring for elderly parents. They are seen as the people that do that caring role and are at home.' Mary highlights the persistence of traditional public/private boundaries, with women being expected to retain responsibility for the private sphere.

Alison contends that having to combine employment, childcare responsibilities and other time pressures is the 'nature of being a woman', reinforcing the 'double burden' theory (Kremer, 2007). Crucially, local anti-austerity groups neglect to take this into account; as Hazel asserts 'ultimately they exclude women, because they have the meetings in the evening when you've got to put your kids to bed'. Likewise, Charles (1993: 71) draws attention to how trade unions' operation at a local level makes it difficult for women to participate, by holding meetings in the evenings or at weekends and providing no crèche facilities. Indeed, Phillips (1991: 21) contends that: '[i]n societies where the division of labour is ordered by sex (that is, every society we know), time becomes a crucial constraint on women and meetings an additional burden'. Charlotte demonstrates this, speaking of a postcard 'that said "I wanted to change the world but I couldn't find a babysitter" and I think I feel a bit like that at the moment'. Similarly, Beth says:

> There is not really any sphere of public life that isn't gendered. So even when you have well-meaning people maybe meeting under a Marxist banner to oppose cuts to the NHS or whatever it might be, they are usually still typically run by men and you need to have people involved that go 'hang on, if we have this meeting at this time on a Sunday evening, then these women won't be able to come'.

Beth draws our attention to the key point that activism tends to be dominated by men and that, because of this, women's concerns are forgotten, which leads to gendered exclusions from activism. In fact, Charles (1993: 75) suggests that when such barriers to participation are removed (by holding meetings during work hours in the case of trade unions, for example), women attend as much as men do.

Participants suggest that social media can help to overcome time pressures associated with caring responsibilities and the subsequent difficulty of attending meetings. Hazel says:

> So, a lot of women don't have access to the internet at home because they can't afford broadband, but most people have mobile phones so when your children are in bed at 8, 9 pm, you're at home, by yourself. So you'll clean your house, you may make some meals so that all the work's done for tomorrow, but you'll not necessarily want to go straight to sleep so you'll have the time to read or to think or to do something. And if it's stuff that people can do on Facebook, on Twitter, through

their phones then they're more likely to get involved than if they have to physically attend a meeting when they're supposed to be putting their kids in bed.

Notably, there is a class element here, with Hazel speaking about women who cannot afford broadband. Like Hazel, Charlotte says 'why I think it's [social media] great because like, you can lie in bed breast-feeding and look at stuff on Facebook'. Demonstrating this, Beth speaks about her friend setting up a now large Facebook group for local feminists: 'So it's like, techno-grassroots in that sense (laughs), it was just like she made it probably like feeding Mika in one hand and like, at 5 o clock in the morning or something, he was new-born so, (laughs).' It appears that social media is a way to combine caring and activism, enabling women to do both at the same time and reducing the time costs of activism that act as a barrier to participation. However, Charlotte also goes on to say 'but yeah I would like to do a bit more sort of active', hinting at a distinction between online and offline action and suggesting that the latter is more 'active' and perhaps preferable, an attitude that I will explore further in unpacking the ideal activist identity in Chapter 6.

Participants highlight gendered exclusions within anti-austerity campaigns, drawing attention to their lack of intersectionality and omission of women's issues. There are two problems here; first, white working-class men tend to dominate activist campaigns, and secondly, there is a preoccupation with class to the neglect of intersecting issues such as gender, race and disability. We can perhaps draw on Brown's (1999) discussion of 'Left melancholy' to explain these problems. Brown (1999) argues that many on the Left are in a state of melancholy, unable to overcome the loss of certain Left ideas and to adapt to the current state of events in the world. Notably, this Left melancholy is manifested as a rejection of cultural or identity politics, which are perceived to 'not only elide the fundamental structure of modernity, capitalism, and its fundamental formation, class, but fragment left political energies and interests such that coalition building is impossible' (1999: 23). Similarly, Bassel and Emejulu (2018) highlight the problems with the Left's single-axis focus on a unified working class that tends to be implicitly white and male and makes it impossible to raise claims for specific oppressed groups. This reflects Hall's (1988) criticism of the Left's traditionalism, which combines with this Left melancholy not only to prevent the acknowledgement of gendered and racialised differences but also to actually reinforce sexism and racism.

Combined with postmodernism, which throws into question the possibility of an absolute truth and objective grounds for Left norms, this results in the continuance of an attachment to what is perceived to have been lost, or Left melancholy. Crucially, the consequence of this is the failure to 'apprehend the character of the age and to develop a political critique and a moral-political vision appropriate to this character' (Hall, cited in Brown, 1999: 19). As Brown (1999: 24) asserts, this 'failure results, as well as from a particular intellectual straitjacket – an insistence on a materialism that refuses the importance of the subject and the subjective'. This Left melancholy, then, can help to explain why some organisations ignore intersecting issues such as gender and race (which are seen as a threat to Left traditionalism), and focus on class instead.

Emejulu and Bassel (2015) draw attention to the ways in which issues of racial oppression, as well as gender oppression, are ignored and reinforced by anti-austerity activist cultures. Emejulu (2017) reveals that minority women activists were often excluded from anti-austerity movements when they attempted to raise gendered and racialised critiques of austerity, and contends that there is an incompatibility with a movement that constructs itself as populist and relies on ideas of a unified people. Moreover, dominant structural oppressions were not only ignored but actively reinforced by anti-austerity activist spaces, with women reporting many instances of racism and sexism (Maiguashca et al, 2016).

While I have attempted to consider the places at which gender and class intersect, there is an obvious absence of race within this study. This reflects the lack of racial diversity within local anti-austerity activism – only three of my participants identify as BME. Participants recognised this lack within their movements and attempted to increase diversity, with little success, raising questions about the invisibility of BME individuals within local anti-austerity activism. Similar to the neglect of gender within local anti-austerity campaigns, race has been forgotten despite the fact that ethnic minorities are disproportionately affected by the public spending cuts.

However, in contrast to Maiguascha et al's (2016) and Emejulu's (2017) analyses, the local People's Assembly did place issues of racism at the centre of their protest activities, often organising events to highlight and resist racism, both in terms of local racism and more global issues, the latter showing how immigrants and refugees are constructed and treated in racist terms. This perhaps reflects the close links between Stand Up to Racism, Unite Against Facism and Stop the War Coalition and the Trades Union Congress (TUC), which the People's Assembly had grown out of, with many of the same Stop the War activists being organisers of the movement and TUC representatives. However, while there was a focus on issues of race, these tended to be one dimensional and focused solely on racism rather than recognising how race intersects with other forms of oppression. Moreover, despite the movement being about resisting austerity, the racialised and gendered elements of austerity's impacts were not recognised. As Forkert (2018: 102) asserts, there seems to have been 'little interaction or co-ordination between anti-austerity campaigns and migrants' rights campaigns. These have largely been treated as single issues.'

Rather than acknowledging and paying attention to the ways in which struggles interlock, these dominant activists rank struggles in a hierarchy. Dermot explains:

> So, the oppressions interlock, our personalities interlock, so the point of intersectionality is that *all* struggles need to address *all* these issues ... because if you don't acknowledge that, you end up with trying to combat one form of oppression by advancing a different form of oppression, so you get a lot of, anti-capitalist people who are really really sexist without realising it and who are setting back the women's struggle because they don't acknowledge the fact that they're linked struggles.

Dermot draws on literature concerning 'intersectionality' (hooks, 2000), a term that was introduced in the 1980s by Kimberlé Crenshaw (1989) to draw attention to how gender and race interact to form particular experiences of oppression. Initially, intersectionality was concerned with making black women's experiences visible. Emphasis was placed on the intersection of race and gender, which was often ignored by a predominantly white feminism. Further, first wave feminism was criticised for ignoring class differences and how these intersect with race and gender (for a more detailed discussion of these debates see Charles, 1993). The concerns of 'getting out of the home' are considered to be middle class, with this experience being portrayed as representative of all women, thus neglecting working-class women who did work, as well as how the home was often a haven for black women facing racism in society, rather than a place of confinement (as it has traditionally been conceptualised within feminist literature). Therefore, intersectionality is useful for thinking about how multiple differences interact to produce different experiences of oppression, including race, class, disability, gender and sexuality. Admittedly, it is difficult to develop fully intersectional research in the context of limited studies that by definition have to focus on particular aspects of experience. Therefore, while I attempt to draw on other key studies that explore race in this book, the main focus of the original research, and thus this book, is gender and the points at which this intersects with class. As I will discuss in Chapter 6, issues of representation are important, and I would rather admit the limitations of this study in relation to race than draw conclusions based on inadequate data from individuals with lived experiences of racism. This is an important area that has been researched in the studies I refer to, and would inform future research in this context.

Within the context of austerity, class is clearly an important element to consider; however, many participants have an ambivalent relationship with class, which reveals itself to be a complex topic. Half of my participants identify as working class, reinforcing the underlying class dimension of austerity, while a further eight were raised in working-class families but were now considered to be middle class through education, occupation or marriage. Regardless of their current class status, these participants still identified with their working-class roots as a basis for understanding the impacts of austerity, as we will see in Chapter 6. Although being working class was central to some participants' identities, the context of increased insecurity and the related changing definitions of class have resulted in participants conceiving of class as problematic.

Further, it may be the case that because of the dominance of class to the neglect of gender in the People's Assembly, class is strategically minimised as an issue in order to move gender to the fore, and specifically, women's voices. Of course, it is not a case of one or the other (gender or class) as the two intersect; both class and gender can be understood as traditional social cleavages, although the latter has been paid less attention (Charles, 2000). However, participants were keen not to let class overshadow other aspects of experience, which Charles (2000) identifies can be the case when class acts as a dominant social cleavage and thus prevents other conceptualisations of movements and participants (such as gender and race) from emerging.

Reflecting the persistence of traditional links between working-class politics and masculinity, several other participants criticise anti-austerity activism's focus on white men's class struggle. Hazel, a white working-class single mother, chooses to distance herself from these campaigns because of the ways in which male privilege dominates and goes unchallenged. She asserts that while women lead many campaigns they often do not get support or credit for doing so, reinforcing research that demonstrates men's privilege and visibility in social movements to the neglect of women's contributions (Thorne, 1975; McAdam, 1992; Jacobsson and Lindblom, 2012). Bobel (2007: 156) remarks that 'there is often a conventional division of labour in social movement communities (e.g. women behind the scenes/men in front of the cameras), a split that obscures women activist's contributions'. Likewise, Brown and Pickerill (2009: 31) contend that 'there is a lingering machismo within autonomous activism which persists in ignoring how the behind the scenes "emotional work" of activism is often left to women'. Notably, these divides reflect gendered differences in the type and status of paid work which women do, compared to men. As Charles (1993: 57) identifies, 'As well as being clearly demarcated, men's and women's work is valued differently; men's is consistently more highly valued than women's and is regarded as requiring a level of skill which most "women's work" does not.'

While participants did not find that they were assigned gendered roles, they did remark on the prestige given to men compared to the visibility afforded to women. It appears that traditional notions of the public sphere being a male and masculine domain, and the related gendered divides in the workplace, are carried over into alternative political spaces. Further, attitudes and behaviours within these spaces reflect ideas of women being seen as a 'liability' to politics, demonstrated by the treatment of women politicians within party politics (Ross, 2011). Therefore, despite movements' attempts to establish themselves as different to party politics, the same gender inequalities persist, suggesting deeply embedded gender structures and divides.

For several participants this reflects a wider societal lack of concern with women's issues. Alison says how 'stuff like raising kids, so that would be seen as something that women do and I would see that as everyone's business and I think because it is a female role it is kind of not seen as very important'. Likewise, Charles (1993: 76) notes that 'women's issues' were not given attention or deemed important by trade unions whose male delegates considered issues such as childcare to be individual problems for women to solve outside work. Instead, Alison asserts that 'the things that happen to women personally are something that politics should be concerned with', drawing on the feminist notion that 'the personal is political'. For Alison, the way to increase the profile of traditionally women's concerns such as childcare is to reconceptualise it by degendering unpaid caring roles within the family:

> If dads did that role more then it would be given a higher status and so that, it is like with anything, so women's work, stuff like caring work or whatever, it's normally women that do that, but if more men did that then you know the status would rise of that kind of work.

Alison's comments draw on the suggestion that valuing care in its own right degenders it, resulting in men and women being freer to make choices about their caring roles (Kremer, 2007). In this vein, Fraser (1994) proposes the 'universal caregiver' model, where men take on care and paid work, degendering caregiving and sharing the care burden.

Especially relevant here is the ways in which such a model encourages the notion of 'universal citizenship', where wider community and public forms of care are also degendered and shared equally between men and women. However, Alison's solution gives the power to men, reinforcing the current dynamic rather than attempting to challenge this and change the position and power of women. Although Kremer (2007: 38) contends that 'when men perform a specific task, its status will increase', there is the risk that rather than redefining care, men who take on caring roles will instead be perceived as feminine, and the gendered nature of care will be further reinforced, along with damaging connotations of femininity and masculinity.

Participants also highlight implicit ways in which activism is gendered, classed and influenced by subtle forms of oppression. Helen draws attention to the 'paradox of participatory democracy', where participatory intentions lead to greater exclusion as only certain people are able to participate fully:

> You say 'everyone come to the planning meeting, we'll all contribute', but people's confidence in how to contribute, people's ideas aren't always, either they're not seen in the same way by other people or they simply just don't have the confidence to contribute their ideas or the space to do it, where it might take a lot more time to develop. And that's the thing with people who were working with limited time, the times I've seen that kind of horizontal thing work really well is in things like occupations, where you've got all the time in the world because everyone's just sat around, so you can have a two-hour meeting every day and gain consensus. Whereas if you're looking at people who are working, campaigning alongside other things, it's the four people who have got the time and the energy who actually end up directing what goes on.

Here we see the issue that even if people can and do attend meetings, 'informal impediments' (Fraser, 1992: 119) exist that prevent people from participating in discussion. Fraser (1992: 126) contends that 'participation means being able to speak in one's own voice', which is not possible when classed and gendered modes of communication are discredited or ignored. Jared demonstrates an awareness of this, asserting that people need to 'feel safe enough to have their voice and safe enough to attend there. 'Cause if there's not then you're preventing a lot of people really taking an active role if they wish to in the movement.' Therefore, even when initial access barriers are overcome, further barriers remain that can prevent people from fully participating. Indeed, participants draw attention to a general atmosphere of 'aggressive machismo' in activist circles that makes spaces feel unsafe for women to participate in. Anna notes how in mixed gender groups 'very often the men have [a] very aggressive argumentative style of arguing and they haven't got rid of all their patriarchal tendencies to speak over you and to shout you down and patronise you'.

In response, participants suggest that social media is a medium that erases 'informal impediments' that prevent less privileged individuals from having a voice in the public sphere by affording the anonymity and distance to speak openly and freely (Fraser, 1992). Beth says that 'social divisions get a little bit blurred with social media in a way that I think's great' and speaks of technology being 'a great leveller'. Hazel reinforces this, contending that social media acts as:

> [T]hat bridge between people who don't have resources and people who do have resources and everybody's more equal. Because on the internet you don't know how skint somebody is, if they've managed to get access to the internet, for that time, they're on an equal footing with you.

We are reminded of Habermas's (1989) original ideal of the public sphere where inequalities are 'bracketed', creating open debate between people with statuses removed so that the emphasis is on the content of the argument, rather than the speaker. However, before jumping too quickly into a romanticised notion of the internet as an ideal public sphere, we should remember that the use of technology creates new exclusions, particularly for those without experience of or access to technology. Hazel states that 'we need to become more welcoming of the internet without leaving older activists behind'. Helen draws our attention to the potential exclusion of groups that do not have the skills or technology required to remain in the loop:

> You must be careful about who you're excluding through doing that. Particularly with NHS things quite a lot of people who get involved are older people who might not necessarily be internet users ... groups of young people who don't have access to the internet and the way that they're digitally marginalised do they call them? Or digitally deprived? So those same groups of people aren't getting this access necessarily.

As Castells (1996) contends, we now live in a world where information and access to it are the new and highly valued form of capital, where a key divide is between the information rich and the information poor. Jack demonstrates how the use of technology can be exclusive, recalling a time when:

> They sort of done a Twitter meeting where you were supposed to use a hashtag and, but for whatever reason, I don't know, my computer at the time just wasn't fast enough, and I thought so that's me out, I can't engage in this discussion because my computer isn't quite up to it.

Furthermore, status and inequalities are not entirely 'bracketed' on social media sites such as Facebook where users' names are visible and assumptions about their gender are likely to be made. Alison highlights gendered risks to participating politically online, saying women are sometimes the recipients of 'negative attention. They get rape threats, that kind of stuff, so it's a double-edged sword, isn't it?' Beard (2014) asserts that where women do speak out they are punished for doing so, reinforcing the traditional boundaries between the masculine public and feminine private spheres.

Therefore, social media does not necessarily erase offline divides; in fact, Loader and Mercea (2012) claim that offline divides in political participation are reproduced and reinforced online. The very qualities that make the internet so appealing – temporal, spatial, and emotional distance and anonymity – can also be used negatively by individuals to create new barriers. Mel highlights this by speaking about the issue of online 'trolls' who deliberately attack individuals. While on the surface there may appear to be an emotional distance from what is said online, in reality this is not necessarily the case and words written online can often have damaging effects on individuals. Local activist and writer Hope (2014) draws attention to how social media can reinforce and even heighten barriers and exclusions rather than overcome them:

> Words slung carelessly at each other can be violent and oppressive — not just to the recipients, but to some onlookers too, until the atmosphere becomes so toxic that those of us who are sensitive cannot breathe in it and we start to entertain serious thoughts of giving up activism, leaving the Internet.

Moreover, participants' narratives highlight how the gendered nature of care-work creates not only structural availability barriers but also emotional and psychological barriers to doing activism. Helen speaks about this in relation to caring for her terminally ill mother:

So I started taking a lot of caring responsibilities and I think that that makes a huge difference to the way that you interact with the public sphere. Not just because of time restraints, because obviously they exist, but also because of your level of confidence [...] feeling like you're socially excluded in some way, you don't have an identity that's formed by your work, makes it more difficult I think to have the confidence to campaign externally. So, people would come by and shout at you 'get a job, don't do this', and you would be able to say 'actually, I am contributing to society, I have a job which is a valuable public sector job, I feel like I'm doing something really valuable for society'. And although I don't hold views that say unemployed people aren't contributing towards society, you can't help but be affected by that kind of discourse around you in terms of your levels of, sort of self-esteem.

Helen reminds us of the cumulative effect of such 'micro-cracks' that are affectively experienced (Hitchen, 2016: 117). She also draws our attention to the way in which unpaid care is not recognised as legitimate 'work' or as contributing to wider society. This negative portrayal of unpaid care and its relationship (or lack of) to citizenship is evident in the way that Helen's role as carer made her feel unable to participate in the public sphere. Helen's experience demonstrates the tension between private and public caring roles. Although caring is described as central to activism and participants' motivations to do activism, private caring roles (such as for one's mother) and activist roles appear to conflict with each other, with the implication being that women can only truly succeed at mastering one of these roles. Leonie demonstrates this, speaking about how she is perceived to be a 'dreadful mother' because she is an active activist. Here, general perceptions of motherhood, and what it means to be a 'good mother', impact negatively on women's ability to participate in activism.

At the same time, other participants confirm the 'motherhood effect', where being a mother encourages political participation. Several participants speak about feeling an emotional and moral responsibility as mothers to 'create a better future for our children' as well as to ensure that they 'grow up in a society that has the services that people need'. Rather than care just being the motivation for activism, as we saw in Chapter 4 concerning empathy, here we see activism itself as a form of caring, reflecting a feminist 'ethic of care' and ideas of 'universal citizenship' (Fraser, 1994).

Furthermore, the notion that *as mothers* these women harness a specific knowledge and understanding of activism demonstrates a feminist standpoint of women having a distinct perspective that is not only different to others but also privileged. Here, women's experiences differ structurally from men's because of the type of work that they do, notably reproductive labour, which involves all of the activities that help to sustain and reproduce individuals or citizens. It has been argued that women's dual position as central and marginal within social relations affords them a privileged viewpoint from which 'relations which are invisible from the dominant position become visible' (Tanesini, 1999: 142).

Notably, the one occasion where Notts People's Assembly explicitly addressed the gendered impacts of austerity was when they supported the Jarrow Mother's March for the NHS and held a women-only platform of speakers for the rally. While the March was a positive women-led initiative, the cynic could note that supporting it is a fairly easy way for the People's Assembly to present an image that shows them to be concerned with and addressing women's issues despite evidence of gendered exclusions. It appears that traditional tropes of femininity and gender (such as mothers protecting their children) are strategically used, whereas more complex and subtle everyday issues concerning gender are obscured and ignored. Therefore, while such tactics can enable women to do activism, they can also be damaging by reinforcing traditional gendered roles and constraining the ways that women can participate politically. Indeed, critics of the 'motherist frame' contend that it uses dichotomous roles of men and women, which 'limits the cultural frames of resistance available to movement participants' (Kuumba, 2001: 19).

Women participants' experiences as carers and activists demonstrate the tensions involved in negotiating these two identities and provokes debate about how the identity of activist could be redefined in terms of care, especially given the emphasis that participants place on empathy as the foundation of activism. Reflecting a feminist standpoint, Hazel suggests that women are actually better activists because they 'care more than men'. Significantly, gender facilitates rather than blocks activism here. Participants thus attempt to subvert gendered exclusions and barriers by reinterpreting gender in positive ways.

Although we have seen that Leonie and others struggle to reconcile the roles of activist and mother, this appears to be because of how they feel the public perceives them rather than their own beliefs about the compatibility of the two roles. This suggests the possibility and fruitfulness of reconceptualising activism in terms of care, and combining the roles of mother and activist, with the former acting as a motivation for the latter. However, as well as reinforcing traditional gender roles and notions of femininity, there is the additional risk that women without children become excluded, as well as the danger that women may again be defined primarily by their role as mothers (carers) first and foremost, with everything else branching from this. It becomes clear that we need to carefully consider the relationship between care and activism, particularly in terms of gender.

So far we have seen that participants perceive local anti-austerity activism to be dominated by male activists who neglect women's concerns, resulting in gendered exclusions and barriers to activism. Having explored these in detail, I now turn to consider how women have responded to such barriers and exclusions by forming their own resistance to austerity.

Overcoming gendered barriers: women–only activism

In response to the male dominated environment of wider anti-austerity groups and their neglect of women's issues, participants propose women-led and women-focused activism within women-only spaces. Hazel says 'there's a lot of male privilege in them [activist groups], which is why I specifically set up my own, with other women, to collectively work against austerity as women'. Participants' narratives reflect findings that women's experiences within mixed gender movements differ from men's and that women's concerns are not listened to by men, leading to frustration and women breaking away to form women-only groups. Similarly, Bassel and Emejulu (2018: 77) demonstrate how minority women developed 'strategies for survival in informal spaces: self-help groups, DIY networks and grassroots community organisations'.

While participants recognise the function of women-only spaces as safe places for domestic abuse victims and survivors, they suggest that these spaces also provide women with a place to do activism where their voices are heard. Charlotte speaks of the difference between meetings where men attend and those that are women-only, 'I think there is something to be said about that sort of female space that's respectful and calm', contrasting participants' accounts of mixed gender meetings that we saw earlier where male voices dominate and women often feel uncomfortable speaking. Beth suggests that the physical presence of the Women's Centre is a source of legitimacy for women's concerns and acts as a 'port in the storm', indicating the significance of tangible, material space.

Women activists organise within women-only spaces to provide practical support to women who are bearing the brunt of the austerity measures. Following the People's Assembly's failure to provide childcare at a conference or listen to women's concerns when this lack of childcare was raised, one of my women participants set up a local group of 'women coming together to do something for women'. One of the group's initiatives is a regular 'swap-shop ... a practical thing to swap toys, clothes, and books'. Demonstrating the intersection of class and gender, Alison says: 'That was really good because that is very hands on, it is what people need in times of austerity. I think maybe that is what she was thinking coming from quite a working-class background, she was thinking about that and the stuff that working-class women need.'

We see here this notion that 'practical' 'hands-on' help is key; Alison talks about the importance of providing 'real' help for women who 'need a home because they are fleeing', providing them with resources that are no longer publicly provided. This focus on providing everyday support reinforces Dodson's (2015) contention that women activist groups tend to be concerned with the particular and the everyday, suggesting that we need to consider the kinds of activism that women do.

This form of women-led activism that provides care within communities has historical roots with women traditionally providing charity, education and guidance for those in poverty through philanthropic work. However, this type of care has a classed dimension, with such duties enabling Victorian women to invent themselves as middle class by providing support to the working classes. Furthermore, there was a paternalistic (or perhaps in this case maternalistic) element to such support, whereby these women saw it as part of their duty to 'civilise' those below them in the social hierarchy and to spread the morals and values of the Empire project. Significantly, the Swap Shop in Nottingham was set up by a working-class woman who stressed the importance of providing support for other working-class women, showing a difference in the class dynamics from such earlier projects. However, it is not as simplistic as this as, in practice, women who identify as middle class or have an ambivalent relationship with class also participated. Crucially, many of these women had working-class roots and drew on these as reasons for participating, signifying that there remains a class dimension to women's activism that intersects with this gendered dimension.

However, while this response demonstrates a feminist resistance to austerity and empowers women, it is problematic given that women end up shouldering the additional care burden created by the public services deficit. This confirms the Fawcett Society's (2012) 'triple jeopardy' thesis in which women are losing services, their jobs providing these services, and being expected to pick up the resulting work unpaid. This expectation reflects underlying assumptions about the gendered nature of care and carries with it the risk that issues of public concern are being quietly pushed back into the private domain, along with women and their voices, thus reasserting traditional boundaries between the public and private spheres.

Rather than this being an unintentional side effect of austerity, McRobie (2012) suggests that it reflects the political objectives of 'a Conservative vision of women primarily as mothers and carers'. Similarly, Bramall (2013: 112) suggests that austerity practices such as being 'thrifty' are 'coded as work for women' by drawing on associations with femininity and qualities of the 'austere housewife [...] (such as patience, care, altruism, and the ability to be organized and to multitask)'. Thus, austerity itself is gendered along traditional gendered divides in roles and norms. Moreover, and especially relevant here, Bramall (2013: 136) notes that there is a risk that those who provide such services become 'complicit with the imposition of austerity', thus reinforcing what they are fighting against. Therefore, women are not only disproportionately affected by austerity, but are excluded from mainstream anti-austerity activism and through their resistance practices, problematically, are reinforcing the gendered impact of austerity and its continuation.

Such responses feed into the Conservative idea of the 'Big Society', whereby individuals and groups within communities undertake voluntary work to provide required services. As Levitas (2012: 322) notes, this idea is a continuation of the New Right and New Labour focus on communitarianism and creating the 'good society', and is 'little more than an attempt to get necessary social labour done for nothing, disproportionately by women, by pushing work back across the market/ non market boundary'. Drawing on this history, Gilbert (2014: 137) asserts that such responses are always problematic because effective progressive reform of public services requires funding. Indeed, Levitas (2012) notes that such policies neglect the necessity of material conditions that encourage and allow such community service provision. Hazel reinforces this:

> Because there's this idea of 'Big Society', which has always been there. And it's very interesting that it's supposedly a Tory ideology when it was the Tories who decided that we don't need society and society is dead and community is dead. So, now that they've *killed* communities and people don't have toy libraries and baby clothes swaps, and stuff, now they want to bring it back, decimating public services to do so (scoffs). I don't know how they expect women and families to go out and help each other plant things, grow things, share things, without any public spaces or services to facilitate that.

Hazel stresses the need for state funding for communities to provide support to individuals, with this being a joint responsibility that the state has pulled out of and which individuals are unable to perform because working-class communities have been destroyed. Likewise, Levitas (2012: 335) contends that 'Many of the conditions of working class organisation have been eroded. It depends on relatively stable work and relatively stable local or work-based communities: social policies from Thatcher on have undermined these material bases of self-organisation, resilience and sociality.'

However, Levitas (2012) argues that reading ideas of the Big Society through a 'hermeneutics of faith' (Ricoeur, 1981) enables us to trace the kernel of appeal and potential within such ideas, explaining why they have had some purchase among those who are not served by Coalition policies. Significantly, Levitas (2012) asserts that there *is* something that has been lost and that individuals value, which is why the Big Society narrative and its appeal to community values has purchase. Hazel reflects this attitude, lamenting the erosion of working-class communities:

> Years ago there used to be, particularly working-class communities, toy libraries, much like book libraries, so you could go and loan toys. These things don't exist any more. There's also not the same level of community whereby you could go to your neighbour and swap clothes, baby clothes, and stuff with people that aren't family.

Using a hermeneutics of faith, then, enables us to grasp the positive and appealing aspects of influential discourses; however, it does not remove the negative impacts and uses of these discourses, such as the Big Society, as highlighted above. Taking the next step is to ask the question, as Levitas (2012: 331) does, 'what are the economic and social conditions under which these ideas [of the Big Society] would cease to be repressive, moralizing claptrap?' Levitas's (2012: 336) answer is to rethink what counts as production and to value 'human flourishing and well-being; promoting equality; addressing the quality of work; revaluing care, and thinking in terms of Total Social Organization of Labour; universal child benefit and a guaranteed basic income'. By providing a wage for social labour, the conditions needed for the Big Society to work would be put in place and the value of care would be recognised. Further, this would address gender inequality as 'recognising the care of vulnerable others as a skilled craft involving practical and emotional labour [...] would radically alter the gender settlement in terms of both redistribution and recognition' (Levitas, 2012: 338). Likewise, Pearson and Elson (2015) suggest putting into place a feminist 'Plan F' that recognises the vital role of social reproduction and invests in this as an alternative to austerity. In fact, Pateman (1987: 259) contends that 'only public or collective provision can provide a proper standard of life and the means for meaningful social participation for all citizens in a democracy'. This returns us to considerations about the role of caring within wider society, and suggests that we need to consider care not only as a public matter but also a collective one, recognising the contribution caregiving makes to social life. In this vein, Herd and Harrington Meyer (2002) define care work as civic participation, and call for it to be recognised as such by social theorists.

It is clear from participants' narratives that there is a need for feminist anti-austerity activism that mitigates the gendered barriers and exclusions that we have seen within local anti-austerity activism, especially given that austerity disproportionately affects women. Hazel contends that 'until society isn't sexist and patriarchy doesn't exist, there will always be a need for women-only spaces. Particularly in any form of austerity fight-back, activism, anything like that.' Beth remarks that the feminist angle of anti-austerity campaigning is often ignored but needs to be taken into account because women are 'undoubtedly' hit the hardest:

> I think even the most hard-pressed neoliberal economist wouldn't be able to deny the evidence that this is the case. That cuts in services affect women and children first and foremost … it should be shouted from the rooftops. Because women and girls are more than 50 percent of the population, it's systematic discrimination.

Similarly, Dermot remarks that 'the people who are getting hit hardest are women. That's just the statistical truth […] so austerity is a women's issue which means it is a feminist issue.' Specifically, participants speak about cuts to women's services and public sector jobs, which tend to be part time and occupied by women: 65 per cent of public sector jobs are done by women, with nearly 40 per cent of women's jobs being in the public sector (Fawcett Society, 2012). Alison, a mother who had left her job in a women's service because of austerity, reinforces this: 'it is the double thing, isn't it, of the public sector, which is mostly women that work in the public sector, and the welfare cuts that massively affect women […] women are the victims, the first victims, because gender specific services are the first ones that go'. In fact, as we have seen, women face a 'triple jeopardy', which is tied to wider gender norms and assumptions about women as unpaid carers. Moreover, minority women are hit especially hard, with race, gender and class intersecting to produce heightened impacts of austerity. Yet this racialised dimension was absent from most participants' narratives, reinforcing Bassel and Emejulu's (2018) claims that minority women are often erased from conversations and political action around austerity.

Given the fact that women bear the brunt of the austerity measures, and that austerity is recognised by participants as a feminist issue, we would expect there to be a gendered focus in local movements such as the People's Assembly, with women activists being part of this. However, we have seen that this is not the case, raising the question of why this gendered dimension is absent. I contend that this shortfall is the result of the gendered exclusions and barriers to activism that have been explored in this chapter, and which will be further outlined in regards to the ideal activist identity in Chapter 6, which explores the gendered barriers not only to doing activism but also to being an activist.

A central feature of participants' arguments for feminist anti-austerity activism is the notion that lived experiences constitute a more authentic motivation for activism. Here, feminist standpoint theory resurfaces, with its emphasis on women's lived experiences and the way these experiences provide the basis for a distinct epistemological position. Anna emphasises this:

> I very strongly believe in women-only spaces, I think we need them just like I think that black people for example need black-only spaces. Because it doesn't matter how much someone is in solidarity with you, there's sometimes things that they don't quite experience in the same way as you, they don't quite feel in the same way as you.

Anna stresses the affective dimension of activism in relation to lived experiences, which other participants draw upon. Several male participants suggest that they cannot call themselves feminists, despite sharing the same values, because 'I can't speak from the same, I don't have the lived experience'. Here, lived experience is seen as distinct from 'academic understanding' because it is 'lived and felt'. Jared reinforces this, suggesting that men are not affected in the same way by patriarchy and feminist issues and that only those with the experience of being a woman can claim the label of 'feminist'. This raises similar questions about who can legitimately and authentically claim the label of activist, as well as issues of representation in terms of who can and who should speak about certain issues. It is to these questions that I now turn.

Part II has focused on the enabling and constraining factors to doing activism. It has demonstrated how emotion, morals and relationships motivate and sustain political participation, as well as how the costs of activism and gendered barriers and exclusions prevent those who are the most affected by austerity from doing activism. Part III explores the activist identity, focusing on the question of who can and who should be an activist.

PART III

Being Activist: The Activist Identity and its Problems

Having explored in Part II what it means to do activism and the complexities involved, Part III focuses on what it means to be an activist. It considers the ways in which the activist identity is constructed and upheld within the local anti-austerity activist culture and uncovers its problematic, damaging consequences, illuminating what I have called 'the dark side' of activist culture. Chapter 6 explores the two main constructions of 'activist'; the 'authentic' and 'ideal' activist. Chapter 7 uncovers the negative aspects of activist culture, and particularly the gendered dimension of the ideal activist identity and its damaging emotional effects.

6

The Authentic and Ideal Activist Identities: Having the 'Right' Motivation and Doing 'Enough' of the 'Right' Type of Activism

We have previously seen how participants conceptualise activism as a moral duty that everyone should do, and that empathy is a key motivation for this, where the imagined experience of another's pain or suffering moves individuals to action. However, participants' narratives reveal that there are limits to empathy as a motivation for activism, which will be explored in this chapter. Furthermore, it seems that not all motivations for activism are considered equal, and that having lived experiences of an issue is perceived to be a more authentic motivation for doing activism. Reinforcing Bobel (2007), it appears that there is a difference between 'doing activism and being activist', raising the question of what defines some people as activists and others as simply participating in activism.

This chapter explores the ways in which the activist identity is constructed and negotiated within local anti-austerity activist culture. It begins by establishing the shared meanings and context-specific nature of the term before discussing in more detail the two main constructions of the activist identity that came out of participants' narratives. The first is the 'authentic' activist who has the required lived experiences to possess the authority to speak about certain topics. Having explored barriers that prevent individuals and groups from doing activism under the question of who *can* do activism in Chapter 5, this chapter considers the question of who *should* do activism, according to participants. Lived experience is conceived of as a legitimate basis for being an 'authentic activist', an identity that is valued and constructed in opposition to its inauthentic other.

The second main construction of the activist identity that this chapter explores is the 'ideal activist', defined by the type and amount of activism one does. In order to be considered an ideal activist, individuals must do 'enough' of the 'right' type of activism (direct action rather than online activism). I have labelled this identity 'ideal' to reflect how participants construct it as the 'gold standard' of activist, which is the goal to aim for. The use of the word 'ideal' also reflects the reality that this standard is not often achievable, despite its prominence in participants' narratives. This chapter demonstrates that the ideal activist identity is underpinned by the distinction participants draw between talking and doing, which feeds into the construction of direct offline activism as the pinnacle of 'real' activism versus online 'slacktivism'. The final section of this chapter interrogates this artificial dichotomy and reveals the enabling features of online activism, as well as the ways in which both forms of activism interact, rather than conflict.

While I have separated the two main activist identity constructions for the purposes of exploring their features in detail, it is important to keep in mind that the two constructions are often combined to produce an overarching activist identity. This implies that individuals need to have relevant lived experiences, be motivated by the 'right' things and do 'enough' of the 'right' type of activism in order to achieve the 'activist' label. Clearly, the bar is set high, which has repercussions that will be explored in Chapter 7.

The shared meanings of 'activist' in activist culture

Participants' narratives underline the distinction drawn between doing activism and being activist, though there is ambivalence around exactly how the activist identity is defined. As Brown and Pickerill (2009: 25) assert, 'the concept of who is 'activist' and thus 'non-activist' is contested and fluid [...] in reality activist identities are complex, multi-layered and hybrid'. Alex contends that 'activist' is used within particular networks where a shared critical understanding of the label exists: 'if I'm talking to people like, that I observe and I know that they get what we're talking about, I'm happy to refer to being an activist or activism and things like this with that kind of knowledge of it's problematised, yeah.' Likewise, Portwood-Stacer (2013: 40) says 'several interviewees remarked that they would identify as an anarchist or not depending on whom they were talking with'. Therefore, 'the degree to which they claimed and performed an anarchist identity depended on the context in which they found themselves at any particular moment' (2013: 40). The context-dependent and shifting nature of identity is reinforced; we also see this notion of a distinct activist community that holds an unspoken shared understanding of particular roles and identities, which we can conceptualise as an activist doxa (to recall Bourdieu, 1992).

While it is the case that for several participants this shared understanding of 'activist' enables them to claim the identity within some contexts, there are individuals who resolutely refuse the label. Some participants have personal issues with the term, including Hazel for whom the label of 'activist' evokes notions of men in Left organisations who have sexually harassed women; she states that activist 'means rapist' to her. She associates 'activist' with violent and aggressive macho behaviour that she does not wish to associate with. While Hazel's reaction to the term activist is extreme, it reveals women's concerns about sexism and suggests that 'activist' refers to the male body, which will be discussed further in Chapter 7. Furthermore, for Hazel, the identity of working-class woman takes precedence, demonstrating how individuals negotiate and prioritise various identities.

Significantly, despite Hazel's strong reaction to the label 'activist', within conversation she still speaks 'as an activist' – implying that on some level she also accepts the shared definition and understanding of the term. Here, we start to see the complex and ambivalent nature of the activist identity as well as how identities are fluid, changeable and contextually driven. Like 'anarchist' in Portwood-Stacer's (2013: 37) study, 'activist' appears to be 'a floating signifier, in that it means different things to different people in different contexts'. As hinted at by Alex above, a key aspect of whether an individual claims the identity of 'activist' depends on who defines and gives the label. Cortese (2015: 224) reflects this, noting that individuals' responses to the question 'are you an activist?' are situational and will change depending on who is asking, what they perceive the asker's likely conception of 'activist' is and whether the individual wishes to be associated with or match that conception.

Nevertheless, participants' narratives reveal two dominant constructions of the activist identity that are shared and maintained in the local anti-austerity activist culture, despite their contradictions and negative impacts. The first of these, the authentic activist identity, contradicts participants' earlier suggestion that everyone and anyone should do activism, and raises questions about the limits of empathy as a motivation for activism.

Who should do activism/be activist?

Participants emphasise the need for anti-austerity activism to be led by and for those who are the most affected by austerity. Dermot asserts that 'it's individual people in individual circumstances who need to lead their struggles' and Martin contends that 'really it has to come from people themselves and they have to realise through their own experience what works and what doesn't'. However, as I have shown, those who are the most affected by austerity are not necessarily in a position to participate in activism, which problematises the suggestion that anti-austerity activism should be led by those who are most affected. Furthermore, while participants suggest that a key part of anti-austerity activism is making the 'truth' and 'reality' of living in poverty known to the wider public, there is also a wariness present about becoming a 'case study of being skint' (Hazel) or the 'poster-girl for intersectionality' (Lily). In this respect, participants value lived experiences as the basis for knowledge but are aware of the danger of these experiences being fetishised by others and of being treated as examples of particular conditions rather than as people. There is a careful balancing act to be maintained here, with questions raised about who can legitimately speak about such issues; Alison says 'we shouldn't be speaking for people'.

Hazel contends that only those with lived experiences of the issues can speak about them, and that without lived experiences people's activism is 'inauthentic' and 'fake'. Lived experience forms the basis for a privileged and more 'real' knowledge that has access to the 'truth' of reality. We start to see that there are different types of activist arranged by participants into a hierarchy, where those without lived experiences are less legitimate than those with them, who are considered to be authentic activists. Authenticity is a moral value that reflects desirable qualities such as 'credibility, originality, sincerity, naturalness, genuineness, innateness, purity, or realness' (Grazian, 2010: 191). Invoking this, participants refer to UK Uncut as 'pure' and 'organic'. There is a sense that authenticity is an inherent quality that cannot be earned, yet it is paradoxically something that is defined and attributed by others. Authenticity is ascribed, not inscribed; other activists decide who is 'authentic' or not, it is not a quality that is self-declared. Speaking about the relationship between authenticity and music, Moore (2002: 213) notes that authenticity is identified 'by an honesty to experience'. Here, 'artists speak the truth of their own situation; that they speak the truth of the situation of (absent) others; and that they speak the truth of their own culture, thereby representing (present) others' (Moore, 2002: 209). This parallels how participants construct the 'authentic activist' identity, with emphasis placed on speaking honestly about lived experiences and of representing others with these shared experiences.

Notably, 'authenticity is so often associated with hardship and disadvantage' (Grazian, 2010: 192), which is reflected by the 'authentic activist' who is typically from a working-class or disadvantaged background and has experienced 'real' life and hardship. Similarly, Forkert (2018: 146) remarks that 'one's credibility within the labour movement is judged not by one's actions [...] but instead by the legitimacy of claims to authenticity'. In this context, rather than creating solidarity, class struggle instead 'becomes about classifying and judging individuals in relation to authentic experience' (Forkert, 2018: 146).

The authentic working-class activist is amplified by the contrast participants draw between it and its inauthentic other – the 'middle-class activist type'. Participants paint a caricature of a relatively wealthy, young activist who at best is out of touch with ordinary people's lived realities and at worst is a 'champagne socialist' who should step aside to make room for 'real' activists, who are actually affected by austerity. Hazel says:

> It's all well and good to pitch a tent in market square for a few months and claim that you're against capitalism and when you decide you've had enough, go home to your parents. It's not the same as people that have to live with these decisions, day in, day out.

Hazel draws attention to issues of privilege by highlighting the way in which such 'middle-class activist types' have the choice to participate in actions and then walk away, not having to live the issues in the same way that those who are affected by austerity do. Therefore, while empathy is emphasised by participants as a motivation for activism, it appears that there are limits to this, and that to have a 'true' understanding of certain realities one must have lived experience of them. In this respect, a distinction is created between the person experiencing the problem, austerity, and the person who seeks to alleviate it out of empathy or compassion. Berlant (2004: 4) summarises this relationship, emphasising the divide that is created between the two individuals: 'the operation of compassion describes a social relation between a sufferer and a compassionate one. In alleviating the pain of others – who are *over there* – the compassionate enact their social privilege.'

Furthermore, there is a concern here about the authenticity and thus legitimacy of not only the activist but the type of action too, with it being presented as a superficial display of resistance. Participants recount the origins of UK Uncut as being spontaneous and born on Twitter, preferring to distance themselves from the alternative origin story (involving a group of Oxbridge graduates), which contradicts this spontaneous emergence. This move is deliberate and perhaps can be explained by participants' disdain of this middle-class, relatively wealthy young activist 'type'.

Graeber (2013: 252) also touches upon this middle-class activist stereotype within the US context, speaking of 'trust fund baby activists', but, unlike my findings, Graeber suggests that it is a perception held by the media and general public rather than by other activists. We begin to see how the identity of activist (in this case the 'authentic activist'), is constructed and upheld within the activist community.

Clearly, lived experiences and feelings are central to this construction of the authentic activist and its opposite. Helen suggests that individuals should speak about what they know and what personally affects them:

> If I was speaking I would usually speak about something that I had a particular perspective on, so at the time I was working in a college with kids who had been excluded from school or had been youth offenders, and would try and narrow down to the effects on the specific people that I knew something about. And speak personally.

Phillips (1991: 114) contends that 'political aims and objectives should be grounded in personal experience and, instead of occupying a distinctively "political" terrain, should arise out of and speak back to each individual's life'. Similarly, Bobel's (2007: 153) participants contend 'that an issue must literally be "lived", in this case materially embodied, for true activism to take place. And what is important about embodiment? [...] if an issue is woven into the everyday, lived reality of an individual, it is inescapably personal.'

Significantly, participants interpret personal experience as providing a more honest and authentic basis for activism, problematising who can and should represent people who are the most affected by austerity, especially when we consider that the most affected often face the biggest barriers to being politically active.

Issues of representation

Participants demonstrate unease about speaking on behalf of other groups. James notes how 'It is all well and good me saying well people are suffering, but I don't feel it in the same way that a lot of people do ... fundamentally we weren't the people bearing the brunt of austerity.' Will argues:

> Well, I only think you can represent yourself. You can support those, so yeah about the disability cuts you can go along and

support the action, I couldn't go there and speak personally about it because I wouldn't know, I'm not personally being affected by it, but I would go there to support those who are being affected.

However, unlike Hazel who contends that only those with lived experience of issues can speak about them, Alex argues that limiting activism in this way is problematic as it creates divides between 'insiders' and 'outsiders':

I don't like this idea of insiders and outsiders as far as things are concerned because if you go down that path then people in comas perhaps should be the only people who can advocate for people in comas. You know what I mean? So, we have to be, we have to have solidarity with each other. And that's not about co-opting and taking over people's movements when you pretend to have, to know their interests more than they do, shouldn't be doing that. But as far as supporting, according to what people wish you to support them in then yeah, I'm all for that but yeah, I don't wish to speak for other people.

Here, then, solidarity is distinguished from empathy as it does not require one to understand or feel another's experience. Similarly, Todd (2004) draws on Levinas (1969) to suggest that ethically we have a responsibility to the other *even when we cannot understand their experiences*. This point is crucial, because empathy assumes that through imagination we can understand the other's experience, which may not necessarily be the case. In the absence of this understanding, we still need motivation for reducing the other's suffering, which can be provided by such responsibility. Thus, we can have solidarity with another because we recognise our shared humanity, vulnerability and the possibility that the other's suffering could be experienced by ourselves, all of which are underlined by the responsibility that we each have to the other (Levinas, 1969). By drawing on a shared human condition and vulnerability, solidarity does not position or privilege one individual above another (the 'onlooker' or the 'compassionate one' above the 'sufferer') or invoke pity, which compassion arguably does or can do.

For Alex, others can advocate on behalf of those affected but it is important that they do not speak over them. Alex makes a distinction between supporting individuals and speaking *for* them, with the emphasis being that one shouldn't try to co-opt or lead movements but to offer support for causes. Adrian reinforces this, contending that he will stand up for people who are being attacked or are suffering but is keen to qualify that this does not mean that he is 'speaking for them'. Likewise, Jared says that individuals can support groups that they do not belong to and 'aid their voice' but that they cannot speak for them. The key point is respecting others, their experiences and feelings, and being aware of one's own position by being careful not to assert authority over someone else, particularly someone in a more disadvantaged position, reminding us of the issue of privilege.

However, there is a danger of putting too much emphasis on difference and lived experience as a source of authority or of 'clinging to marginality' (Tanesini, 1999: 148). This logic can be reversed to imply that marginal groups can *only* speak about marginality and that what they have to say is only relevant to their own group, thus meaning they will be ignored by everyone else. Further, the focus on oppression as a basis for a 'truer' knowledge, as demonstrated by Hazel, provokes debate about whether someone loses their insight if they stop being oppressed; and there is the risk that concerns about representation devolve into an 'oppression hierarchy' whereby individuals become preoccupied with establishing who is more oppressed (Letherby, 2003: 47).

We are reminded of the ways in which 'checking one's privilege' has become a damaging discourse within activist communities. Participants privately refer to the problem of 'oppression top trumps' that exists within activist cultures, where individuals try to 'out-oppress' others in order to prove that their standpoint and views are more legitimate. Difference and disadvantage become the basis for a process of one-*down*manship, in which the most oppressed is perceived to be the most authentic and therefore has the most authority to speak. There is a careful balancing act to perform between recognising and respecting difference and becoming preoccupied with 'oppression hierarchy' and standpoint theories, which negate anyone speaking about topics that they do not personally experience.

In contrast to many participants, Anna suggests that, in some contexts, not having a lived experience of the issues can afford the speaker more legitimacy:

> I mean I don't represent them [Muslim students] as coming from that community but ... the way they put it to me was that ... if they spoke about it because they are the people who are actually directly affected by it, they can be dismissed. I mean if you think as a woman or as a feminist, sometimes it can be dismissed 'oh, that's your subjective experience', you can't speak. Whereas there is this kind of assumption that if you're

the white person who happens to be Muslim, you're maybe more objective, maybe you've heard more than one story.

Anna's comments about how subjectivity is dismissed reveals how emotion has traditionally been pitched in opposition to reason and perceived to be an inadequate basis for argument or 'truth'. Notably, this perspective is gendered, with men tending to be associated with the rational side of this dichotomy and women with the emotional and subjective which become linked to irrationality, suggesting that this (feminine) type of knowledge is inferior. Feminist theory challenges this position by arguing for the legitimacy and value of feminist knowledge that emerges from women's lived experience.

Nonetheless, Anna draws our attention to the importance of context, noting that this occurred in the immediate aftermath of 9/11 when Muslim students were very often:

> even scared to speak for themselves. So they would come and tell me and then I would have to represent them because they would think that a non-Muslim person would be heard better than they would be heard in terms of what was happening.

This is problematic as it reinforces the notion that only particular voices can speak and will be listened to, and prevents attempts to actually change that. However, given that it was the wishes of the particular students that she was representing and that these students actually felt scared to speak, this was perhaps the only solution available. We are reminded of Joe's earlier suggestion that individuals can use their privilege to draw attention to the views of oppressed groups who would otherwise be ignored. Indeed, there is the problem not only of who can speak but also of who gets listened to; as Mary remarks, 'there are a whole sort of tranche of people there who I think have been disproportionately affected and who haven't got the voice to be able to do anything about that'.

For many participants, a key problem is that those affected by the issues are not in a position of power where they are listened to and that those who are in power lack the lived experience to understand the issues. Participants demonstrate concern with this democratic deficit and its impacts. Hazel contends that there is a massive gap between 'those at the top and those at the bottom,' and attributes this to the fact that those in power do not understand 'the real world' because they have always lived a life of privilege. Crucially, mainstream politics is not representative; Mel claims that 78 per cent of politicians are millionaires and thus out of touch with people's real lives. Lily remarks that 'parliament doesn't even reflect the make-up of this country. That's the sad thing' and Jared contends that 'the representatives, political representatives, are representing the minority – they're generally from public schools and have attended Eton and are from very privileged backgrounds'. Often, participants suggest that the neglect of the real effects of policies on people's daily lives and particularly on vulnerable groups is caused by this lack of representativeness within government. For Dana, unlike Hazel who suggests that austerity is a deliberate attack on poorer people, this gap between the powerful and 'ordinary people' is to blame for the resulting negative impacts on particular groups:

> And that's not probably happened because somebody thought 'oh sod them', it's happened because the people in that room had no insight into that, it's happened because there was nobody in that room to say 'wait a minute, before we go any further with this how will this impact, I mean not just women in vulnerable positions but anybody in a vulnerable situation' … this is why parliament needs to be representative of the people and it bloody well isn't.

Problematically, participants contend that this problem of representativeness and access is mirrored within the activist community, a point that is demonstrated by the neglect of gendered and racialised concerns.

The central argument made by participants is that those who are the most affected by austerity need to be listened to and not dictated to. Hazel states that people should 'shut up and listen'. Similarly, Mel contends that we should listen to people about their lived experience as they are the experts of their situation and should be the ones to bring about change. Jared and Owain contend that the people who are affected have to be involved *because* they are directly affected, therefore others need to listen to both understand better and to know what change those who are affected want and need. For Owain, this means that activists should concentrate on connecting 'basic issues of bread and butter questions' to wider politics in order for people to feel that politics is relevant to their lives. Henry notes the importance of 'feeling that you are being listened to'. Furthermore, Dana acknowledges that issues are not 'black and white' and asserts 'I don't know what the answer is but for god's sake it's not to stop listening'. A key aspect of this 'listening' is paying attention to others who have lived experiences that you do not, as Dana points out: 'Where women of colour are talking about their experiences of sexism and racism intersecting, I let them talk. It's not for me to comment 'cause I've not experienced it so I won't very often comment at all except to say thank you and I'm listening.' Again we see the importance of intersectionality and personal lived experience for having the authority to speak about a certain issue. However, there is also the implication here that even in this situation Dana is the one with the power as she is able to allow others to speak and to choose to listen (or not), again drawing our attention to the role played by privilege in issues of representation and voice.

The 'ideal activist' identity: doing 'enough' of the 'right' type of activism

It might be assumed that individuals reject the activist identity because of its negative connotations; however, it is often because 'activist' is held in such high regard, and defined by distinctive criteria, that individuals do not accept the label. Participants' narratives reinforce Stuart's (2013: 170) suggestion that 'the more positive stereotype of the high level committed activist could function as a high-bar perceived requirement where some individuals may feel they fall short'. In response to being questioned about what 'activist' means to her and whether she identifies as an activist, Beth says 'I don't do enough [activism]', and others suggest that they cannot claim the activist title because they 'only do little bits' (Anna). Yet both Anna and Beth had been involved in various forms of activism over at least four years, including anti-austerity, feminist and human rights activism, which has involved taking on organising roles, attending events and protests, and managing online groups. Both therefore had a long-term history of activism, yet still felt unsure about whether they fulfilled the criteria for being an 'activist'.

Similarly, Bobel (2007: 150) suggests that the 'perfect standard' of activism 'effectively places the label "out of reach" for many social movement actors who deem themselves unworthy'. Referring to the anarchist identity, one of Portwood-Stacer's (2013: 38) participants remarks: 'it's a funny term because you feel like it's an impossibility [...] You feel like there's a bar that's set really high and you can never really be that so why even bother identifying yourself that way.' Stuart (2013: 105) notes how this focus on the ideal activist is demotivating, as participants use it 'to make relative judgements about their own identity or abilities. The implication is that when these self-judgements fall short, this may result in inaction or uncertainty about how to take action.' Therefore, such conceptions about the 'right' amount of activism required to be an activist often act as a barrier to doing activism. Moreover, the key question arises of how much would be enough.

At one point Charlotte directly asked me 'am I doing enough?', suggesting that 'activist' is a label to be granted by somebody else. In this respect, the activist identity works via the Althussian (1971) concept of 'interpellation', where a subject comes into being when hailed by someone who has authority. Charlotte implies that I have the authority or expertise to decide what counts as activism given my role as researcher, indicating that what counts as enough is relative to others' activities and is not openly discussed in activist communities. Indeed, participants appeared to use the interview situation as an opportunity to freely discuss their anxieties about the activist identity and role. There is a sense, then, that participants are seeking not only guidance but also reassurance from someone qualified to give it, that what they are doing is enough to be deemed an activist. Notably, when speaking of doing enough, participants are nearly always referring to enough to be considered an activist, rather than to create social change; as we have seen, participants suggest that small acts are enough to make a difference (although the ideal activist identity's criteria of doing the right type of activism complicates this).

Dana reinforces the idea that rather than being a self-identification, 'activist' is a title to be earned and awarded by somebody else:

> I remember somebody when, just before I got involved properly with No More Page 3 and I'd done a couple of the demos that was all and somebody tweeted me or included me in a tweet saying 'oh looking for local feminist activists' and they included me! And I thought, is that me?! I thought God, I suppose it is! Blimey, I'm a feminist activist, who knew!

Dana's comment shows that the 'activist' label is regarded as a badge of honour. It became clear that the title is held in high regard by participants and functions within the local activist culture as a form of symbolic and social capital (Bourdieu 1986). Those who are awarded it are granted status and a good reputation as well as possessing links to others with authority in activist circles.

What is more, it appears that there is a discrepancy between what participants perceive the social definition of activist to be and what it actually is. While there is no clear definition of what is enough activism to be deemed worthy of the activist title, participants' response to others' perceptions of them reveals a probable gap between what others actually think and what they perceive others to think. Dana demonstrates this; despite being pleased to receive the activist title, Dana implies that she had perhaps not yet done enough to earn it, stating 'I'd done a couple of the demos that was all'. Likewise, Stuart (2013: 104) notes that 'one pattern of occurrences was where the ideal person [activist] was described as quite extraordinary – highly capable, knowledgeable and skilled, but their [participants'] own self-description did not match this ideal'. This self-judgement according to imagined standards results in individuals making harsher judgements of themselves than others perhaps would. However, as Stuart (2013: 98) contends, 'what others *really* think is not directly relevant, but rather the assumption made by the individual is'.

It emerges that the ideal activist's criterion of doing the 'right' amount of activism is tied to the criterion of doing the 'right' type of activism, as demonstrated by Charlotte: 'I think I'm a lot more active than most people but I don't think I'm active enough, I don't in terms of, you know, I haven't gone and handcuffed myself to a power station or anything like that.'

Therefore, despite participants emphasising caring in their narratives about activism (speaking about empathy as a motivation for activism and conceptualising everyday activism as a form of care), it appears that the ideal activist identity is defined not by caring but by *doing* (as suggested by the often repeated question 'am I doing enough?'). Activists' symbolic capital thus appears to be defined by direct action, which is described as '[a]n action where you actually go out and *do* something, where you go out and let's say shut down a shop, close a street' (Will). Wieck (n.d.) demonstrates this distinction between talking and action in his analogy of indirect versus direct action:

> If the butcher weighs one's meat with his thumb on the scale, one may complain about it and tell him he is a bandit who robs the poor, and if he persists and one does nothing else, this is *mere talk*; one may call the Department of Weights and Measures, and this is *indirect action*; or one may, talk failing, insist on weighing one's own meat, bring along a scale to check the butcher's weight, take one's business somewhere else, help open a co-operative store, and these are *direct actions*.

The importance of *doing* something about the issues rather than merely talking was a common theme in participants' narratives. Helen notes:

> There is a tendency among a lot of people involved in the Left to do this kind of navel-gazing. There's a lot of factionalism, there's a lot of people arguing about which specific brand of social awareness is the one that you should be buying into. So you end up with organisations that either splinter or spend

so much time talking about theory and tactics that they don't get a fat lot done.

UK Uncut is contrasted with other Left organisations that are criticised for being 'talking shops', placing talking above action. In particular, participants criticise the People's Assembly:

> I don't see what they're doing, I can't see that they've made any difference. They've had a really good couple of meetings and had a couple of high-profile authors and politicians speak, it's always nice to hear people speak … but they're not doing anything. They're not helping, on the ground … PA are just talking, they've been talking for a year so. (Hazel)

> The problem is in terms of sheer organisation a lot of the meetings tend to be talking shops, they tend to talk about stuff that is wrong, then they don't talk about what they need to do to change it and they don't commit to doing it. (Owain)

Many participants assert the importance of doing something 'practical' and highlight the embodied nature of such actions, speaking of being 'hands on' and 'actually going down with my feet, and doing stuff'. Mel suggests that rather than just talking, people need to 'go off and do something practical instead'. Emphasis is placed on providing practical 'on the ground' help that is relevant to people's everyday lives. Participants criticise talking without action, saying 'don't whinge, change it' and that 'talking is too much hot air'. For Joe, doing something practical is central to how he defines activist: 'someone who recognises that there is a need for political change and then doesn't sit on their arse and do nothing about it. Someone who actively, yeah, someone who actively campaigns for change, hence the term activist.' Likewise, Alison states 'I think it is also important to actually do something, apart from just talk about it.' Owain asserts: 'actions speak a lot louder than words'. Clearly, actions are placed above talking, with the sharp distinction that is drawn between the two suggesting that participants do not conceive of talking as a form of acting, but something entirely separate and even antithetical to doing. This contradicts participants' comments (see Chapter 4) about the discursive elements of doing activism. Perhaps, while talking can be a part of doing activism, it is not sufficient by itself and does not make someone an activist, again emphasising the distinction between doing activism and being activist.

The 'real' and the 'virtual': online versus offline activism

Participants draw a sharp distinction between online and offline activism, often defining the two in opposition to each other, referring to online as 'armchair' or 'soft' activism and offline as 'direct action', which involves 'actually *doing* something'. Again, the distinction is made between talking and action, with participants contrasting the virtual to the 'real' and suggesting that offline direct action is a more valid and legitimate form of activism. This hierarchy of activism is demonstrated by the very language used to describe online activism, with words such as 'slacktivism' and 'soft' (as opposed to hard) denoting online activism's lower position. Henry remarks that 'slacktivism is a sub-category of activism'. Notably, online activism is perceived to be less worthy than offline activism.

In contrast, participants refer to offline activism as 'actual', 'real' and 'actually physically going out'. Adrian speaks about how most of his anti-austerity activism is online, and contrasts this to times when he offers 'physical support'. He suggests that the tangibility of offline spaces and actions is significant, a theme echoed by other participants who emphasise creating protests around the tangible:

> I think it's simple. I think people can get it. And they had something physical to look at and deal with as well, they had somebody's shop which they could stand against, which they could say was a ... was the force they were acting against. I think that's something people lack in a modern society is that the structures of power are kind of opaque, so you sort of know what the government's responsible for but you can't really get at them, and a lot of the rest of it happens, you say well it's international banking well what can you do to international banking? Or the exploitation that you're angry about might be the exploitation of somebody who's in another continent because those jobs have been moved out of your community, so you don't witness it every day. So you don't have many opportunities to stand next to the thing that you're cross with and shout at it and I think that having people's physical shops to do that to, made the issue more kind of understandable and concrete. (Helen)

Amin reinforces this, arguing that translating abstract concepts (such as justice and equality) into concrete, tangible issues and targets is particularly important in a postmodern context rife with uncertainty. There is perhaps a latent concern here about visibility, with offline tangible actions being more visible when compared with potentially anonymous and less visible online activities.

For participants, a key strength of offline activism is how it helps to build relationships between activists. Henry asserts that relationships are easier to build face to face because 'it comes down to what's called common grounds which is being able to create mutual discourse with someone and a shared understanding of things'. Likewise, Jack says 'there is a level of trust that's built up' through 'real-world shared struggles'. Participants reflect critics' concerns that so-called 'slacktivism' is ineffective because of how social media forms 'weak ties' between people rather than the 'strong ties' that are required for activism (Gladwell, 2010). While Beth claims that Facebook 'makes it quite an intimate friendship in a way … you almost feel like you're living their life, with them', she immediately contends that it is important to have 'the physical meet-ups' because that is when 'people are made real and that you actually get to know them'. Again, we see this distinction drawn between the virtual and the 'real', with the latter being seen as more authentic and thus better than the former.

A key criticism of online activism is that it is not 'real' activism, as Gladwell (2010) remarks when comparing the current context of social media activism with the Civil Rights Movement in the US: 'we seem to have forgotten what real activism is'. Crucially, for Gladwell (2010), such 'real' activism is defined by risk and is 'not for the faint of heart'. Again, we see the idea that 'proper' activism is dangerous and requires an extraordinary individual to be able to carry it out. This is problematic as it again puts up barriers to who can do activism and be an activist, privileging an implicitly masculine version of activism, where 'real' activism is risky, tough and concerned with fighting long and hard for one's cause. Halupka (2014: 117) remarks that a line is definitively drawn between 'meaningful engagement and unsubstantial engagement, a line that holds that political change must be hard-fought'. Reinforcing this, Morozov (2009: 185) suggests that meaningful activism must be risky, authentic and demonstrate a deep commitment. Here we see the combination of authenticity with the criteria of doing the 'right' amount and type of activism, thus producing even higher standards for earning the activist title. Reinforcing the notion that direct action is tougher and because of this more noble, Beth suggests that online activism is often perceived to be 'cowardly' as it is not directly confronting the problems and people who are causing them.

Participants' narratives reflect the denigration of online activism in relation to offline, 'real' activism. Jared says that he cannot be called an activist because he 'only' does online activities, which do not count as 'real activism'. Similarly, Anna says that she is 'only the clicktivist, I have to say', suggesting that to be a 'real' activist one must participate in direct action. Significantly, Anna was unsure about whether she fulfilled the criteria to be interviewed about activism because of her recent focus on online participation, despite having been involved in many forms of activism throughout her life (which emerged during the interview). This raises key questions concerning who can legitimately call themselves an activist and whether online activism 'counts', in the eyes of participants. Beth remarks:

> I get a bit frustrated because I have felt a little bit sometimes like some people in the group, I won't name any names, say enough of this talking we need more action and so on, and I think well … when am I going to have time to do the action? It's, because I'm not attending these meetings mean that what I think isn't valid?

We again see this idea that some types of action are perceived to be more 'valid' than others, leaving those who cannot participate feeling guilty and frustrated. In fact, the distinction drawn between online and offline activism, with the latter being deemed to be more valid and authentic, is deeply problematic as it creates further barriers for those who are already restricted from doing activism.

What's more, online activism is conceived of as a threat to traditional forms of political engagement. In this respect, participants and critics of so-called 'slacktivism' worry that individuals will substitute their offline activism with online activities because they are less costly but still provide satisfaction. Adrian asserts that the problem with social media is people becoming armchair activists and 'just sticking behind a computer and believing that is the only way to change the world'. Similarly, Jared contends that the difference between online and offline activism is being 'active versus passive' and links this to the contemporary 'lazy' consumer culture that he and other participants believe we currently live in. Owain refers to 'the sapping effect' that social media has and Jared contends 'it [social media] makes us do things in a different way, we often do things with our fingertips rather than our feet and our voices'. Notably, Jared says that social media *makes* us act in certain ways, reifying the technology and suggesting that it has a power of its own. He also demonstrates the crux of this 'substitution thesis' – that people do things online *instead* of offline. Like Owain and Jared, Morozov (2009) dismisses 'slacktivism' as 'the ideal form of activism for a lazy generation' who do not want 'to get their hands dirty' (Christensen, 2011). Slacktivism is perceived to be easy, and despite being ineffective (according to its critics), it alleviates the guilt that individuals feel for not participating politically and fulfilling the duties of active citizenship (Morozov, 2009).

Conversely, other participants challenge this assumption as well as the notion that so-called 'keyboard warriors' are ineffective, asserting that social media has scope to reach wider audiences. Alison says:

> I guess they are pretty savvy on social media, which I think I, you know people kind of laugh about keyboard warriors and stuff but you reach a lot of people. I think it is a really good change as well from when I was younger because you didn't have that power to reach people.

Like Alison, Dermot questions the disparaging of 'keyboard warriors', claiming that although they are sneered at they actually play an important role: 'people do underestimate this sort of, people: 'oh, you, you're just a keyboard warrior', somebody's got to spread the ideas'. He contends that while previously, ideas were spread using books, 'we now live in the internet age so why not do it through the internet as well?' and draws comparisons to popular political thinkers and writers such as Orwell and Chomsky:

> Well he [Orwell] wasn't that active really, the reason people like him, and I like him is because of the ideas he spread ... people absolutely love Noam Chomsky, and I do, I think he's brilliant. But he's not out there doing things, he's speaking and writing. And so how is it any different to me sitting at home doing that on the internet, it's a different audience and it's elitism ... it's okay for him to do it 'cause he's an intellectual white man but not when other people do it.

Dermot draws our attention back to issues of privilege and the notion that only certain people are in a position to speak and be heard within the public sphere. He also implies that online writings are perceived to be inferior to published books, reminding us of the distinction that is often drawn between 'high' and 'low' culture. Notably, though, despite claiming the significance of people spreading ideas, Dermot still defines and separates this from action and being active by separating doing from speaking and writing. This position mirrors traditional Marxist theory concerning the distinction between base and superstructure, where the former is concerned with the modes of production and the latter concerns culture. In this formulation, the superstructure can influence the base but ultimately the base determines the superstructure and predominates.

The disparaging of so-called 'slacktivism' for being 'easy' and 'lazy' reveals an underlying concern about how the activist identity is defined, with individuals appearing protective of the title. Henry demonstrates this, stating 'It's too easy for people to say they're an activist now'. We are reminded of how the activist identity is seen as a title to be earned, with the implication being that those who do online activism do not *deserve* to have the honour of the activist label. Dermot demonstrates this point, admitting that he personally finds it frustrating when people 'only' do online activism given that he is doing direct action and putting himself at risk when they are not. Again, 'real' activism is equated with risky activism. Ironically, there are echoes here of a current dominant discourse that anti-austerity activism attempts to challenge – that of 'strivers versus skivers' (Valentine and Harris, 2014). This discourse repackages the historic 'deserving' and 'undeserving' poor distinction within the context of neoliberalism and austerity. Here, strivers are seen as hard-working, moral and good people who deserve the fruits of their labours and are pitted against those who are not deemed to work hard enough or be worthy of any 'benefit'. In relation to activism, it seems that so-called 'armchair activists' are perceived to be the lazy individuals who are unworthy of the 'activist' title in comparison with those who are working hard doing dangerous and 'real' direct action. Clearly, this is problematic, especially when we consider the ways in which online activism is often done by more vulnerable individuals for whom direct action is inaccessible. Contradictorily, such attitudes reinforce the dominant discourses surrounding austerity that these same activists are seeking to undermine. However, Dermot is aware that such concerns about who receives the activist title are 'irrational and childish', concerned with 'getting credit' for the activism that one does. Again, then, we see the influence of the ego and individual interests in doing activism, as well as the importance of the visibility of actions, with the need for individuals to be witnessed doing direct action in order to feel validated.

We need to carefully consider how online and offline forms of activism interact, rather than merely dismissing the former as 'slacktivism'. Gladwell (2010) emphasises how 'real' activism involves boycotts and non-violent confrontations, but forgets the fact that nowadays, as is the case with UK Uncut, these are often organised and coordinated online. Therefore, while participants and theorists may construct online and offline activism in opposition to one another, we need to consider the interaction between the two forms of activism and realise that online activism constitutes *another* form of activism that should not be assessed according to the criteria of offline activism. Beth comments 'I guess the problem is that, well the question to me is does online activism, in the long run will it change like gender norms? And so far, I think it will, and it can do, but not without the physical activism as well.' Rather than prioritising offline activism over online activism, Beth suggests that there needs to be an interaction between the two. Participants speak about online and offline activism in terms of a feedback loop, with each propelling and reinforcing the other. Though Dana still draws the distinction between 'real physical' activism and social media activism, she demonstrates how the two interlink:

> Now it's a whole lot easier for people to shout because of social media and it has such a bigger resonance because it sort of feeds itself if you know what I mean, so it will start on social media and then it will become a real physical thing and then that will resonate through social media and it's so easy to get a message out and about really quickly.

Moreover, we need to recognise that online activism involves more than merely changing one's Facebook profile picture; it includes signing petitions, organising events offline, discussions, group formation and the sustaining of individuals' activities offline, as we shall see throughout the rest of this chapter.

It becomes clear that we need to carefully consider the purpose of online activism as well as critically reconsider how we define 'success' within this context. Crucially, there is no robust evidence that confirms the substitution thesis, meaning that while individuals involved online will not necessarily become involved offline, they also do not replace offline activism with so-called 'slacktivism'. It may be the case that online activism provides opportunities for individuals to become active in a way that they would never have otherwise been. Dana demonstrates this:

> Murdoch tweeted in response to a tweet from a woman who had only joined Twitter the week before, and she was just some woman at home and we decided that day to get everyone tweeting Rupert Murdoch and he replied to her tweet and we got goodness knows how many tens of thousands extra signatures on the back of that, and obviously, our whole petition is online and everything so.

Dana suggests that social media gives individuals a voice because the speed and ease of platforms such as Twitter enable participants to fit activism around their daily routines. In particular, she draws our attention to how such opportunities presented by social media may help to overcome gendered barriers to activism, as discussed in Chapter 5.

Anna demonstrates how Facebook has helped her to politicise others and reach those who would not otherwise be concerned with politics: 'I believe Facebook is my propaganda channel, so I say. And it works!' She speaks about how her friends have become politicised by reading and commenting on her Facebook posts and articles that she shares. Similarly, Charlotte speaks of how the internet has helped to spread information and make political issues more understandable through the use of graphics and videos that simply explain situations such as the Israel/Palestine conflict. Beth also speaks of translating facts and figures into 'bite-size, Facebook friendly' pieces that can be shared with friends and family to increase their knowledge and understanding of politics. Moreover, Dana asserts that it is easier to read articles and blogs online compared with finding time to read books, again demonstrating how the internet makes activism more accessible by overcoming the time costs associated with it. Charlotte says:

> I think that's the thing, people can in the privacy of their own home, in their own time, read things that they might not have read otherwise because it wouldn't be in the kind of newspaper that they would pick up, so I think it is really useful and also, obviously there's the tweeting and just the fact that you can sign a petition in seconds, I think it's a really powerful thing.

Several participants suggest that social media is a way to involve individuals who do not or cannot usually do activism and has the ability to cross barriers and divides between people, making activism more inclusive and representative of vulnerable and disadvantaged individuals and groups. Beth suggests 'that's the role that it has played for me, putting me in touch with people with very diverse backgrounds and experiences ... that kind of access to people, and their life, I don't think we've ever had that before'. Likewise, Riftkin (2009: 551) remarks that the exposure to diverse people that the internet enables results in an 'empathic surge'.

Furthermore, Alison contends that while the media has traditionally been owned by the 'ruling classes', 'now they don't have that control so I think that makes a massive difference because people do get their voices heard and real minorities get their voices heard and do end up having that kind of influence and power'. Mel reinforces this, saying how despite her disability 'I can still be an activist, I can be an armchair activist because I'm a laptop activist'. The term 'armchair activist' implies that those who engage mainly online are a different type of activist; significantly,

Mel sees this as empowering rather than derogatory, which is how many participants use the term.

Similarly, for several women participants, the internet acts as a way of claiming a voice and feeling that they are 'doing something rather than nothing'. Anna and Amanda speak of being a 'clicktivist' and how signing petitions makes them feel that they have a voice, even if their campaigns are ineffective: 'I'm a bit of a clicktivist … I spend a lot of time signing petitions, lots of them. No, I don't think petitions make any difference, I think that just makes me feel like at least I get counted as disagreeing with something' (Anna). Likewise, Charlotte remarks 'I think it's [social media] changed activism and made people feel more able to do something', drawing our attention to the ways in which being active online can empower individuals. While participants acknowledge that online actions may not impact upon policy, they ascribe other value to them. Indeed, Halupka (2014: 117) asserts that disregarding political acts because they are different to traditionally held ideas about what constitutes activism is a mistake. For even if it requires limited effort, online activism has relevance for the individual. We have seen how doing activism and being activist is a key part of some participants' self-understanding, with activism taking on a meaning in itself. However, this raises questions about the purpose of such activities. While it is important not to minimise activism to purely instrumental aims and instead to recognise the diverse emotional, social and moral aspects that comprise doing activism and being activist (which this book attempts to do), it is also important that we do not solely define activism in individualistic terms that do not reflect the wider impact and significance of political activities.

Moreover, Dana suggests that social media is a way of seeing 'around' mainstream media and is in some ways more truthful and honest, providing the potential for people to become enlightened, empowered and to mobilise:

> It could potentially be the basis of a revolution, perhaps not a revolution with, you know, guillotines and stuff but a revolution that sees people taking the red pill instead of the blue pill, not just in terms of feminism but in terms of oh my god, these people have been getting away with this shit for years! How did we let this happen?! And that comes from reading things outside of mainstream.

Here, Dana is referring to the film *The Matrix*, and the protagonist's choice to take either a pill that would reveal the 'truth' and reality or a pill that would allow him to remain in ignorance about the real world. This analogy implies that individuals have a choice and alludes to ideas of 'reality' versus a false consciousness, which, in Dana's eyes, social media and activism can help to free individuals from. Also relevant here is the fact that the 'red pill' is presented as the choice to embrace the often painful truth of reality, whereas the blue pill reflects blissful ignorance. Therefore, we get a sense that to choose to be a part of Dana's 'revolution' is not necessarily the easy or comfortable choice, reflecting the strains that activism places on individuals. While it is not the easy choice, it is implied that it is the 'right' choice morally, highlighting the centrality of morality throughout participants' narratives, especially in terms of motivations for doing activism.

Reinforcing Dana's and other participants' assertion that social media has radically changed the political landscape, Mel suggests that we are now living in the 'Facebook generation' and speaks about activism in terms of 'before' and 'after' Facebook. She contends that social media has transformed activism, with events being organised and publicised online and people networking through social media. She compares this with 'before Facebook', when people would meet at protests and face-to-face meetings and find out about events via leaflets. Likewise, Dana speaks of 'before' and 'after' social media in activism, saying how now you can be involved in activism by sending 'one or two tweets while sitting having your sandwich at lunchtime', emphasising the way in which social media makes activism accessible by fitting it into people's routines. She goes on to note that 'in the past you'd have had to put posters up or done a letter writing campaign, goodness knows how long it would have taken and things happen in like hours now'. Jack summarises: 'the cost of organising things has plummeted, the time cost, the money cost, the effort cost, it's just, it's gone'. Mary remarks: 'You can use social media without doing ... you can use it by setting up groups or coordinating and organising things in a very quick way because you know that everybody is always on. You just send somebody a message and they will pick it up.'

However, while many participants perceive the ubiquity of social media to be a positive attribute, others recognise the risks of this. Dana remarks that social media 'sort of infiltrates everything because it's all, a lot of it's social – you know, online activism, it goes with you everywhere in your pocket doesn't it (picks up mobile phone) so, I'm never away from it, quite literally never away from it'. Significantly, she highlights the psychological strain activism places on people, noting that it's 'probably really bad for me isn't it? I'll probably have a nervous breakdown.' Alison also alludes to the ubiquity of social media commenting:

> Although I am not, you know, some people I know are just
> constantly you know, so I am not like people on, I don't
> know, some activists I know are on Twitter constantly and
> social media constantly and it can't be as big a part of my life
> as that, you know.

Interestingly, Alison compares herself and her own level of activity to others, suggesting that anxiety about doing enough is also present in terms of online activism. We see how individuals internalise other activists' judgements about the type and amount of activism one does, resulting in participants policing and criticising themselves based on how they live up to the ideal activist standard. Moreover, social media does not remove this barrier but actually heightens it, with the anxiety of not doing enough being compounded by the fact that individuals are constantly exposed to the activities of other activists via social media.

Although participants extol the virtues of social media and speak about the need for both online and offline spaces, as well as the interaction between the two, they tend to still consider offline activism to be more important than online activism. Beth speaks of online activism as 'supplementary' to offline and Joe says that 'grassroots campaigning [offline] is much more important' and that online activism 'will always be ancillary to grassroots campaigning, in person, in the real world, in meet space'. In fact, despite being heavily involved in a campaign that is 'nearly all online ... and doesn't have a physical office, we have a virtual office as a Facebook page and run the campaign entirely out of that space', Dana says that the campaign leaders 'still need to get together obviously to keep that bond', echoing Beth's and others' earlier comments about the need for face-to-face meetings in order to foster strong ties. Therefore, while social media offers opportunities to overcome certain barriers to activism, particularly those of time constraints and accessibility to meetings, it also introduces new exclusions and produces anxiety about 'doing enough' of the 'right' type of activism, which underlies the ideal activist identity.

This chapter has explored the ambivalent and contradictory ways in which participants construct the activist identity. It began by asserting how the local activist culture creates shared meanings of the term before exploring in detail the two main constructions of the activist identity: the authentic activist who has the required lived experience and the ideal activist who does 'enough' of the 'right' type of activism, direct action. The emphasis placed on lived experience as an authentic motivation for activism reveals limits to empathy as a motivation for doing activism, while the emphasis placed on 'doing enough' of the 'right' type of activism contradicts participants' conceptualisation of activism as care and the assertion that 'doing what you can' is all that matters. This chapter has further explored how the emphasis on direct action is underpinned by a sharp distinction drawn between talking and doing, and maintained through constructing online activism as its ineffective opposition (or 'slacktivism'). This chapter has considered some of the ways in which this construction of the activist identity is problematic given the barriers it introduces to becoming an activist and its negative emotional effects on participants. Chapter 7 further elaborates on this negative impact by exploring what I have called the 'dark side' of activist culture and bringing to light its hidden gendered dimension.

7

The Dark Side of Activist Culture and its Gendered Dimension

As Alexander (2013: 1) asserts in reference to modernity, 'there has always been a dark part that offers a kind of counterpoint to the light part'. Alexander (2013: 3) speaks of modernity as 'Janus-faced', both forwards- and backwards-looking at the same time, remarking that 'even when you're moving through something, you're also drawn back into the chaos'. Alexander's analysis of the messy, ambivalent nature of modernity is well suited to understanding the complexity of meanings and experiences of 'doing activism and being activist'. In Chapters 3, 4, 5 and 6, I have explored the distinction made between activist and non-activist, and how the activist identity is constructed within the local anti-austerity activist culture. This chapter begins by acknowledging that the activist identity is constructed outside activist culture, as well as inside, and explores how the activist culture produces barriers for non-activists. However, it is the internal constructions of the 'ideal' and 'authentic' activist identities that are enforced and maintained by this culture, and which have negative implications for those within the activist field. This chapter explores how these identities are enforced through practices of activist shaming and how such judgements become internalised, with individuals policing their own activities, especially in relation to the ideal activist's criteria of doing enough of the right type of activism (direct action). Finally, this chapter reveals the hidden gendered dimension of the ideal activist identity and its negative consequences.

Given the pervasiveness and severity of these negative impacts, combined with the way in which this dimension tends to be hidden from public view, I contend that these behaviours and their consequences constitute the dark side of activism. Furthermore, there are two layers to this. The first is recognised negative behaviours, such as activist shaming, through which individuals police other activists' behaviour; while the second, deeper layer is largely unnoticed by participants and consists of subtler negative impacts, including the gendered guilt and anxiety that arise and the insidious self-policing that runs rife.

While the ideal activist is constructed within the local anti-austerity activist culture as an abstract individual, this chapter argues that it is actually the white, able-bodied male, given the criteria that define it. Therefore, this identity is easier to achieve for men than women, and the negative emotional consequences of not achieving the identity are more likely to be experienced by women. The criterion of doing the right amount of activism excludes those who cannot commit to constantly doing activism; women tend to face structural availability barriers to political participation, often related to caring responsibilities. The binary construction of direct action as 'real' activism versus online 'slacktivism' minimises online activism, which is a form of accessible activism that women can combine with caring responsibilities. This construction is also damaging for people with disabilities, those who cannot afford the costs of activism and others who are excluded from the normalisation of the ideal activist as white, able-bodied male, and for whom alternative methods of political engagement are often the only way of participating politically.

While women participants identify and challenge gendered barriers and exclusions to local anti-austerity activism, the implicit gendered nature of the ideal activist identity and its damaging gendered consequences are not recognised, resulting in women feeling guilt and blaming themselves for their perceived failure to adequately perform the identity. This chapter thus reveals the complex ways that spaces of resistance can reinforce dominant gendered power structures, while ostensibly fighting against them. Utilising a feminist approach establishes the importance of paying attention to the gendered differences between activist experiences in counter-hegemonic movements and contributes to understanding the complexities of the activist identity in the context of anti-austerity activism. By exploring the contradictory and problematic ways in which this activist identity is constructed and negotiated within activist cultures, and the obscured negative implications of this, I hope to illuminate this lesser seen dark side of activism.

Constructing the activist identity: outside as well as in

Chapter 6 highlighted the two main constructions of the activist identity that occur within the local anti-austerity activist culture. However, participants are also aware of how the activist is constructed and perceived outside this context. In contrast to the construction of the identity inside activist culture, where the activist label is highly valued and functions as a form of symbolic and social capital, participants suggest that activist is perceived as overwhelmingly negative outside this context. Lily and Adrian suggest that the term tends to be associated in the public imagination with violence, aggression and the risk of arrest. These perceptions can act as barriers to individuals becoming involved in activism.

Jared suggests that activist passion can come across to non-activists as aggression and 'put people off'. He recognises that a confrontational approach does not work for everyone but that it tends to be the dominant approach within activism and that this can therefore make people shut down, producing another barrier. Again it is more likely to be vulnerable individuals who are excluded because the tone of aggression creates a space that is not safe or comfortable to enter. Hope (2014), a local activist and writer, contends that 'this has become an access issue – only those with robust mental health and low sensitivity or trauma that's so entrenched they've dissociated from it, need apply'.

Another negative activist stereotype external to the activist culture that participants speak of is that of the young person who has not yet 'grown out of it'. Charlotte says 'it's seen as something that you do when you're a young person, a younger person'. Similarly, Harry notes that:

> I think people have got a very limited view of it [activism], I think when they hear the word activist that they think of tabard-wearing Oxfam clipboard users, that an activist is a gap year thing, that it's something that you do between the ages of 18 and 21 if you're middle class and you don't have to work, and that it's something that you grow out of.

Here, we see the notion of the middle-class activist type again, along with the notion that the definition of 'activist' needs to be widened, particularly within the public consciousness. Indeed, Morris argues for the normalisation of protest, saying:

> This is something that I did want to say, that's important. Because there is perhaps a perception that there's some sort of nutter who goes out and does this and we're some sort of strange weirdos. The people I know certainly aren't, they're well adjusted, ordinary, normal people from many walks of life. I can count civil servants, teachers, single mothers, unemployed people, family people, self-employed people,

tradesmen, and professional people amongst us. And none of
them, possibly apart from myself, are particularly eccentric
or different. I think the big point that I wanted to get across
is that a lot of people do things in their spare time. People
might restore old cars, they might go to church, they might
play sport, people do things in their spare time. And society
that wants to preserve its status quo, has really said to go and
protest in your spare time is the activity of cranks, you know?
Go and play football! Go and do something else, go fishing, it
doesn't matter, but don't protest. Normal people fish, normal
people play football, normal people go to the gym, go for a
run, cranks go and protest. Well, I'm sorry, but in a democratic
society everybody should be, people should be protesting!
It is, it is a, doing it in a non-violent way, I do stress, going
and throwing bricks at the police isn't particularly helpful.
But going and making a point, in a non-violent way, that
you don't overly inconvenience people, is part of a vibrant
democratic society. And to me it's no more weird doing this
than it is going sitting by the Trent and catching some fish.
It's possibly a lot less antisocial than going out and getting
absolutely hammered and having a fight.

Morris attempts to challenge common misconceptions about who does
activism, as well as what being an activist means. Notably, he stresses the
need for 'non-violent' action and compares it with other social activities,
highlighting the social dimension of activism (as we saw in Chapter 5).
However, despite speaking positively about activism, Morris seems to
imply that activism is, or at least is perceived to be, 'anti-social behaviour'
by comparing it with other socially undesirable behaviours and remarking
that it is 'possibly a lot less anti-social' than these. Significantly, though,
Morris's comment returns us to this notion that activism is something
that anyone can and should do.

Like Morris, Chatterton (2006: 261) contends that there is a need
to 'transcend the role of activist' in order to foster dialogue between
so-called 'activists and their others'. Here, the role and label of activist
act as a barrier to interactions between activists and the public. Jared
contends that the activist community is not welcoming to 'outsiders' or a
friendly environment for non-activists to ask questions and learn. He and
Adrian refer to 'Left activist elitism', where particular language is used
that excludes those who are not knowledgeable about political theory and
those who do not already move within activist circles. We are reminded
of the problem of telling others to 'check your privilege' and how it is

tied to an exclusive activist mentality. Lamon (2016: n.p.) suggests that this attitude perpetuates 'a form of bigotry on its own because it alienates and 'otherises' those who do not share their ways of thinking and speaking about the world'. Adrian suggests that this attitude is 'condescending and egotistical' and 'excludes huge portions of people who don't read theory'.

While being part of a close-knit community can help to sustain participants' activism, it can also act as a barrier to other people getting involved. Phillips (1991: 125–6) acknowledges that 'For those already involved, the absence of formal structures, the informality, the shared jokes and references, were a part of what the [women's] movement was about. These very same phenomena could seem mysterious and exclusionary to those not yet accepted as friends.'

Participants were aware of how the core group of Notts Uncut could be seen as 'a bit cliquey' (Will), which was a barrier that the group struggled to overcome. While participants argue that Uncut was inclusive, they also acknowledge the need to attract new activists and that they were often failing to reach outside the group, resulting in a lack of diversity. Participants refer to the 'activist bubble' as a space that can be 'quite insular' and accuse it of 'talking to itself sometimes', resulting in concerns that activists are 'preaching to the converted'. Some participants suggest that social media increases the divide between activists and non-activists by perpetuating this bubble. Morris acknowledges that social media is 'certainly a very good tool, we use social media a lot, we communicate ourselves on it', but points out:

> Don't you ever notice that we've got our own little bubble? You know, we talk to the political people, they talk to us, we all exist within that little bubble. If social media is going to become an effective tool we've got to get out of that bubble.

Similarly, Lydia suggests that groups exist within their own bubbles online and that non-activists are unlikely to be mobilised online:

> If I wasn't interested in sort of politics, left wing politics and that sort of thing, I would be able to just completely ignore it. It wouldn't even sort of come up and it wouldn't even show up on my radar ... so it's useful if you already have an interest in something.

Joe reinforces this: 'people tend to follow sources of information on Facebook which they already want to, so they're not going to have their belief system challenged'. Here, we see this notion that the internet merely produces radical enclaves rather than wider public debate. Sunstein (2001: 16) contends that such fragmentation can lead to more dangerous 'group polarization' where people encounter less diverging opinions and instead remain within their own corners of the net 'listening to louder echoes of their own voices'. Indeed, this 'activist bubble' is accused of creating and perpetuating an 'activist false consciousness', whereby individuals believe that the majority of people think and feel the same way that they do. Alison reinforces this, saying that it can be hard to know what the 'general opinion' is when she is surrounded by activists. Participants appear to reify this 'bubble', treating it as an external object that almost has a life of its own, thus distancing individuals from their actions and removing responsibility. Moreover, while this section has focused on the negative impact of activist culture on those outside this culture in how it functions as a barrier to getting involved, there is another side to the negative effects of activist culture that occurs within the boundaries of this field. It is this internal dimension that is the focus of the rest of this chapter.

Being policed by others: activist shaming

Being and feeling judged by other activists' values is central to the dark side of activist culture, with such judgements determining who can claim the activist identity. Participants feel that they do not qualify as activists because they do not do 'enough' activism or because they 'only' do online activism, reflecting the criteria of the 'right' type and level of activism. Significantly, this judgement comes from within the activist community. Jared claims that there is a 'level of snobbery among activists' where some activists hold the opinion that 'I'm more of an activist and more anti-oppression than you'. Conflict over the salience of particular values, notably veganism, feeds into this attitude and reveals a potential downside to considering all oppressions as equal and interlocking, for activists are penalised when they neglect one that other activists consider to be central. Certainly, for Adrian, Dermot and Alex, animal welfare and veganism form the basis of their activism, as Adrian proclaims, 'because I think it sets the tone for the rest of exploitation that occurs'.

However, participants contend that 'white vegan males' tend to be particularly aggressive about their views and judgemental of others. Anna recalls having been told that she is 'an evil, bad person' for not being vegan and reports occasions where:

> Some of them go as far as to say well if you're not a vegan
> you have no right then to speak about the oppression of

women, I mean some of them literally say stuff like that, they don't imply it they actually say it, or you have no right to talk about peace and to talk about anti-violence because you kill and eat animals.

This militant veganism acts as a barrier to many getting involved in activism as it 'puts people off'. Portwood-Stacer (2013: 9) notes how within anarchist cultures lifestyle practices 'become targets of self-righteous moralizing and other forms of social policing', which she terms 'politicking over lifestyle'. She draws on veganism as a key example of such politicking and warns that this judgemental practice can 'fracture bonds of solidarity among activists who make different lifestyle choices'. Anna remarks: 'out of all of the 'isms' it's [veganism] quite … I don't know whether it's the people propagating it but it's kind of quite forceful in a way that I've never experienced before'. In this regard, individuals compete over symbolic and cultural capital within the activist field.

In a similar fashion to Portwood-Stacer (2013), Jacobsson and Lindblom (2012: 49) assert that informal hierarchies exist within movements that are based on 'moral evaluations and distinctions'. Here, 'activists construct a moral hierarchy in which actions are ranked by their morality and activists are assigned different positions closer to or further from the sphere of "the sacred"'. Having a high position in this hierarchy enables one to lay claim to an activist identity. Anna reflects this, speaking of an 'evangelical' activist mindset:

They have this look on their face that they've seen the truth and you can't see it. But they're actually patronising you in a way, without even realising that their belief system is quite egotistical. Some activists are actually exactly like that, they have seen the truth, they know about capitalism and patriarchy and all of the rest of it and 'oh poor you', and I think that's a horrific, it's a massive, actually obstacle to activism.

We are reminded of previous discussions about the way in which activists position themselves as more knowledgeable, and hence more privileged, than other people. Likewise, Portwood-Stacer's (2013: 42) participants refer to a 'holier-than-thouism' attitude among activists. Portwood-Stacer (2013: 34) remarks: 'Whether anarchists intend to or not, they may give the impression that their rejection of norms is done to demonstrate their intellectual superiority to the masses who aren't sophisticated enough to have developed a political critique of mainstream culture.'

Anna claims that this attitude is ego-driven and selfish, reflecting the very individualistic values that such activists claim to be against (as we saw in Chapter 5). Furthermore, this attitude then acts as a barrier to doing activism because it excludes individuals with less knowledge or experience of activism and also deters other activists from participating because they do not wish to be associated with these attitudes. Hope (2014) summarises the damaging effects of this 'competitive capitalist activism', which has created an environment:

> Where people who could be working together are constantly jumping down each other's throats. Please note: this kind of crass telling off is not the same as challenging – challenging is good, but doing it in a way that the person can hear, rather than in a way designed to put a person down and make them feel so small they instinctively want to fight their way back up.

This 'crass telling off' links back to earlier discussions about the damaging way in which 'check your privilege' has been used by activists to police and shame others. Portwood-Stacer (2013: 42) notes that without a critical interrogation of what being a 'real' anarchist means, 'holding people accountable can easily be mistaken (or actually devolve into) self-righteous moralism and arbitrary boundary policing'. Jacobsson and Lindblom (2012: 53) contend that, paradoxically, 'we are both moral and social creatures, which entail a need to put significant effort into being viewed as moral by others – which in itself is a non-moral activity'. There appears, then, to be a dark side to the motivating force of morals, for while morality is concerned with what is 'good', the activities that we undertake to be considered moral and how this morality is then enforced within communities can become destructive.

Notably, the pressure to conform comes from other activists rather than outside the activist community, with such performances of morality being inward-facing, directed towards other activists, rather than outwards-facing to the public. Again, we see how local activist culture constitutes a field with its own doxa and habitus and, within which, individuals compete over the attainment of symbolic capital, as well as the value and definitions of such capital. Participants' narratives reveal that these values are upheld, and the moral hierarchy enforced, through the practice of activist shaming. Jack demonstrates this, referring to a time when he was called a 'chicken' by other activists for not wanting to occupy a store with only five people:

This is something that we, when I was first involved, would call moralism, and it's when you sort of try and use, turn protesting into a morality and then try and use it against people who aren't willing to do these things. And I sort of felt like well this is more akin to religion than it is to politics, it's sort of making judgements about people.

Jack reveals the dark side of groups with strong bonding social capital (Putnam, 2000), where part of the group's strength and cohesiveness is rooted in excluding the 'other' that does not conform to the group's norms. In other words, 'we are united and confident in our identity because we know what we are not, and that which we are not is to be expelled':

> The Left looks more like a religion now, it's got the interpretation of texts, so what did Lenin say, and people will go into long arguments about what that really means and it's got that sort of element of moralism and cultism and do you believe this as fervently as I do and if not, get out of my group. (Jack)

Again, we see activism referred to as a 'religion', reflecting earlier comments about activists' evangelical fervour, devotion and desire to be near 'the sacred'. Morris criticises people for holding up certain theorists and texts as 'sacred cows'. It seems that, for some, activism is like a secular religion, which provides meaning and a clear set of moral values within what is deemed to be a corrupt world. Moreover, in terms of group definition and boundaries, there are similarities with anarchist cultures and more conventional identity-based movements such as LGBT groups, where there is 'endless infighting about who has the right to claim membership in identity categories and who has the right to speak on behalf of the oppressed' (Portwood-Stacer, 2013: 37). This was raised in Chapter 6 regarding issues of authentic representation and its relation to lived experiences of oppression; what is key is the ways in which close groups work to maintain definitions of what being a member of that group means. While close friendships help to sustain activism for many, there is a dark side where 'the other side of the coin is the infamous moralism that political movements so often produce' (Phillips, 1991: 113). Portwood-Stacer (2013: 42) speaks about the 'sectarian' attitude among anarchist groups who are 'closed off, cliquey, dogmatic or even elitist'. Despite anti-austerity activism being a more horizontally organised, 'networked' movement, such features of group politics are still present, demonstrated by participants' comments.

This attitude and type of activist is considered to be such a barrier to activism that Anna distances herself from the label 'activist' because of it:

> I think that's why for a very long time I even didn't like to use that word activist because I always used to associate people who call themselves activist have such kind of a personality, way of conducting themselves, and I never wanted to be associated with those people and I still hope I'm not.

Similarly, Stuart (2013: 170) remarks that 'the negative stereotype functions as a barrier if people do not want to be seen to be associated with 'self-righteous', 'extreme' protestors'. Further, she (2013: 115) draws our attention to the similarities between the activist and feminist identity, given the ways in which stereotypes of the two create barriers to participation, demonstrated by so-called 'I'm not a feminist, but...' literature.

Nevertheless, Anna asserts that:

> This is a very small minority of people also, I'm not sure whether it's worth demonising them too much. And I'm not sure they make a great disservice, like some people think 'oh it makes a disservice to the movement', not really, I don't think so, I think that's silly.

Despite concentrating on the issue of activist judgement and shaming for a large proportion of the interview and admitting that these practices have damaging impacts on individuals, Anna minimises their effect here. This could be out of loyalty to the movements that she is involved in and a desire to protect them from negative attention or perhaps a way of removing the power from these activists through asserting their irrelevance. Although Anna highlights that it is a small minority of people who act in this way, it is indisputable that this minority has a loud voice given that almost all participants referred to it. Such activists and their judgemental behaviours may not be visible to the general public but they certainly have an impact on those within the activist community. Participants appear to internalise such values and judgements, resulting in self-policing and negative emotions.

Critically, judgement from the wider activist culture and its resulting constant self-policing create anxiety for participants about whether they are 'doing enough', resulting in feelings of guilt for not doing the 'right' amount of the 'right' type of activism. Beth says 'I don't do enough' and Dana feels guilty for not having the time to attend meetings for campaigns other than the one she is currently focused on: 'it's just there's quite a lot going on, you know?'. Jacobsson and Lindblom (2012: 52) assert that 'the imperative to act often gives rise to guilt feelings among activists. The interviewees for this study expressed that they felt guilty for not doing enough, with guilt propelling them into further action.' Whereas Jacobsson and Lindblom contend that these feelings of guilt encourage activists to be more active, I argue that this negative emotional impact often has the opposite effect of paralysing activists. Moreover, it becomes clear that this negative emotional impact is in fact gendered, bringing our attention back to the gendered barriers and exclusions to activism that exist. The next section of this chapter reveals how alternative spaces of resistance inadvertently mirror the gendered power dynamics of the dominant spaces they seek to resist. This is demonstrated through uncovering the implicit ways that the ideal activist identity and its negative emotional effects are both gendered.

The gendered dimension of the 'ideal activist' identity and its negative impacts

Although portrayed as an abstract, genderless individual, the 'ideal activist' is, I argue, a white able-bodied male, given its criteria of doing enough of the right type of activism, which excludes women and people with disabilities. Similarly, Coleman and Bassi (2011: 216) draw attention to how anarchist movements' emphasis on 'DIY politics' and individual agency 'conceals a very specific subject and a specific body: the white, male able-body'. Their allusion to the racism and ableism at play in constructing the ideal activist identity is particularly relevant in the case of anti-austerity activism where ethnic minorities and people with disabilities are disproportionately affected, alongside women; and, of course, these intersect. The implication is that the white, male body is the ideal and 'normal' body whereas the ethnic, female body is lacking and less 'able' than the male. Thus, it is important to look closely at the implicit ways in which activism and the activist identity are gendered as well as racialised, and the ableism underpinning these constructions. As previously explained, this book focuses especially on the gendered element given the research context that it draws on, and the lack of BME participants prevents me from drawing conclusions about the racialised experience of political participation. However, it is highly likely that the ideal activist is not only able bodied and male but white also, given the traditional ways in which the Left has constructed a unified (white) working-class identity. Bassel and Emejulu (2018) provide an in-depth analysis of minority women's experience of anti-austerity spaces, which demonstrates the ways in which such spaces reinforce racism and either exclude or limit the possibilities for minority women's activism.

The ideal activist identity's criterion of doing the right amount of activism (protesting tirelessly) excludes those who do not have the time or ability to commit to doing activism around the clock. As Bobel (2007: 156) asks, 'Who can afford to devote nearly every waking hour to their chosen cause? And while this mythic activist is off doing the good work, who, after all, is caring for the children, preparing meals, washing laundry, paying the bills?' More often than not, it is women who care for the children and maintain the household. Again, we are reminded of the continuing presence of structural availability barriers that prevent women from participating politically. Moreover, we start to become aware of implicit and often invisible gendered barriers and exclusions to doing activism and being activist.

The criterion of doing the 'right' type of activism – direct action – adds a further implicitly gendered exclusion. The binary construction of direct action as 'real' activism versus online 'slacktivism' is problematic because it minimises online activism (an umbrella term that includes many different activities such as signing online petitions, organising events, sharing information, among others), which women's narratives reveal as being a central form of activism that they can combine with caring roles.

While direct action is often associated with traditionally masculine traits such as physical confrontation, toughness and aggression (Sullivan, 2005; Coleman and Bassi, 2011), it should be noted that it is not inherently masculine; indeed, the Suffragettes were renowned for their direct action. However, because of the way in which participants construct direct action in opposition to online activism, thus denigrating a central form of women's activism, the gendered barriers women face in participating in direct action, and how this combines with the criteria of constantly protesting, it is argued that this results in the ideal activist identity being implicitly gendered, which has negative gendered consequences.

Women's guilt?

While all participants were asked about how they understood the activist identity and whether they personally identified as an activist, it was only women's narratives that revealed anxiety and guilt about whether they were 'doing enough' to be considered an activist. Male activists spoke about activist shaming practices, referring to activists' judgement and criticisms for not doing enough direct action. However, they did not speak about being personally affected by these attitudes or question whether their activities met the criteria of the ideal activist identity construct. Only one male participant referred to feeling guilty about how much he did, and this was at the end of the interview as an afterthought. The only female participant who did not feel uncertainty about the activist identity was someone who was involved more peripherally, perhaps because she was not as embedded within and influenced by the local activist culture's values and expectations. Likewise, Kennelly (2014: 249) found that while both men and women commented on the intense expectations of activist cultures, 'it was women who appeared to take these expectations in and transform them into self-debasing emotions such as guilt or feeling selfish'.

It could be argued that men are less likely to speak openly about their emotions (and thus do feel the same as women but do not express it in the same way), but this does not seem to be the case as they spoke openly about other emotions such as empathy and caring. It could also be argued, then, that men are more likely to speak about positive emotions rather than negative ones that could be perceived as 'weakness'. However, this does not appear to be the case either as men were forthcoming in speaking about other emotions that could be perceived to be weak, such as being upset and being 'in really shit disempowered kind of positions'. Moreover, while empathy is portrayed as a positive emotion, participants closely link it to 'caring about others', which has often been considered a feminine activity. Yet both men and women spoke about activism as a form of caring for others. Finally, given the time I spent as a participant attending groups' meetings, events and protests, I built a good relationship with many of my interview participants and so they spoke openly and honestly with me about personal topics. Therefore, I believe that the absence of guilt within male participants' narratives reflects the gendered nature of the ideal activist identity and its effects.

Women participants' anxiety and guilt about whether they do 'enough' of the 'right' type of activism (direct action) raises questions about whether this is specific to activism or part of a wider issue of 'women's guilt'. Beth suggests that this guilt is just part of being a woman. Reinforcing this, Greer (2013) notes that women are socialised to feel guilty from a young age, drawing our attention to a recent Spanish study that discovered women are more susceptible to guilt than men. Likewise, Bartky (1990) suggests that guilt is a deeply gendered phenomenon that occurs because of gendered structures and socialisation. Kennelly (2014: 243) contends that the repeated occurrence of guilt within women's narratives says less about the individual women that are interviewed and more about the wider social and cultural contexts within which these women are positioned.

While shame is concerned with group norms and is used to hold individuals to the group standard, 'guilt's role is to hold individuals to their own standards' (Jacquet, 2015: 11). I have discussed how interlinked social and individual conceptions of identity are. Indeed, Jacquet (2015: 51) notes that guilt occurs where 'the [group] norm has been internalised and is self-enforcing'. Therefore, it is not so simple as to separate the two emotions and their causes. However, guilt is 'inherently individualistic' (Jacquet, 2015: 58); in the context of anti-austerity activist culture, it seems that guilt is a private individual emotion that arises from and contributes to individuals' self-policing. Because of its individualistic nature, Benedict (2006) asserts that guilt is a distinctly Western emotion that emerges within a context that emphasises the individual and that its prevalence has recently risen. It is here that we see the influence of the current context of neoliberalism that fosters an environment of individualisation and responsibilisation.

In the neoliberal context, individuals are perceived to be both capable and responsible for their own actions and success. If one should fail, this is interpreted as a *personal* failing, and the fault of the individual rather than any external or structural factors. Kennelly (2014: 245) notes that neoliberalism is 'a form of political governance that makes a merit out of individualism, flexibility, and forms of self-regulation that decrease reliance on the state while increasing individuals' sense of responsibility for themselves'. While I discussed the ways in which such neoliberal discourses of individual responsibility are transformed by participants into positive motivations for activism in Chapter 5, we see here the dark side of the internalisation of these values. Women participants tend to blame themselves for not living up to the ideal activist standard, perceiving this to be a personal failing and thus turning these negative emotions against themselves. Although Kennelly (2014) does not refer specifically to the activist identity, she ties feelings of guilt to the context of neoliberal responsibilisation, remarking that 'amongst the women, I noted professions of an overwhelming – at times even crippling – sense of responsibility and culpability' (2014: 243). Crucially, in order to feel guilty for failing to reach a benchmark, one must believe that such a benchmark is achievable and that it is entirely within one's own power to achieve it.

However, a key question arises about why this particular negative effect of neoliberal ideology is gendered, especially as we have seen the ways in which participants of both genders engage with the notion of individual responsibility. According to Kennelly (2014), there are two aspects to consider here. First is the gendered nature of responsibilisation discourses under neoliberalism, and second is the impact of the concurrent 'retraditionalisation' of gender norms. Kennelly (2014: 243) draws on post-feminist literature and argues that 'reflexivity under neoliberalisation needs to be understood as a gender-differentiated practice, with particular kinds of inducements to self-interrogation experienced by young women'. Gill (2008) demonstrates that it is women more than men who are required to regulate themselves and work on the project of the self, thus making neoliberalism always already gendered. Women therefore experience more pressure to both change and govern the self.

At the same time, Kennelly (2014: 243) follows feminist critiques of the 'detraditionalisation' thesis (Beck et al, 1994), which assert that gender 'has been *retraditionalised* under current neoliberal regimes'. Here, traditional gender norms and roles are reinforced, along with the binary between men and women, resulting in the restriction of women's opportunities to participate politically. We have seen in Chapters 2, 4 and 5 how the traditional boundary between the private and public domains and their associations with women and men respectively is problematically being redrawn in the current context of austerity. Within the context of gendered neoliberal responsibilisation discourses and the retraditionalisation of gender structures, it is women who 'bear the burden of that 'choice' [to change the world] as an overwhelming and impossible responsibility' (Kennelly, 2014: 250). In fact, Greer (2013) contends that women are 'loaded with responsibility for other's behaviours' since childhood. Similarly, Brown (2015) draws attention to how women are uniquely positioned under neoliberalism as responsible for both themselves and others, highlighting the contradictions present in neoliberal logic that assumes all individuals to be wholly independent and accountable, and obscures the reproductive labour that goes into sustaining an 'independent' individual, which is usually carried out by women. Therefore women accept and place responsibility for social change on themselves but at the same time feel that 'their efforts can never be enough'. In this respect, 'guilt belongs to women under retraditionalised forms of gender in modernity' (Kennelly, 2014: 246). We see, then, how guilt becomes a gendered emotion that is influenced by the cultural and structural context of the society within which individuals are doing activism. Because of this, Kennelly (2014: 243) argues that guilt is a 'gendered structure of feeling', in the vein of Raymond Williams (1977).

Notably, the phenomenon of gendered guilt is not specific to anti-austerity activism but found in other political contexts too. Maddison (2007) discovered from interviews with young women involved in the Australian Cross Campus Women's Network that feelings of inadequacy were a common theme. Maddison (2007: 402) remarks:

> The pressure that some of these young women place on themselves is, at times, quite extraordinary. For example, Fiona feels that she is active on a personal level but feels guilty that she does not 'do more' and 'would like to be more active on a political level'.

It appears that students are also influenced by the same sort of pressures and feelings that other women activists encounter. Fiona personally feels active but believes that her level of activism does not match social expectations, whereas my participants did not personally feel active 'enough'. However, Fiona still goes on to say she would like to do more, implying that she is not entirely satisfied with her performance and demonstrating the negative emotional impacts of these doubts about the amount of activism one does.

While it has been suggested that young women in particular are affected by guilt because of their position as the 'ideal neoliberal subject', it emerges that this is not always the case. The Women's Liberation and After in Nottingham (WOLAN) project, which collected interview data from women who are and/or had been active in the local women's movement over the past 50 years, reveals a similar attitude regarding older women's feelings about their level of activity. Picot (2016: 18) remarks that: 'Marion Davis who spearheaded [Women Against Violence Against Women] describes her mother who at 87 years of age still actively campaigns and is in the Jewish Women's Peace Group saying "her activism puts me to shame really".'

Again, we see how women compare their own activities with others who are deemed to be exceptional. Picot notes that this activist modesty was a common theme in the WOLAN interviews, but interprets it as 'a collectivistic humble act of other's achievements over one's own' (2016: 18). While this assessment may be correct, I contend that there is also a gendered element here regarding women's socialisation to be less assertive regarding their successes (for fear it be considered arrogant and 'unwomanly'), as well as the element of gendered guilt that we have seen is present throughout my and Kennelly's (2014) data.

Although participants recognise the gendered dimension of austerity and highlight gendered exclusions and barriers to doing anti-austerity activism, they do not recognise the gendered dimension of the ideal activist identity. Thus, despite being male, the ideal activist is accepted as a universal abstract body. In this respect, activist cultures reflect the wider societal doxa of masculine domination, highlighted by Bourdieu (2001), where masculine behaviour and forms of thinking are afforded a higher status but taken for granted as 'natural' because of how embedded and inscribed in our daily activities and discourses they are. The obscuring and naturalisation of the gendered nature of the ideal activist identity masks the structural causes of women's perceived failure to achieve the identity and instead places full responsibility on the individual, leading women to blame themselves for their perceived *personal* failure to live up to the identity's criteria. This results in 'symbolic violence' (Bourdieu, 2001) where 'the internalized experience of pain or suffering that results from social conditions [...] is misrecognized by the subject as somehow of their own making' (Kennelly, 2014: 250). This is problematic as it obscures the presence of further gendered barriers and exclusions to political participation, with the result being that women are more likely to disengage from social movements. By ignoring such internal power relations, resistance politics 'may shore up the status quo even as it undermines it' (Coleman and Bassi, 2011: 205).

The influence of this masculine doxa is reflected by the 'very slowness of [gender's] revelation' in research studies of activism (Kennelly, 2014: 242). Kennelly (2014) admits that gender only emerged once she searched her interview transcripts for the word 'guilt'. Likewise, while I had paid attention to explicit gendered barriers and exclusions to activism, as well as discovering the presence of anxiety and guilt about the amount and type of activism individuals did, it was not until I returned to my interview transcripts with gender in mind regarding guilt that I discovered that it was a distinctly gendered phenomenon. The majority of studies regarding activist experiences and especially the ideal activist identity do not consider the gendered dimension of these aspects, with the exception of Bobel (2007), who notes the explicit gendered aspects of the ideal activist identity. It is therefore important to pay close attention to gendered differences in experiences of activism in order to uncover and challenge the power relations between activists, which are often neglected when focusing on movements that seek to resist elite power.

So far, we have seen that considering the activist identity as an ideal to strive towards is problematic because of the resulting feelings of anxiety and guilt that occur when one does not measure up to this standard. Within the activist field individuals feel constant pressure to either achieve or maintain perceived ideal activist behaviours, which in the case of anti-austerity activism are interpreted in terms of the type and amount of activism one does. Though this could encourage people to be active, as suggested by Jacobsson and Lindblom (2012), it can also result in individuals undervaluing their contribution and clearly has a negative emotional impact that is especially felt by women.

Critically, as previously alluded to, the question of 'how much is enough?' remains forever hanging over the heads of participants, with the attainment of 'enough' perhaps always being just out of reach. This results in the constant pressure to 'do more', while never feeling like one is 'doing enough'. Kennelly's (2014: 248) participant demonstrates this, saying 'I always feel that an expectation in activism is to be more involved to do more. To do more. To do more. To do more. You know?' Ironically, this attitude reflects the capitalist logic of perpetual accumulation, revealing the ways in which such ideologies are internalised even while one is attempting to resist them. Furthermore, the question is raised here of whose expectation it is to 'do more'; in Kennelly's quotation, her participant attributes it to 'activism', both reifying activism and removing responsibility from others for this attitude (though it is clear she has internalised these values). Similarly, Holyoak (2015: 133) notes that her participant, Katie, struggled with 'a persistent sense that she should do more [...] "I don't know if I should be doing more [...] I feel under pressure to do more which is my own pressure".' Here, then, Katie is aware that the pressure is her own, but rather than recognising this as a widespread feeling that she has internalised, it appears that she blames herself for this pressure, reinforcing Kennelly's (2014) argument about symbolic violence. This constant pressure to always 'do more' can lead to 'activist burnout' where activists push themselves too far, resulting in negative impacts on their health and the inability to do further activism. Burnout has been studied since the 1970s as a condition that is mainly associated with workplace stress within the environment of person-centred occupations (Maslach and Schaufeli, 1993), but is a term that has become part of activist discourse. It is these negative consequences, including burnout, that make up another, more explicit, element of the dark side of activist culture, to which I now turn.

Doing enough or doing too much? The negative effects of activism and activist burnout

Like participants, Brown and Pickerill (2009: 27) draw attention to the ways in which the 'perfect standard' of activist:

> Can be deployed by some self-identified 'activists' to police the boundaries of their social and political networks [...] one of us [researchers] has been accused by activist acquaintances of not having sacrificed enough to claim that identity [...] such accusations are loaded with an emotional impact (whether guilt, anger, despair or frustration) on those against whom they are levelled which in turn affect the individual's capacity to sustain activism.

Brown and Pickerill demonstrate how the activist identity is defined by the amount of work and dedication one puts in, as well as how this construction is enforced by activists through the practice of activist shaming (as discussed earlier). Moreover, and the key focus of this section, they highlight a central feature of the dark side of activist culture, namely the emotional, psychological and physical strain of doing activism and the negative impacts of this on activists. Significantly, it is again those who are the most vulnerable and/or disadvantaged who are at the greatest risk.

Several participants speak about the detrimental effect activism has had on their health as well as its impact on other areas of their lives. Anna remarks 'I think activism's taken a very bad toll on my physical and mental health'. Likewise, Adrian says 'it takes a toll personally' and remarks: 'It's like I think I can handle so I'm going to take it on board. And I think sometimes that has become overbearing and I've had to take myself out of it because I can't, and just not do anything for a while because it's tiring.'

We start to see the negative impacts of trying to meet expectations to do a certain amount of activism, as well as one of the key consequences, namely that individuals withdraw from activism. Leonie remarks:

> Things are a little bit different for me since then [since Notts Uncut started]. I am now a single parent, I have got some health issues as well and I don't think that I can devote as much to it as I used to and to be honest I don't feel that I want to devote quite as much to it as I used to. Not because it is not worthwhile but because it had such a massive impact on my life, most of it positive, some of it not. I don't necessarily want to give that much of myself right away. Maybe at some point in the future but not right now, I am still kind of in recovery (laughs).

This statement in particular emphasises the personal strain of activism, with Leonie comparing activism to giving part of herself away, which requires a period of 'recovery'. Graeber (2009: 252) contends that '[t]he trick to staying involved over the long term is to find a way to resist the temptation to overcommit. Relatively few, in my experience, successfully manage to do this.' For many participants, activism was a huge part of their lives but also an activity that they couldn't always take part in because of its all-encompassing nature. In response to looking through pictures of Uncut actions, Helen says:

> I had a lovely megaphone, which I got for my 30th birthday, it was my special 30th birthday present, a big one and this part

was red on it. It's indicative of where I am at the moment that
it's broken and I haven't gotten it fixed. So it needs repairing.

Notably, the negative impacts of activism on Helen and Leonie's personal
lives were partly related to their role as carers or mothers, highlighting
gendered barriers to activism. While male participants speak about the
strains of activism and activist burnout, again it is a more prominent theme
throughout women participants' narratives. Like Leonie and Helen, Dana
draws our attention to the all-encompassing nature of activism, remarking
'it's [activism], you know, a big chunk of my life is taken up with this …
probably as much of my life as my job does, if not more … it sort
of infiltrates everything'. Furthermore, Amanda notes that the constant
'chipping away' at the system is 'tiring' and can begin to feel 'futile'. Mel
asserts that 'people feel like they're endlessly, endlessly protesting' and
warns that this leads to burnout. Charlotte proclaims 'you have to be
careful, you don't want to get burnt out'. A significant risk of the criterion
of 'doing enough' is that individuals might overstretch themselves and do
too much. Indeed, Kennelly (2014: 248) notes that the 'capacity to say
no is often only achieved after reaching breaking point'.

In order to avoid such negative impacts, participants suggest that activists
need to prioritise and 'be careful not to spread yourself too thinly'; Alison
and Anna speak of the need to choose an issue to focus on in order to
be able to sustain their involvement. Anna states 'I just thought (sighs) I
need to, as a human being for my own sanity and well-being, I need to
kind of focus on a few things', drawing attention to the strains of activism
on her personal life and health. Likewise, Martin notes how his partner
chooses to focus on 'single issues rather than the bigger stuff, the wider
picture' because 'the big stuff seems too much, too big, too like there is
no way I can take on this'. However, this is problematic as it can result
in individuals feeling that they do not live up to the criterion of 'doing
enough'. As Stuart (2013: 196) contends, 'those highly committed to
their movements can be equally troubled by not doing "enough" as they
are by doing "too much"'. Furthermore, Bobel (2007: 155) notes that
her participants speak about how 'there's a lot of pressure to be big, the
stuff I do all feels so little'. Significantly, participants' concern is not solely
about the *amount* of activism that they do but also the *type*, with 'big'
activism tending to be associated with direct action. Holyoak's (2015: 76)
participant Ella demonstrates this: 'people look at bigger things, like 'let's
shut down this coal plant or this nuclear plant". This problematises the
extent to which the individual 'small actions' that participants emphasise
are perceived to actually 'count' as activism, casting doubt on participants'
earlier assertion that 'doing what you can is all that matters'.

Moreover, activist burnout is detrimental not only to individuals but also to the activist community, given that it prevents key players from participating. Leonie suggests that the reason the local activist scene is currently quiet is because of the strains activism places on individuals and the resulting occurrence of burnout:

> I think it needs somebody to say 'right let's do this, let's get on with it' and so far none of us are putting our heads out of the parapet. I have got a feeling, I mean we have privately between individuals some discussions about 'right, we need to get back out there, we need to be doing something about this or something about that' but we haven't actually done it yet and I think some of us are a little bit wary. I certainly am a little bit wary about getting caught up in it to the same degree as I was before because I just don't have the time or the energy.

The word 'parapet' has connotations of a defensive wall that protects soldiers, reflecting how activism tends to be described using masculinised metaphors of fighting, and drawing our attention to the link between direct action and visibility. Leonie implies that in order to sustain involvement it is vital that activists take 'time off' to recover (perhaps becoming invisible to the activist community). Similarly, Cox (2009) draws attention to the need to consider the 'problem of personal sustainability in social movements', especially emotional sustainability, and to situate this within specific contexts. Brown and Pickerill (2009: 28) assert:

> Following a period of burn-out, social movement actors need to engage in reflection about their emotional needs and priorities before negotiating the terms of any potential re-engagement in activism; not least of all to minimise the reoccurrence of burn-out and to better balance activism with other demands on their time.

Amanda reinforces this:

> Just on a personal level I needed some time off, my work is supporting women which can be futile, can feel futile, there's the activism which can feel futile, and sometimes you do, you get so tired, or I do anyway, get so like running on empty, you know? Can't keep hitting your head against a brick wall can you, so I think you need time, on a personal level, I just need

time off. Hang out with friends or hang out on my own just, ahh, a break from it all.

Similarly to Leonie and Amanda, Mary speaks of the need for 'a bit of recovery before getting on with the next thing'. Stuart (2013: 155) reinforces this, noting how 'the theme of protecting oneself, or balancing demands, was stressed as necessary to avoid burnout – however balancing demands was also described as something that had to be learnt the hard way, through experience', as in Leonie's case.

Significantly, as we have seen in relation to guilt, burnout is perceived to be the outcome of an individual's *personal* failing, thus placing the blame for and responsibility to avoid burnout on the individual. Furthermore, like guilt, because it is perceived to be an individual problem there is also the sense that it is a private issue that, while acknowledged among activists, is rarely spoken about in terms of personal experience. Perhaps, on some level, an individual may feel ashamed about suffering from burnout because it implies that they are not good enough at being an activist and have therefore failed. The typical response to activist burnout is to disengage from activism and to leave the activist community for a time until one feels 'strong enough' to return (implying that burning out is weak).

Yet, as Holyoak (2015: 131) asserts, 'crucially, burnout does not result from individual failings of "over-sensitivity" but rather is a response to "situational stress"'. In this vein, Brown and Pickerill (2009: 34) switch the focus to the *situation* rather than the individual, asking the question: 'how can we better understand why people suffer burn-out and how it can be "treated" as a collective failure of activist situations?' Similarly, Cox (2009: 3) contends that we need to 'view sustainability as both a collective, political and an individual issue and problematic'. King (2005) emphasises the need for 'practices of emotional reflexivity' within activist spaces, whereby individuals 'check in' with how they are, monitoring themselves and others' emotional well-being in order to avoid anyone reaching the point of burnout. However, as Holyoak (2015: 134) points out, 'while seemingly effective, these practices remain ones that are undertaken at the individual level', which thus reinforces the 'sense of individualised responsibility for managing one's own emotional wellbeing'. Furthermore, there is the added risk that caring for others becomes an additional responsibility and burden, which is more likely to fall to women as the traditional carers and emotional labourers within movements.

Moreover, the need for collective treatment of activist burnout is problematic when part of the cause of such strains is the pressures that come from within the activist community. There is a need, then, to intervene before the stage of burnout and to prevent contributing factors such as activist judgement and shaming. Participants emphasise fostering a supportive and inclusive activist environment; Mel speaks about the importance of receiving continued support from other activists, even when one is not actively engaged, and has created a Facebook group for this reason. Holyoak (2015: 134) asserts that 'what is required are collective responses to stress and trauma that are embedded within the very emotional culture of movements'. In order to avoid caring being tied to femininity and being interpreted as 'women's work', Holyoak (2015: 138) suggests that caring be reframed as solidarity. Here, she draws on work by feminists regarding the 'ethic of care' and the need to emphasise 'interdependence' over independence. By politicising care and emphasising the importance of emotional well-being and support for sustaining activism, it is hoped that care acts will be redefined as those of activists rather than women. Such collective notions of care as activism, including interpersonal care *within* activist culture, contrast with the neoliberal responsibilisation discourses that especially target women.

Similarly, Kennelly (2014: 244) draws on notions of 'relational agency' and 'affective solidarity' alongside the work of Arendt (1998) to assert that a 'web of relations', which perceives agency to reside in collectives rather than the liberal individual, 'can enable political action through the capacity to share with others the burden of this otherwise individualised experience' (Kennelly, 2014: 253). Crucially, Kennelly is not referring to sharing the caring burden in the way that I referred to earlier as problematic, where women potentially will end up shouldering more responsibility, but in terms of fostering a space of communication where individuals can speak openly about their experiences and feelings. Here, then, Kennelly tackles the issue I raised earlier of guilt and burnout being perceived as not only individual problems, but also private ones that activists cannot speak openly about but must suffer with alone (usually by withdrawing from activism). Moreover, this 'web of relations' is reproduced by such acts of sharing experiences and serves to sustain solidarity and action, while also unburdening the individual. Kennelly (2014: 254) remarks that:

> In Suzie's [participant] case, telling her story to others hooks her back into the web of relations, reducing her internalised sense of crippling responsibility and enabling her continued involvement in social movement organising. It is thus a political act in the Arendtian sense, creating the conditions of possibility for further action in the public sphere.

However, many participants speak about the need for a 'break' from activism and, significantly, other activists. Anna speaks of having a non-activist partner:

> I find it's a bit like my sanctuary actually. In some ways, it's nice to switch off once in a while. So it's nice that you can be upset and have a hug and cry and someone will comfort you without launching into a big debate with you, if that makes sense?

Likewise, Jared notes that while it is important to have friends 'on the same wavelength ... it can be very intense to socialise with people with those, with the same sort of political interests because everything ends up a debate or intense discussion, even the jokes do as well'.

Dana emphasises the need for a break from activism, saying 'The running helps ... I think that's part of why I do the running I think because it just stops you, you tune out and tune into something else for a while, yourself and the actual world.' Dana implies that the activist 'world' is separate from the 'actual world', reminding us of Bourdieu's (1992) conceptualisation of fields as little worlds, and that it is important to reconnect with this reality and stay grounded to prevent burnout. Similarly, Anna suggests that her partner and non-activist friends provide a 'sanctuary' from the constant discussion within the activist community and that this escape is needed in order to sustain her involvement. Certainly, participants speak about the need to take time away to be replenished. While this may change if activist cultures were to transform themselves in relation to care and how burnout is understood, it is likely that the activist community and individuals' other parts of their lives would still constitute two separate spheres, or fields, between which individuals would still desire to move at different times (as Dana demonstrates). Perhaps these two worlds would collide and merge if activism was redefined in terms of the mundane and quotidian; however, as we have seen, such understandings of 'activist' clash with the ideal activist identity that participants construct.

Although the notion of self-care places responsibility of an individual's welfare into their own hands, and thus risks reinforcing neoliberal responsibilisation discourses and removing the structural and communal elements of care that are important, participants demonstrate that it is a necessary way of protecting oneself from the damaging impacts of activist culture. However, this is spoken about privately, rather than being part of the wider activist discourse, signifying that it is a personal issue and also perhaps separating it as a form of private care, rather than the public care activists speak about when defining activism as care that is enacted through everyday acts in the local community. This boundary between private and public forms of care needs to be challenged, and compassion shown publicly not only to others but also to oneself. Hesitance in doing so might reflect participants' desire to distance themselves from neoliberal capitalist individualism that places the individual above the collective and that they perceive to be characterised by 'selfishness'. However, just as the neoliberal responsibilisation discourse has been subverted, it is perhaps possible to do the same in relation to self-care. Similarly to how Holloway (2010) constructs resistance as success, Bassel and Emejulu (2018: 81) draw on Sara Ahmed and Audre Lorde to suggest that we can interpret 'self-care as warfare', especially when it bolsters minority women and those who face a daily struggle to survive a system that is inherently hostile to them.

This chapter has explored what I have called the dark side of activist culture, in the vein of Alexander's (2013) assessment of modernity. This involves how the ideal activist identity is upheld through shaming practices, its negative emotional effects and the problem of doing too much in striving to do 'enough' of the 'right' type of activism to achieve the identity. This results in activist burnout, which is damaging both for the individual and the activist community. It has been argued that the ideal activist identity is easier for (white, able-bodied) men to achieve than women, which results in women feeling guilty about not doing 'enough' activism to merit the 'activist' title. Therefore, women are more likely to experience not only barriers and exclusions to doing activism and being an activist in the first place, but negative emotional impacts from not fulfilling the criteria to be deemed an ideal activist and from perceiving this failure as personal and individual rather than structural, gendered and beyond their control. Thus, the activist field is not an equal playing field, despite its presentation as such; the ability to achieve the activist identity and its associated rewards is weighted in favour of men, while the negative emotional consequences of not achieving the identity are more likely to be experienced by women.

Overall, this chapter demonstrates the importance of paying close attention to the gendered differences in experiences within counter-hegemonic groups in order to identify how dominant power relations might be reinforced by the spaces that seek to resist them. It also highlights the subtle, implicit ways that gendered structures affect women's experiences of political participation. It is hoped that this will contribute to our understanding of the complexities of identity within anti-austerity activist culture and encourage individuals who do activism to widen their understanding and definitions of activist to incorporate other, inclusive, forms of activism, thus minimising the exclusive and damaging gendered effects of the ideal activist identity.

PART IV

Concluding Remarks

The final part of this book, Part IV, draws together the strands of a key theme that has been threaded throughout this book: the ways in which anti-austerity activism interacts with the wider neoliberal capitalist context and the tensions present here. This includes how activists subvert and re-invent neoliberal discourses as well as the ways in which neoliberal capitalism restricts the space for resistance and political action. It demonstrates the ambivalence and complexity of anti-austerity activism and reaffirms the importance of in-depth 'thick description' (Geertz, 1973) that reveals the contradictions, tensions, and strengths of activist cultures and how they interact with the wider political context.

8

Subverting/Reinforcing Neoliberal Capitalism: The Complex Ambivalence of Anti-Austerity Activism

This book has attempted to weave a rich tapestry that portrays the complex, dynamic and ambivalent space of a local anti-austerity activist culture. In doing so, I have revealed several underlying contradictions within this context that are held in tension by participants' narratives. In particular, there is a contradiction between the centrality of empathy as a motivating and sustaining factor for doing activism and the notion that only those with lived experiences can truly understand the issues and therefore be authentic activists. Another problematic contradiction is that between the assertion that 'anyone and everyone can and should do activism' and the reality that this is not always the case, which is compounded by how the activist identity is constructed and the existence of a hierarchy of activism.

Throughout, I have demonstrated the ways in which anti-austerity activism interacts with the wider neoliberal capitalist context and the tensions present here. We have seen how participants subvert and at times unwittingly reinforce the neoliberal capitalist values that they seek to resist. This has included the hidden ways that spaces of resistance reinforce dominant oppressive structures of gender and race, as well as the creative ways in which activists reinvent neoliberal responsibilisation discourses to provide a rationale for doing activism. In this respect, anti-austerity activism represents both a hermeneutics of faith and suspicion (Levitas, 2012).

The ideal activist identity typifies this ambivalent relationship between neoliberal capitalism and its resistance, demonstrating the insidious ways

181

it infiltrates all areas of social life, including the spaces that fight against it. The ideal activist identity functions as a key form of symbolic and cultural capital within the local anti-austerity activist culture, with individuals valuing it and wanting to earn the title that is ascribed by others. In order to become the ideal activist, individuals compete to do 'enough' of the 'right' type of activism (direct action). Inherent to this criteria, but not recognised, is its gendered, ableist and likely racialised, dimensions; the ideal activist is actually the white, able-bodied male who also enjoys a position of dominance in the wider political context of neoliberal capitalism. Ironically, the ideal activist is perhaps actually the neoliberal capitalist activist, with criteria informed and defined by the conditions of neoliberal capitalism.

As Brown (2015) observes, neoliberalism is not solely destructive but also creates new subjects and relations. Problematically, the ideal activist reflects the neoliberal capitalist values that anti-austerity activism seeks to resist, and reproduces the sexism, ableism and racism that are embedded within this wider structural and political context. The drive to constantly do more activism in order to reach an undefined bar of 'enough' reflects the inherent capitalist logic of continual accumulation; while the desirability of the ideal activist identity introduces competition between individuals in the activist field. Drawing on Weber's (1930) notion of 'ideal types' can help us to better understand the construct of the ideal activist within the neoliberal capitalist context. Weber (1930) identifies the Protestant work ethic, which valorises and perpetuates values of hard work, discipline and frugality, as an 'ideal type' that emerged out of, was made possible by and was perpetuated by the wider capitalist context. Here, ideal type provides a conceptual model of an aspect of social reality from which the extent of empirical deviation can be studied. Significantly, 'ideal' does not mean desirable or normative but refers to how the concept is a construct of the social scientist to be used as an analytical tool. Weber's (1930) theory of the Protestant work ethic identified central tendencies across Protestants that, taken together, could promote a strong capitalist mentality because of an elective affinity between their qualities and those needed to succeed in business enterprises. In a similar way, the activist ideal type appears to be the individual who possesses the qualities valued within a neoliberal, patriarchal, capitalist society, which enables a certain type of individual to flourish in activism during times of economic austerity.

The presence of such contradictions and tensions might leave us feeling hopeless that any solutions to existing barriers and exclusions to doing activism and being activist can be realised. Admittedly, the preceding chapters have painted a pessimistic picture, and it is perhaps because of this resulting pessimism that the dark side of activist culture is hidden so well; for bringing it to light risks undermining the positive, enabling features of doing activism and being activist, and could function as a further barrier to individuals becoming politically involved. Instead, it is hoped that illuminating this side of activist culture will enable spaces of communication, sharing and care to be created and that, in line with a feminist research practice, the groups and individuals involved can use this information to challenge problematic features of activist culture.

Harnessing the hopeful attitude of participants, I contend that the grounds for improving experiences of political participation lie within activist culture. In this respect, we can perhaps draw on Habermas's (1992: 429) argument that despite its downfalls and exclusions the public sphere contains within it the potential for 'self-transformation'. Here, the public sphere's grounding in universalist discourses of equality and rights provides the platform from which inequalities can be challenged. Although I have identified the need to be wary when assuming 'universal abstract' categories because of how this assumed universality can often mask inherent inequalities and ignores difference, there remains a kernel of potential in this argument that I believe can be applied to activist cultures. As Kohn (2003: 8) argues, theorising about democracy 'can be understood as a dialectical process whereby the normative core of the concept and its particular manifestations continually transform one another'. I have demonstrated that the normative ideals of equality, empathy, common humanity and activism as a form of care are present within the local activist culture; therefore, the seeds for change already exist but require nurturing in order to grow into actualisation.

In response to gendered barriers and exclusions to activism, I have explored how women form their own feminist resistance to austerity, providing practical support for other women affected by the cuts and utilising women-only spaces to do so. I have shown that while this may be empowering, it is also problematic as it reinforces the 'triple jeopardy' thesis and contributes to the retraditionalisation of gender roles and norms. Despite this, it is important to recognise the significance of women-only spaces where women feel that their voices are heard and which enable women to positively reinterpret gender as facilitating, rather than blocking, political participation. Participants invoke a feminist standpoint, suggesting that women actually make better activists than men because they are innately more caring and possess a different, and privileged, type of knowledge. Again, this solution is problematic as it reinforces the traditional gender binary and associated behaviours upon which women are constitutively excluded from the public sphere and political action. However, this approach does contain the seeds of a potential solution to barriers and exclusions to activism, namely by stepping outside the strictly defined 'activist' role and redefining activism in terms of the everyday and, particularly, as a form of care.

Redefining activism as caring could potentially widen our understanding of activism and degender care by making it a collective activity that activists do, rather than one that women do. The grounds for doing so are present within participants' narratives, which draw on the centrality of empathy as a motivating and sustaining force. Here, we can draw on a feminist ethic of care that combines feelings of empathy for the other with a moral duty to act, resulting in the practical act of providing care for others. Vitally, such notions of care need to be extended within activist culture, alongside related ideas concerning the importance of collectivism above individualism in order to prevent activist burnout from being considered an individual weakness and problem for the individual to solve, and to prevent the pressures that result in such burnout. This would benefit the collective as a whole, as well as individuals, by eliminating the need for key activists to remove themselves from activist culture and its stresses; thus strengthening the community and providing better support to individuals who would be less likely to interpret struggles as personal failings.

However, we must be careful that caring for others does not become an additional gendered responsibility and burden. One way to prevent this is to reframe 'caring' as 'solidarity', so that it becomes part of the activist habitus, redefining caring acts as those of activists rather than women. Another solution is provided by Kennelly (2014), who suggests fostering a space of communication within activist culture where individuals can speak openly about their experiences and feelings, including negative ones, and which in time becomes part of the activist habitus. Achieving this requires efforts to create an open and honest space where individuals feel safe to display vulnerability without fear of negative judgement. This may seem idealistic, but the courage to be vulnerable has the potential to transform our relationships and experiences (Brown, 2013). Furthermore, it involves embracing imperfection, rather than continually striving to cover up feelings of inadequacy and to attain unattainable levels of perfection in our activities. Brene Brown's work (Brown, 2013, 2018) on the paralysing power of shame, and the importance of 'daring greatly' by embracing vulnerability, is a useful starting point for considering how to put such ideas into practice within activist culture. While much has been said about so-called 'safe spaces', it is perhaps more apt that we seek to develop 'brave spaces', where those who face discrimination and oppression can freely speak out, given that the majority of space is safe for the dominant groups in society (Craddock. 2019).

However, it is vital that fostering a culture of caring and communication is combined with actively breaking down the hierarchies of activism and removing the shaming practices that maintain these hierarchies within activist culture. Again, this requires a widening of our understanding of activism and what it means to be an activist to include more accessible forms of activism, not solely direct action. As Bassel and Emejulu (2018: 14) assert, we need to redefine 'what counts' and who enjoys the identity of 'activist' in order to 'extend the moniker of "activist" to as many women as possible' (2018: 9).

This book contributes to the development of a gender-focused SMT by utilising a feminist approach to explore the ways in which gender influences the cultural processes of political engagement, both explicitly and implicitly. This is a key theoretical contribution; as Roseneil (1995), Taylor (1999) and Charles (2000) outline, there is a need for mainstream SMT to incorporate feminist analyses of movement activities and for a distinct approach to studying social movements that takes full account of the role of gender in political participation. Anti-austerity activism is an important example given the disproportionate impact of austerity on women and the triple jeopardy that women face (Fawcett Society 2012). Furthermore, as a movement that does not explicitly define itself as feminist (in the local context at least), anti-austerity activism provides an interesting setting within which to explore the role of gender in social movement participation more generally, in a context that is not overtly concerned with gender politics (though participants within the movement recognise the gendered nature of austerity). As Bassel and Emejulu (2018: 8) state, in relation to minority women and anti-austerity activism, the responsibility to recognise and advance social justice claims should not rest solely on feminists' shoulders.

By utilising a feminist approach, I have revealed the obscured ways in which the activist identity is gendered and the negative gendered consequences of this, which are linked to the neoliberal context and its prevailing, gendered, responsibilisation discourses. Here, I have shown how the ideal activist, though presented as an abstract individual, is actually the (white) able-bodied male, and how the ways in which activism is constructed prioritise traditionally masculine ways of thinking and acting over feminine ones, reflecting the traditional public/private and related male/female binary constructions. The result of such constructions is that women feel guilt and anxiety for not doing 'enough' of the 'right' type of activism and, critically, turn these negative feelings against themselves, misrecognising the consequences of gendered structures as personal failings. These negative emotions and the misrecognition of their source results in gendered symbolic violence (Kennelly, 2014).

Despite women participants identifying as feminists and drawing attention to the explicit gendered barriers that exist to doing activism, as well as the feminist dimension of anti-austerity activism, participants do not recognise the gendered nature of the ideal activist identity and the associated negative emotions that emerge from failing to meet this standard. This reveals how insidious such gendered constructions and their effects are, and reasserts the urgent need for research that explores and reveals the role of gender in contemporary political participation. The hidden nature of the gendered negative impacts of how activism and the activist identity are constructed within activist culture is deeply problematic as it obscures the presence of further gendered barriers and exclusions to political participation, meaning women are more likely to disengage from social movements, and their reasons for doing so are unlikely to be addressed. This book therefore exposes the power relations and imbalances within practices of resistance that are often neglected and obscured in studies of social movements that are perceived to be counter-hegemonic. Making this visible opens up possibilities for challenging and overcoming such imbalances. I have demonstrated the ways in which neoliberalism infiltrates spaces of resistance to it and how dominant power relations and gender structures are replicated within alternative spaces of political action. This book therefore builds on the foundations laid by NSMT in terms of recognising the need to address the wider historical and political context within and out of which social movements emerge.

Moreover, I have shown that in the current context we are actually witnessing a retraditionalisation of gender roles and norms, rather than the perceived detraditionalisation of gender structures that has been theorised. Here, explicit traditional gendered barriers and exclusions to doing political participation, such as those related to women's caring responsibilities, are reaffirmed and heightened in the context of austerity, which places a further unpaid caring burden on women, and anti-austerity activism, which prioritises implicitly masculine forms of activism. There is a real risk that the traditional gendered boundaries between the public and private spheres are being redrawn and solidified. This is a critical contribution at a time when gender roles and norms are perceived to have less relevance and when women, under neoliberalism, are perceived to be autonomous, free agents, more so than ever before. This book therefore firmly asserts the continuing need for feminist theorising and activism, and the importance of paying close attention to the hidden ways in which gender structures and inequalities operate, even within spaces of resistance.

While I have demonstrated that participants of anti-austerity activism, unlike NSM, are largely working class, I have also revealed the ambivalence surrounding class within the current context. I have shown that although participants perceive their working-class roots to be an authentic basis for anti-austerity activism, participants' class identifications are not straightforward. The majority of participants possess high levels of cultural capital in the form of education and qualifications but are in an uncertain employment situation, or acknowledge that while they may now technically be 'middle class', identify more with their working-class heritage, and the two categories of middle class and working class seemingly clash uncomfortably for participants, creating ambivalence around class. Further, by exploring the intersections between gender and class, I have revealed that women participants tend to strategically prioritise gender over class in the current context, being influenced by traditional associations between working-class politics and men, which they wish to overcome. This reinforces Charles's (2000) contention that the dominance of class as a social cleavage in the UK has traditionally prevented struggles from being framed in terms of gender. This book therefore reaffirms and begins to answer Charles's (2000) call for a SMT that explores both gender and class, and how they intersect.

Additionally, this book contributes to the building of a body of in-depth studies of the impacts of austerity and its resistance within specific local contexts, which, alongside large-scale studies of anti-austerity movements, improve our understanding of the complex and varied experiences of women fighting austerity in the everyday (see also Coventry Women's Voices project outputs). I have demonstrated the value of invoking culture, emotions and gender as an approach in its own right, rather than as an addition to existing theories. This approach enabled me to uncover the centrality of emotions and how they combine with morals in motivating and sustaining political participation. This has contributed to the development of an understanding of activism as a form of care and care work as activism, which further adds to a feminist theory of social movements.

By centring on participants' lived and felt experiences of activism, I have uncovered how the activist identity is fraught with contradictions and the crucial implications of this for political participation. I have also shown the importance of paying attention to differences between activist experiences. My findings reinforce the contention that women's experiences within mixed gender movements differ from men's and that women's concerns are not listened to by men, resulting in women breaking away to form women-only groups for doing activism. Therefore, while anti-austerity activism attempts to establish itself as separate to party politics and the wider dominant neoliberal structures, the same gender inequalities that are present in these contexts persist in this alternative space, suggesting deeply embedded gender structures and divides that are not recognised by activists and that need to be highlighted by SMT.

Drawing on Bourdieu's (1992) theory of practice to explore local activist culture has enabled me to cast light on the lesser-seen dark side of activist culture, revealing the ways in which individuals involved in anti-austerity activism compete over symbolic and social capital, and how the activist field within which this competition occurs creates and reinforces a hidden, taken-for-granted, masculine doxa that obscures the implicit gendered barriers and exclusions that exist not only to doing activism but also to being activist. At the same time, this approach has enabled me to break the 'silence about the sphere of fellow feelings, the we-ness that makes society into society [...] and the processes that fragment it' (Alexander, 2006: 53). I have demonstrated how solidarity and collective identities are created and sustained within the context of anti-austerity activism and networked social movements, as well as how they are threatened. This investigation challenges the shift away from the study of collective identities within sociology that we have witnessed with the rise in theories of reflexive modernisation that emphasise individualism over collectivism. It also demonstrates the importance of paying attention to what sustains political engagement over a long period of time, including during latent periods, rather than solely focusing on the initial motivating factors that enable movements to emerge.

This book demonstrates, therefore, how the local anti-austerity activist culture, reflecting Alexander's (2013) conceptualisation of modernity, is 'Janus-faced', containing both enabling and positive elements that empower individuals and a darker, hidden and damaging side, which I have revealed is distinctly gendered and multilayered. Revealing and exploring this ambivalence demonstrates the value of looking closely at individual and collective experiences of political participation and situating these within the wider social, historical and political contexts.

Finally, this book has demonstrated that despite the seeming failure to impact on policies of austerity, individuals are finding creative ways to become politically active and to sustain this activity, by fostering positive emotions such as solidarity and hope that an imagined better future will be realised. Therefore, it is vital that we pay close attention to the meanings that individuals ascribe to their actions so that we do not miss the nuances that exist here. This also involves a need to reconsider how we define 'success' within the context of such resistance, as it becomes clear that participants do not solely consider success in instrumental terms of ending austerity. Instead, success is reinterpreted as resistance to a hostile, individualistic, neoliberal capitalism that actively erodes core values of human dignity and collectivism. Despite the contradictions and ambivalence present, anti-austerity activism is rooted in ideas about what it means to be human and the importance of caring for and about others. By reinterpreting and subverting neoliberal responsibilisation discourses to emphasise the collective above the individual, reasserting human dignity and reimagining the present in the mould of a better future, activists are not only creating 'cracks' in capitalism, which have the potential to be widened through agitation, but planting seeds of political change within them.

Future directions for research

Any piece of research of restricted scope is bound to have limitations, and this project is no exception. To begin with, it was necessary that I provided boundaries to the research site in order to make it manageable; thus I selected the specific research context of Nottingham. This enabled me to develop rich and detailed data over a set period of time, but the ability to generalise from the findings is limited. Future research into other localities and a comparison between them would enable us to gain a fuller picture of anti-austerity activism as it occurs on the ground throughout the UK, including the similarities and differences between cases, and perhaps provide potential solutions for problems that arise in one area but are either absent or have been solved in another.

A further way in which the research could be built upon and its focus widened is by broadening the research sample, and in particular paying attention to the experiences of people with disabilities, which was a topic that arose during my fieldwork but that I did not have scope to explore adequately, as well as the conspicuous absence of ethnic minority participants in local anti-austerity activism – to what extent is this the case in other localities and why? Both of these groups are important to study in the context of austerity that disproportionately impacts people with disabilities and ethnic minorities. Bassel and Emejulu (2018) demonstrate the need to pay attention to minority women's resistance to austerity, especially given the ways in which Left politics and the dominant political context erase minority women's experiences.

Recent developments at the time of writing (June 2019) suggest that ethnicity has been brought to the fore in local anti-austerity movements, with the rising visibility of Black Lives Matter protests and responses to the increase in racism that has been associated with the Brexit campaign and the decision for Britain to leave the European Union (EU). The local People's Assembly has held several meetings and protests about racism, but whether this will reflect an increase in BME participants remains to be seen. As Bassel and Emejulu (2018) assert, there are dangers that minority women will be constructed one-dimensionally as passive victims; thus it is important for such activism to emerge from and be centred on the lived experience and voices of minority women themselves. I have drawn attention throughout to the lack of race in my analysis of anti-austerity activist culture, which is due to the lack of BME participants in the research study. While I have drawn on other studies that explore race, I have deliberately avoided making claims that are unsubstantiated and, as a white woman, I wish to avoid speaking for or over minority women.

My research was undertaken during a time of disengagement from and distrust of mainstream political institutions, especially party politics, which movements sought to distance themselves from completely. While the election of Jeremy Corbyn as Labour leader suggested a shift in party politics towards a more hopeful anti-austerity mainstream politics, recent events have cast significant doubts on his potential. In light of the momentous EU referendum results, where over half of the votes cast were for leaving the EU, resulting in Brexit, there has been much political upheaval in both the Conservative and Labour parties. The ever-changing party political scene is reflected by the multiple times I have had to rewrite this section over a short period of time. The research took place during the Coalition government. Since then, we have seen a new Conservative party leader and prime minister, Theresa May, who appointed a new cabinet, and at the same time witnessed massive discord within the Labour party with many MPs challenging Corbyn's leadership. At the time of writing, the Conservative party leader and prime minister is Boris Johnson, a controversial figure who has previously made sexist, racist and homophobic comments. Combined with Donald Trump as US president, the possibilities for progressive politics look slim. It is impossible to predict the future, especially at such a tumultuous time when new events are seemingly unfolding every minute. However, one thing that is certain is that we are unlikely to see the end of austerity any time soon, despite Theresa May's recent claims otherwise. Moreover, with an apparent rise in racism and much political uncertainty surrounding the Brexit decision, it may be that concerns about austerity will take a backseat for the time being. Whether these concerns will return to the fore remains to be seen in the coming years.

While it is easy to fall into hopeless pessimism at this time of political upheaval and uncertainty, there are glimpses of more positive aspects of the current moment that it would be fruitful to explore further. Within the context of Brexit, it appears that citizens are becoming more politically active, with many movements and individuals protesting against the leave vote and associated political processes and social attitudes. Thus, the current moment opens up further opportunities to explore how social movements work with or outside 'the system', and how the Brexit decision may have encouraged a turn towards grassroots politics. It would be insightful to see how the changing political landscape impacts upon those who previously rejected party politics, whether they have shifted more towards working within the system and attempting to impact mainstream political institutions, or if there is still tension here.

Furthermore, while this book has focused specifically on anti-austerity activist culture, it is worth remembering that it is one part of a wider, holistic, activist community and vision that combines aligned political causes, with the boundaries of such activist cultures being porous. As previously stated by participant Beth, 'austerity is a thread that runs through many campaigns'. Nevertheless, anti-austerity activism is an intriguing case study given the diversity of its participants, with activists being 'not just the usual suspects' (as one participant explained), and its unique positioning as a movement that is not overtly feminist and yet is concerned with an issue that disproportionately affects women. The transferability of the research findings has been reinforced by my own and others' experiences and discussions of various forms of activism in different localities. Future research could provide rich data about the intersections of race, class, gender and disability within activist cultures that seek to resist neoliberal capitalism and the points at which different causes and movements overlap and interact.

Overall, this book sheds light on a distinct moment in the history of neoliberalism and resistance to it in the form of anti-austerity activism. It has explored the alternative spaces that open up in times of crisis, the alternative imaginaries that are created in these spaces and the tensions and ambivalence that exist here, focusing especially on the role played by emotion. In the context of austerity, which has been interpreted as a 'crisis of care' (Brown et al, 2013), combined with activist responses that emphasise caring and empathy, this book brings to the fore questions about the relationship between activism and care, austerity and care, and the gendered dimension and implications of these debates. It provides a strong foundation for future research into local anti-austerity activist cultures and reaffirms the importance of adopting a cultural, affective and feminist approach that takes into account emotion and gender.

References

Agosta, L. (2011) 'Empathy and sympathy in ethics', *Internet Encyclopedia of Philosophy*, available at: http://www.iep.utm.edu/emp-symp/ [Accessed 5 June 2016].

Ahmed, S. (2014) *The Cultural Politics of Emotion*, New York: Routledge.

Alexander, J.C. (2003) *The Meanings of Social Life*, Oxford: Oxford University Press.

Alexander, J.C. (2006) *The Civil Sphere*, Oxford: Oxford University Press

Alexander, J.C. (2013) *The Dark Side of Modernity*, Cambridge: Polity Press.

Althusser, L. (1971) 'Ideology and ideological state apparatus (notes towards an investigation)', in Althusser, L. (ed.) *Lenin and Philosophy and Other Essays*, New York: Monthly Review Press, pp. 127–89.

Anderson, B. (2013) *Us and Them? The Dangerous Politics of Immigration Control*, Oxford: Oxford University Press.

Arendt, H. (1998) *The Human Condition*, Chicago: University of Chicago Press.

Bakhtin, M. (1984) *Rabelais and His World*, Bloomington: Indiana University Press.

Bartky, S. (1990) *Femininity and Domination: Studies in the Phenomenology of Oppression*, New York: Routledge.

Bassel, L. and Emejulu, A. (2018) *Minority Women and Austerity: Survival and Resistance in France and Britain*, Bristol: Policy Press.

Beard, M. (2014) 'The public voice of women', *London Review of Books*, 36(6): 11–14.

Beck, U., Giddens, A. and Lash, S. (eds) (1994) *Reflexive Modernization: Politics, Tradition and Aesthetics in the Modern Social Order*, Stanford, CA: Stanford University Press.

Benedict, R. (2006) *The Chrysanthemum and the Sword*, Boston, MA: Houghton Mifflin Harcourt.

Benford, R.D. (1997) 'An insider's critique of the social movement framing perspective', *Sociological Inquiry*, 67(4): 409–30.

Berlant, L. (2004) *Compassion: The Culture and Politics of an Emotion*, London: Routledge.

Blyth, M. (2013) *Austerity: The History of a Dangerous Idea*, Oxford: Oxford University Press.

Bobel, C. (2007) '"I'm not an activist, per se, though I've done a lot of it": doing activism, being activist and the perfect standard in a contemporary movement', *Social Movement Studies*, 6(2): 147–59.

Bourdieu, P. (1984) *Distinction*, London: Routledge.

Bourdieu, P. (1986) 'The Forms of Capital', in Richardson, J. (ed.) *Handbook of Theory and Research for the Sociology of Education*, New York: Greenwood.

Bourdieu, P. (1992) *The Logic of Practice*, Cambridge: Polity Press.

Bourdieu, P. (2001) *Masculine Domination*, Stanford, CA: Stanford University Press.

Brah, A., Szeman, I. and Gedalof, I. (2015) 'Feminism and the politics of austerity', *Feminist Review*, 109: 1–7.

Bramall, R. (2013) *The Cultural Politics of Austerity: Past and Present in Austere Times*, Basingstoke: Palgrave Macmillan.

British Sociological Association (2017) 'Statement of ethical practice for the British Sociological Association', available at: https://www.britsoc. co.uk/media/24310/bsa_statement_of_ethical_practice.pdf [Accessed 24 October 2019].

Brown, B. (2013) *Daring Greatly: How the Courage to be Vulnerable Transforms the Way We Live, Love, Parent, and Lead*, London: Penguin.

Brown, B. (2018) *Dare to Lead: Brave Work. Tough Conversations. Whole Hearts*, London: Vermillion Books.

Brown, G., Dowling, E., Harvie, D. and Milburn, K. (2013) 'Careless talk: social reproduction and fault lines of the crisis in the UK', *Social Justice*, 39(1): 78–98.

Brown, G. and Pickerill, J. (2009) 'Space for emotion in the spaces of activism', *Emotion, Space and Society*, 2(1): 24–35.

Brown, W. (1999) 'Resisting Left melancholy', *Boundary2*, 26(3): 19–27.

Brown, W. (2015) *Undoing the Demos: Neoliberalism's Stealth Revolution*, New York: Zone Books.

Bubeck, D. (1995) *A Feminist Approach to Citizenship*, Florence: European University Institute.

Cable, S. (1992) 'Women's social movement involvement: the role of structural availability in recruitment and participation processes', *The Sociological Quarterly*, 33(1): 35–50.

Calhoun, C. and Sennett, R. (2007) *Practicing Culture*, Oxford: Taylor and Francis.

Calhoun, C. (2001) 'Putting emotions in their place', in Goodwin, J., Jasper, J.M. and Polletta, F. (eds) *Passionate Politics: Emotion and Social Movements*, Chicago: University of Chicago Press, pp 45–58.

Cameron, D. (2009) 'Age of austerity speech' delivered in Cheltenham: April 2009, available at: http://conservative-speeches.sayit.mysociety.org/speech/601367 [Accessed 2 June 2016].

Cameron, D. (2013) 'Economy speech' delivered in Yorkshire: March 2013, available at: https://www.gov.uk/government/speeches/economy-speech-delivered-by-david-cameron [Accessed 26 February 2015].

Castells, M. (1996) *The Rise of the Network Society: The Information Age: Economy, Society and Culture Vol. 1*, Oxford: Blackwell.

Castells, M. (2012) *Networks of Outrage and Hope*, Cambridge: Polity Press.

Castells, M., Caraça, J. and Cardoso, G. (eds) (2012) *Aftermath: The Cultures of the Economic Crisis*, Oxford: Oxford University Press.

Charles, N. (1993) *Gender Divisions and Social Change*, London: Rowman & Littlefield.

Charles, N. (2000) *Feminism, the State and Social Policy*, Basingstoke: Palgrave Macmillan.

Chatterton, P. (2006) '"Give up activism" and change the world in unknown ways: or, learning to walk with others on uncommon ground', *Antipode*, 38(2): 259–81.

Christensen, H.S. (2011) 'Political activities on the internet: slacktivism or political participation by other means?', *First Monday*, 16(2), available at: http://firstmonday.org/article/view/3336/2767 [Accessed 3 March 2016].

Clarke, J. and Newman, J. (2012) 'The alchemy of austerity', *Critical Social Policy*, 32(3): 299–319.

Coleman, R. (2016) 'Austerity futures: debt, temporality and (hopeful) pessimism as an austerity mood', *New Formations*, 87: 83–101.

Coleman, L.M. and Bassi, S.A. (2011) 'Deconstructing militant manhood: masculinities in the disciplining of (anti)-globalization politics', *International Feminist Journal of Politics*, 13(2): 204–24.

Corrigall-Brown, C. (2012) *Patterns of Protest: Trajectories of Participation in Social Movements*, Stanford, CA: Stanford University Press.

Cortese, D.K. (2015) 'I'm a "good" activist, you're a "bad" activist, and everything I do is activism: parsing the different types of "activist" identities in LBGTQ organising', *Interface*, 7(1): 215–46.

Cox, L. (2009) '"Hearts with one purpose alone"? Thinking personal sustainability in social movements', *Emotion, Space and Society*, 2(1): 52–61.

Craddock, E. (2019) 'The uncomfortable transformation of discomfort in the neoliberal higher education context', *Social Epistemology Review and Reply Collective*, 8(10): 107–10.

Crenshaw, K. (1989) 'Demarginalizing the intersection of race and sex: a black feminist critique of antidiscrimination doctrine, feminist theory and antiracist politics', *University of Chicago Legal Forum*, 1989(1): Article 8.

Crossley, N. (2002) *Making Sense of Social Movements*, Buckingham: Open University Press.

Culley, M.R. (2003) 'Women's gendered experiences as long-term Three Mile Island activists', *Gender and Society*, 17(3): 445–61.

De Certeau, M. (2011) *The Practice of Everyday Life*, Berkeley: University of California Press.

Della Porta, D. (2013) 'Amoral neoliberalism and moral protests: social movements in times of crisis', paper presented at Consejo General del Trabajo Social, Malaga, November 2013.

Della Porta, D. (2015) *Social Movements in Times of Austerity: Bringing Capitalism Back into Protest Analysis*, Cambridge: Polity Press.

Denning, M. (1996) *The Cultural Front: The Laboring of American Culture in the Twentieth Century*, London: Verso.

Department for Work and Pensions (2015) '2010 to 2015 government policy: welfare reform', available at: https://www.gov.uk/government/publications/2010-to-2015-government-policy-welfare-reform/2010-to-2015-government-policy-welfare-reform [Accessed 30 January 2019].

Dodson, K. (2015) 'Gendered activism: a cross-national view on gender differences in protest activity', *Social Currents*, 2(4): 377–92.

Durkheim, E. (2002) [1925] *Moral Education*, New York: Dover.

Einwohner, R.L., Hollander, J.A. and Olson, T. (2000) 'Engendering social movements: cultural images and movement dynamics', *Gender & Society*, 14(5): 679–99.

Emejulu, A. and Bassel, L. (2015) 'Minority women, austerity and activism', *Race & Class*, 57(2): 86–95.

Emejulu, A. (2017) 'Feminism for the 99%: towards a populist feminism?', *Soundings* 66 (Summer), available at: https://www.lwbooks.co.uk/soundings/66/towards-populist-feminism [Accessed 10 May 2018].

Fawcett Society (2012) 'The impact of austerity on women', available at: https://www.fawcettsociety.org.uk/Handlers/Download.ashx?IDMF=f61c3b7e-b0d9-4968-baf6-e3fa0ef7d17f [Accessed 22 October 2019].

Flam, H. and King, D. (eds) (2005) *Emotions and Social Movements*, London: Routledge.

Forkert, K. (2018) *Austerity as Public Mood: Social Anxieties and Social Struggles*, London: Rowman and Littlefield.

Fraser, N. (1992) 'Rethinking the public sphere: a contribution to the critique of actually existing democracy', in Calhoun, C. (ed.) *Habermas and the Public Sphere*, Cambridge, MA: MIT Press, pp 109-41.

Fraser, N. (1994) 'After the family wage: gender equity and the welfare state', *Political Theory*, 22(4): 591–618.

Fraser, N. (2013) *Fortunes of Feminism: From State-Managed Capitalism to Neoliberal Crisis*, London: Verso.

Fuchs, C. (2005) 'Social movements and class analysis', available at: http://fuchs.uti.at/wp-content/uploads/SM2.pdf [Accessed 3 June 2016].

Gadamer, H-G. (1982) *Truth and Method*, New York: Crossroad Publishing Company.

Gamson, W.A. (1992) *Talking Politics*, Cambridge: Cambridge University Press.

Geertz, C. (1973) 'Thick description: toward an interpretive theory of culture', in *The Interpretation of Cultures: Selected Essays*, New York: Basic Books, pp 3–30.

Gentleman, A. (2015) 'Austerity cuts will bite even harder in 2015 – another 12bn will go', *The Guardian*, available at https://www.theguardian.com/society/2015/jan/01/austerity-cuts-2015-12-billion-britain-protest [Accessed 3 June 2016].

Gerbaudo, P. (2012) *Tweets and the Streets: Social Media and Contemporary Activism*, London: Pluto.

Gilbert, J. (2014) *Common Ground: Democracy and Collectivity in an Age of Individualism*, London: Pluto.

Gill, R. (2008) 'Culture and subjectivity in neoliberal and postfeminist times', *Subjectivity*, 25: 432–45.

Gill, R. and Scharff, C. (eds) (2011) *New Femininities: Postfeminism, Neoliberalism and Subjectivity*, Basingstoke: Palgrave Macmillan.

Giugni, M. and Grasso, M.T. (eds) (2015) *Austerity and Protest: Popular Contention in Times of Economic Crisis*, Farnham: Ashgate Publishing.

Gladwell, M. (2010) 'Small change: why the revolution will not be tweeted', *New Yorker*, 4 October, available at: http://www.newyorker.com/magazine/2010/10/04/small-change-malcolm-gladwell [Accessed 10 June 2016].

Goodfellow, M. (2016) 'A toxic concoction means women of colour are hit hardest by austerity', *The Guardian*, available at: https://www.theguardian.com/commentisfree/2016/nov/28/toxic-concoction-women-colour-pay-highest-price-austerity [Accessed 31 January 2019].

Goodwin, J., Jasper, J.M., and Polletta, F. (2000) 'The return of the repressed: the fall and rise of emotions in social movement theory', *Mobilization: An International Quarterly*, 5(1): 65–83.

Goodwin, J., Jasper, J.M. and Polletta, F. (2001) (eds) *Passionate Politics: Emotions and Social Movements*, Chicago: University of Chicago Press.

Graeber, D. (2009) *Direct Action: An Ethnography*, Edinburgh: AK Press UK.

Graeber, D. (2013) *The Democracy Project: A History. A Crisis. A Movement*, London: Pearson.

Grazian, D. (2010) 'Demystifying authenticity in the sociology of culture', available at: http://works.bepress.com/cgi/viewcontent.cgi?article=1023&context=david_grazian [Accessed 14 May 2016].

Greer, G. (2013) 'Guilt poisons women', CNN, available at: http://edition.cnn.com/2013/03/12/opinion/greer-women-and-guilt/ [Accessed 4 June 2016).

Grenfell, M. (2008) *Pierre Bourdieu: Key Concepts*, Durham, NC: Acumen.

Guardian, The (2018) '*The Guardian* view on the 2018 budget: end austerity for the nation's sake', available at: https://www.theguardian.com/commentisfree/2018/oct/28/the-guardian-view-on-the-2018-budget-end-austerity-for-the-nations-sake [Accessed 31 January 2019].

Habermas, J. (1981) 'New social movements', *Telos*, 49: 33–7.

Habermas, J. (1989) *The Structural Transformation of the Public Sphere: An Inquiry into a Category of Bourgeois Society*, Cambridge: Polity Press.

Habermas, J. (1992) 'Further reflections on the public sphere', in Calhoun, C. (ed.) *Habermas and the Public Sphere*, Cambridge, MA: MIT Press.

Habermas, J. (1998) *Between Facts and Norms*, Cambridge: Polity Press.

Haiven, M. and Khasnabish A. (2014) *The Radical Imagination*, London: Zed Books.

Hall, S. (1988) *The Hard Road to Renewal: Thatcherism and the Crisis of the Left*, London: Verso.

Halupka, M. (2014) 'Clicktivism: a systematic heuristic', *Policy and Internet*, 6(2): 115–32.

Harvey, D. (2007) *A Brief History of Neoliberalism*, Oxford: Oxford University Press.

Herd, P. and Harrington Meyer, M. (2002) 'Care work: invisible civic engagement', *Gender and Society*, 16(5), pp 665–88.

Hesse-Biber, S.N. (2007) 'Feminist research: exploring the interconnections of epistemology, methodology, and method', in Hesse-Biber, S.N. (ed.) *Handbook of Feminist Research: Theory and Practice*, London: SAGE Publishing, pp 1–28.

Hesse-Biber, S.N. and Piatelli, D. (2007) 'Holistic reflexivity: the feminist practice of reflexivity', in Hesse-Biber, S.N. (ed.) *Handbook of Feminist Research: Theory and Practice*, London: SAGE Publishing, pp 493–514.

Hitchen, E. (2016) 'Living and feeling the austere', *New Formations*, 87: 102–18.

Holloway, J. (2010) *Crack Capitalism*, London: Pluto Press.

Holyoak, R. (2015) 'Young women's gendered subjectivity and political agency in social movement activism', unpublished PhD thesis, University of Leicester.

hooks, b. (2000) *Feminist Theory: From Margin to Center*, London: Pluto Press.

Hope, S. (2014) 'The capitalist model of activism and why it sucks, a feminist challenging transphobia', available at: https://feminist challengingtransphobia.wordpress.com/2014/12/08/the-capitalist-model-of-activism-and-why-it-sucks/ [Accessed 29 January 2015].

Horton, J. and Kraftl, P. (2009) 'Small acts, kind words, and "not too much fuss": implicit activisms', *Emotion, Space and Society*, 2(1): 14–23.

Horton, T. and Reed, H. (2010) 'The distributional impact of the 2010 spending review', *Radical Statistics*, 103: 13–24.

Institute for Fiscal Studies (2014) *Autumn Statement Briefing*, available at: http://www.ifs.org.uk/uploads/publications/budgets/as2014/as2014_johnson.pdf [Accessed 3 June 2016].

ITV News (2015) 'Thousands protest austerity cuts in Bristol', available at: https://www.itv.com/news/westcountry/story/2015-05-13/thousands-protest-austerity-cuts-in-bristol/ [Accessed 22 October 2019].

Jacobsson, K. and Lindblom, J. (2012) 'Moral reflexivity and dramaturgical action in social movement activism: the case of the plowshares and Animal Rights Sweden', *Social Movement Studies*, 11(1): 41–60.

Jacquet, J. (2015) *Is Shame Necessary? New Uses for an Old Tool*, London: Penguin.

Jasper, J.M. (1997) *The Art of Moral Protest: Culture, Biography, and Creativity in Social Movements*, Chicago: University of Chicago Press.

Jasper, J.M. (2011) 'Emotions and social movements: twenty years of theory and research', *Annual Review of Sociology*, 37: 285–303.

Jasper, J.M. (2014) 'Feeling – thinking: emotions as central to culture', in Baumgarten, B., Daphi, P. and Ullrich, P. (eds) *Conceptualizing Culture in Social Movement Research*, Basingstoke: Palgrave Macmillan, pp 23–45.

Kennelly, J. (2014) '"It's this pain in my heart that won't let me stop": gendered affect, webs of relations, and young women's activism', *Feminist Theory*, 15(3): 241–60.

King, D. (2005) 'Sustaining activism through emotional reflexivity', in Flam, H. and King, D. (eds) *Emotions and Social Movements*, London: Routledge.

Kiwan, D. (2017) 'Emotive acts of citizenship, social change and knowledge production in Lebanon', *Interface*, 9(2): 114–42.

Kohn, M. (2003) *Radical Space: Building the House of the People*, New York: Cornell University Press.

Kohut, H. (1977) *The Restoration of the Self*, New York: International Universities Press.

Kremer, M. (2007) *How Welfare States Care: Culture, Gender, and Parenting in Europe*, Amsterdam: Amsterdam University Press.

Kuumba, M.B. (2001) *Gender and Social Movements*, Walnut Creek, CA: Alta Mira Press.

Laclau, E. (2005) *On Populist Reason*, London: Verso.

Lamon, B. (2016) 'Why this radical activist is disillusioned by the toxic culture of the left', *The Independent*, available at: http://www.independent.co.uk/voices/why-this-radical-activist-is-disillusioned-by-the-toxic-culture-of-the-left-a6895211.html [Accessed 4 June 2016).

Lampert, K. (2005) *Traditions of Compassion: From Religious Duty to Social Activism*, London: Palgrave Macmillan.

Lasn, K. (1999) *Culture Jam: The Uncooling of America*, New York: Eagle Brook.

Letherby, G. (2003) *Feminist Research in Theory and Practice*, London: Open University Press.

Levinas, E. (1969) *Totality and Infinity: An Essay on Exteriority*, Pittsburgh, PA: Duquesne University Press.

Levitas, R. (2012) 'The just's umbrella: austerity and the big society in coalition policy and beyond', *Critical Social Policy*, 32(3): 320–42.

Lister, R. (2008) 'Citizenship and gender', in Nash, K. and Scott, A. (eds) *Blackwell Companion to Political Sociology*, Oxford: Blackwell Publishing, pp 323–33.

Loader, B. and Mercea, D. (eds) (2012) *Social Media and Democracy: Innovations in Participatory Politics*, New York: Routledge.

McAdam, D. (1992) 'Gender as a mediator of the activist experience: the case of Freedom Summer', *American Journal of Sociology*, 97(5): 1211–40.

McCammon, H.J., Taylor, V., Reger, J. and Einwohner, R.L. (eds) (2017) *The Oxford Handbook of U.S. Women's Social Movement Activism*, Oxford: Oxford University Press.

McCarthy, J.D and Zald, M.N. (1977) 'Resource mobilization and social movements: a partial theory', *American Journal of Sociology*, 82(6): 1212–41.

McGuigan, J. (2016) *Neoliberal Culture*, Basingstoke: Palgrave Macmillan.

McRobie, H. (2012) 'When austerity sounds like backlash: gender and the economic crisis', available at: http://www.opendemocracy.net/5050/heather-mcrobie/when-austerity-sounds-like-backlash-gender-and-economic-crisis [Accessed 10 May 2016].

Maeckelbergh, M., (2013) 'Solidarity economies in times of crisis', *Interface*, 5(2): 98–120.

Maddison, S. (2007) 'Feminist perspectives on social movement research', in Hesse-Biber, S.N. (ed.) *Handbook of Feminist Research: Theory and Practice*, London: SAGE Publishing, pp 391–408.

Maiguashca, B., Dean, J. and Keith, D. (2016) 'Pulling together in a crisis? Anarchism, feminism and the limits of left-wing convergence in austerity Britain', *Capital & Class*, 40(1): 37–57.

Maslach, C. and Schaufeli, W.B. (1993) 'Historical and conceptual development of burnout', in Schaufeli, W.B., Maslach, C. and Marek, T. (eds) *Professional Burnout: Recent Developments in Theory and Research*, Washington, DC: Taylor and Francis.

May, T. (2018) 'Speech to the 2018 Conservative Party Conference', October 2018, available at: https://www.politicshome.com/news/uk/political-parties/conservative-party/news/98760/read-full-theresa-mays-speech-2018 [Accessed 10 December 2019].

Melucci, A. (1984) 'An end to social movements? Introductory paper to the sessions on "new social movements and change in organizational forms"', *Social Science Information*, 23(4–5): 819–35.

Melucci, A. (1989) *Nomads of the Present: Social Movements and Individual Needs in Contemporary Society*, Philadelphia, PA: Temple University Press.

Melucci, A. (1996) *Challenging Codes: Collective Action in the Information Age*, Cambridge: Cambridge University Press.

Moore, A. (2002) 'Authenticity as authentication', *Popular Music*, 21(2): 209–23.

Morozov, E. (2009) 'From slacktivism to activism', *Foreign Policy*, 5 September, available at: http://foreignpolicy.com/2009/09/05/from-slacktivism-to-activism/ [Accessed 10 June 2016].

Mouffe, C. (2005) *On the Political*, London: Verso.

New Economics Foundation (2013) 'Framing the economy: the austerity story', available at: http://b.3cdn.net/nefoundation/a12416779f2dd4153c_2hm6ixryj.pdf [Accessed 11 June 2016].

Niemöller, M. (n.d.) 'First they came for the socialists...', *Holocaust Encyclopaedia*, available at: https://encyclopedia.ushmm.org/content/en/article/martin-niemoeller-first-they-came-for-the-socialists [Accessed 22 October 2019].

Nottingham City Council (2015), 'Your city, your services', available at https://www.nottinghamcity.gov.uk/your-council/about-the-council/your-city-your-services [Accessed 24 October 2019].

Oakley, A. (1981) 'Interviewing women: a contradiction in terms', in Roberts, H. (1981) *Doing Feminist Research*, London: Routledge, pp 30–61.

Oakley, A. (2015) 'Interviewing women again: power, time and the gift', *Sociology*, 50(1): 195–213.

Osborne, G. (2012) 'Conservative Party conference speech' delivered in Birmingham, October 2012, available at: http://www.newstatesman.com/blogs/politics/2012/10/george-osbornes-speech-conservative-conference-full-text [Accessed 12 June 2016].

Papacharissi, Z. (2015) *Affective Publics: Sentiment, Technology, and Politics*, Oxford: Oxford University Press.

Pateman, C. (1987) 'The patriarchal welfare state: women and democracy', in Gutmann, A. (ed.) *Democracy and the Welfare State*, Princeton, NJ: Princeton University Press, pp 231–60.

Pearson, R. and Elson, D. (2015) 'Transcending the impact of the financial crisis in the UK: towards plan F – a feminist economic strategy', *Feminist Review*, 109: 8–30.

People's Assembly (n.d.) 'What we stand for', available at: http://www.thepeoplesassembly.org.uk/index.php/about/what-we-stand-for [Accessed 24 October 2019].

Peterson, A., Wahlström, M., and Wennerhag, M. (2013) 'Is there new wine in the new bottles? Participants in European anti-austerity protests 2010–2012', paper presented to ECPR General Conference, Bordeaux, 2013, available at: http://ecpr.eu/filestore/paperproposal/a1555da5-b8c1-42f4-bda8-68a223a7f2a6.pdf [Accessed 3 June 2016].

Phillips, A. (1991) *Engendering Democracy*, Cambridge: Polity Press.

Picot, N. (2016) *Women's Liberation in Nottingham: A Portrait*, Nottingham: Nottingham Women's Centre.

Polletta, F. (2006) *It Was Like a Fever: Storytelling in Protest and Politics*, Chicago: University of Chicago Press.

Portwood-Stacer, L. (2013) *Lifestyle Politics and Radical Activism*, London: Bloomsbury.

Putnam, R.D. (2000) *Bowling Alone: The Collapse and Revival of American Community*, New York: Simon & Schuster.

Ricoeur, P. (1981) *Hermeneutics and the Human Sciences*, ed. and trans. J.B. Thompson, Cambridge: Cambridge University Press.

Rifkin, J. (2009) *The Empathic Civilization: The Race to Global Consciousness in a World in Crisis*, Penguin: New York.

Rose, H. (1983) 'Hand, brain, and heart: a feminist epistemology for the natural sciences', *Signs*, 9(1): 73–90.

Ross, K. (2011) *Gendered Media: Women, Men and Identity Politics*, London: Rowman and Littlefield.

Roseneil, S. (1995) *Disarming Patriarchy: Feminism and Political Action at Greenham*, Buckingham: Open University Press.

Runnymede Trust (2015). 'The 2015 budget: effects on black and minority ethnic people', July, available at: https://www.runnymedetrust. org/uploads/The%202015%20Budget%20Effect%20on%20BME%20 RunnymedeTrust%2027thJuly2015.pdf [Accessed 2 February 2017].

Scott, J.C. (2012) *Two Cheers for Anarchism*, Princeton, NJ: Princeton University Press.

Sevenhuijsen, S. (2000) 'Caring in the third way: the relation between obligation, responsibility and care in *Third Way* discourse', *Critical Social Policy*, 20(1): 5–37.

Shannon, D. (ed.) (2014) *The End of the World as We Know It? Crisis, Resistance, and the Age of Austerity*, Chico, CA: AK Press.

Shelter (2018) 'How to deal with the bedroom tax', December, Available at: http://england.shelter.org.uk/housing_advice/benefits/how_to_ deal_with_the_bedroom_tax [Accessed 30 January 2019].

Shouse, E. (2005) 'Feeling, emotion, affect', *M/C Journal*, 8(6), available at: http://journal.media-culture.org.au/0512/03-shouse.php [Accessed 3 June 2016].

Sitrin, M. (2012) *Everyday Revolutions: Horizontalism and Autonomy in Argentina*, London, New York: Zed Books.

Slote, M. (2007) *The Ethics of Care and Empathy*, London: Routledge.

Slote, M. (2010) *Moral Sentimentalism*, Oxford: Oxford University Press.

Smith, D. (1988) *The Everyday World as Problematic: A Feminist Sociology*, Milton Keynes: Open University Press.

Solnit, R. (2005) *Hope in the Dark: The Untold History of People Power*, Edinburgh: Canongate Books.

Stuart, A. (2013) 'Being active but not an activist: managing problematic aspects of activist identity by expressing individuality, or taking alternative forms of collective action', unpublished PhD thesis, Murdoch University, available at: http://researchrepository.murdoch.edu.au/22564/ [Accessed 4 March 2016].

Sullivan, S. (2005) '"Viva nihilism!" On militancy and machismo in (anti-)globalisation protest', working paper 158/05, University of Warwick.

Sunstein, C. (2001) *Republic.com*, Princeton, NJ: Princeton University Press.

Tanesini, A. (1999) *An Introduction to Feminist Epistemologies*, Oxford: Blackwell.

Taylor, V. (1999) 'Gender and social movements: gender processes in women's self-help movements', *Gender & Society*, 13(1): 8–33.

Thatcher, M. (1980) Speech at the Lord Mayor's Banquet (10 November), *Margaret Thatcher Foundation*, available at: http://www.margaretthatcher. org/document/104442 [Accessed 24 October 2019].

Thompson, E.P. (1963) *The Making of the English Working Class*, London: Penguin Books.

Thompson, E.P. (1971) 'The moral economy of the English crowds in the eighteenth century', *Past and Present*, 50(1): 76–136.

Thorne, B. (1975) 'Women in the draft resistance movement: a case study of sex role and social movements', *Sex Roles*, 1(2): 179–95.

Todd, S. (2004) 'Teaching with ignorance: questions of social justice, empathy, and responsible community', *Interchange*, 35(3): 337–52.

Todd, S. (2014) *The People: The Rise and Fall of the Working Class, 1910–2010*, London: John Murray.

Touraine, A. (1985) 'An introduction to the study of social movements', *Theory Culture and Society*, 9(1): 125–45.

Touraine, A. (2014) *After the Crisis*, Cambridge: Polity Press.

Trades Union Congress (2015) 'The impact on women of recession and austerity', March, available at: www.tuc.org.uk/sites/default/files/WomenRecession.pdf [Accessed 2 February 2016].

Tyler, I. (2013) *Revolting Subjects: Social Abjection and Resistance in Neoliberal Britain*, London: Zed Books.

Valentine, G. and Harris, C. (2014) 'Strivers vs skivers: class prejudice and the demonisation of dependency in everyday life', *Geoforum*, 53: 84–92.

Walzer, M. (1970) 'A day in the life of a socialist citizen', in Walzer, M. *Obligations: Essays on Disobedience, War and Citizenship*, Cambridge, MA: Harvard University Press.

Weber, M. (1930) *The Protestant Ethic and the Spirit of Capitalism*, New York: Scribner.

Wettergren, A. (2009) 'Fun and laughter: culture jamming and the emotional regime of late capitalism', *Journal of Social, Cultural and Political Protest*, 8(1): 1–15.

Wieck, D. (n.d.) *The Habit of Direct Action*, available at: https://libcom.org/library/habit-direct-action [Accessed 22 October 2019].

Williams, Raymond. (1977) 'Structures of feeling', in Williams, R. *Marxism and Literature*, Oxford: Oxford University Press, pp 128–36.

Williams, Rosalind. (2012) 'The rolling apocalypse of contemporary history', in Castells, M., Caraça, J. and Cardoso, G. (eds) *Aftermath: The Cultures of the Economic Crisis*, Oxford: Oxford University Press, pp 17–43.

Women's Budget Group (2016) 'A cumulative gender impact assessment of ten years of austerity policies'. March, available at: https://wbg.org.uk/wp-content/uploads/2016/03/De_HenauReed_WBG_GIAtaxben_briefing_2016_03_06.pdf [Accessed 2 February 2018].

Websites

https://coventrywomensvoices.wordpress.com/publications/
www.nottinghamwomenscentre.com
www.thepeoplesassembly.org.uk
www.ukuncut.org.uk

Index

www.ingramcontent.com/pod-product-compliance
Lightning Source LLC
Chambersburg PA
CBHW070925030426
42336CB00014BA/2534